BIRD MILK &

MOSQUITO

BONES

BIRD MILK & MOSQUITO BONES

❧ A MEMOIR ❧

Priyanka Mattoo

ALFRED A. KNOPF

NEW YORK

2024

THIS IS A BORZOI BOOK PUBLISHED
BY ALFRED A. KNOPF

Copyright © 2024 by Priyanka Mattoo

LIBRARY OF CONGRESS CATALOGING-IN-PUBLICATION DATA
Names: Mattoo, Priyanka, author.
Title: Bird milk & mosquito bones: a memoir / Priyanka Mattoo.
Other titles: Bird milk and mosquito bones
Description: First edition. | New York: Alfred A. Knopf, 2024. |
Identifiers: LCCN 2023021183 (print) | LCCN 2023021184 (ebook) |
ISBN 9780593320389 (hardcover) | ISBN 9780593314586 (trade
paperback) | ISBN 9780593320396 (ebook)
Subjects: LCSH: Mattoo, Priyanka. | Authors, American—21st
century—Biography. | Motion picture producers and directors—
United States—Biography. | LCGFT: Essays. | Autobiographies.
Classification: LCC PS3613.A8566 Z46 2024 (print) |
LCC PS3613.A8566 (ebook) | DDC 814/.6 [B]—dc23/eng/20230517
LC record available at https://lccn.loc.gov/2023021183
LC ebook record available at https://lccn.loc.gov/2023021184

Jacket illustration by Noémie Cédille
Jacket design by Linda Huang

Manufactured in the United States of America
First Edition

To Mum and Dad

Tchari chhu kand thari peth qarar.

A sparrow is content on its own thorny branch.

—KASHMIRI PROVERB

❧ CONTENTS ❧

BIRD MILK &

MOSQUITO

BONES

Goddess of Destruction

❧ 1989–1995 ❧

If only the house had been swept away in a flood. Incinerated in a conflagration, or leveled in an earthquake. All three were likely, in Kashmir, and a single event might have been easier to explain. But when anyone asks what happened, I say: "It was burned down by militants." I know the blunt force of my words creates a conversational cul-de-sac, one that makes people spin right around and back to . . . well, anything else. Their own revelatory trip to India. The unusual amount of rain we're getting. Whatever we were discussing just before. It's not only a conversation ender, it's a lie. But the truth would take too long.

I was born a Hindu in the city of Srinagar, as was almost everyone in my family, for probably thousands of years. My parents decided to move abroad for work opportunities in the early 1980s, only so that they could gather funds to build their dream house back home. We spent every summer and holiday—four to five months a year—in Kashmir, the topmost region of the Indian subcontinent, nestled into the Himalayas. I was born in Habba Kadal, a neighborhood in central Srinagar, its maze of streets lined with narrow four-story wooden houses.

My parents built our house in the suburban area of Natipora, on the south side of the city. It was lush then, with open fields, fresh air, and an unobstructed view of the foothills nearby. The house we were building would be rough-hewn stone, with a peaked wooden roof—the Platonic ideal of a mountain dwelling. And as we traveled all over the world, we gently, in our hand luggage, carried back decorative items for this future home: carefully sourced porcelain, hand-embroidered linens. There is a Kashmiri phrase, *chhari daud te mahe adij,* "bird milk and mosquito bones," used when someone is describing things so rare and precious that the listener should question their very existence. It comes to mind whenever I think about that little treasury of items we gathered.

Once the house was built, I remember the heavy curtains I wrapped around myself in Natipora, until I dislodged a family of mice. Afternoons cleaning string beans and corn from our vegetable patch. The time my mother told me not to play badminton into the evening, and it got so dark on the lawn that I smacked a shrieking bat into the net instead of the shuttlecock. Once, in the middle of a new-moon night, I woke up and saw the faintest shadow of a bear dancing on its hind legs on the lawn. Nobody believes me about this one, but it happened.

I split time between the Natipora house and my Matamaal—my mother's ancestral home—in a verdant central Srinagar area, where I was the first of eight grandchildren, doted on by a boisterous extended family. I can draw you a detailed architectural map of both homes. I can also recount every moment of our weekend trips to picnic in Pahalgam, a hill town so picturesque it is featured in many Hindi movies. We'd breakfast on chocolate-covered walnuts, tramp through a rushing steam, duck out of the way for people's endless honeymoon shoots—everyone, for an age, honeymooned there. This is all to say: many have waxed poetic on the marvels of Kashmir. "Almost painfully beautiful, like staring at the sun," says a friend's mother. Indian travel posters touted the cliché of "paradise on earth," which sounds like an exaggeration, but it was absolutely all of that. To my nine-year-old self, it was the most extraordinary, joyful place in the world.

At the same time, being Kashmiri has always been difficult. My parents' generation had seen two wars between India and Pakistan over Kashmir, followed by an insurgency against Indian rule and rapid militarization in the winter of 1989–90. When the violence began, many Pandits, as Kashmiri Hindus are known, were targeted and killed by militants. This led to rushed middle-of-the-night departures by most of our community, including my extended family—my parents, brother, and I were living abroad as the house in Natipora was being built, always with the idea that we'd return. I usually rattle off these facts simply and without emotion, as a child would, so I don't cry. But here, I'll say more. Fire was involved, and militants, but our definitive severance came about slowly and strangely.

The first thing that happened was I woke up in the middle of the night, in our apartment in Riyadh, Saudi Arabia, to hear adults speaking in low, serious voices in the living room. I wandered out in my pajamas and was startled to see my grandparents—my father's parents. I hardly recognized them. Papaji's well-moisturized cheeks hung low, like those of a cartoon bloodhound. His eyes tired, no sparkle. Bhabi wore a drab brown salwar kameez—I had only seen her in saris, shades of green to match her eyes. They all sat on the ground, as though, after their flight here, they had run out of energy to raise them-selves to chair level. My parents told me to go back to sleep.

When I remind my parents of this memory, they say it never happened. That Bhabi and Papaji had already been visiting us in the fall of 1989. They say we had just gotten back from another summer in Srinagar, putting finishing touches on the house. The mason who had built our house came over to take a look at the garage, where Dad was thinking of adding a room. The idea was that in a few years he'd have raised the funds to build a children's hospital in Srinagar, and we'd be back full-time. "Is it possible you might not come back?" asked the mason. "Because, if you're not coming back, you might want to sell this place." Dad was surprised—there had been a couple of small blasts in Kashmir that summer, but nothing anyone was worried about. In retrospect, he sees maybe he should have been.

While Bhabi and Papaji were visiting us that fall, we heard that things were getting worse back home. That Pandits were being threatened and targeted, that our community was being advised to leave for a time. Letters had appeared on the doors of Hindu families across town—letters saying we should leave or be killed. Then Urdu-language newspapers started urging non-Muslims to leave, so they did. Bhabi and Papaji left in January 1990, in a truck, in the middle of the night, and made their way to nearby Jammu. Like all the other families who left that month, they traveled with a couple of suitcases and one photo album.

Eventually, they landed in Delhi, where Papaji's company had an office, and Dad went to get them settled in. He was hor-rified to see how they were living. Papaji had rented a single room, in which the three of them slept. Dad asked Bhabi for a glass of water, and she disappeared for half an hour: the one fridge in the building belonged to the landlords, on the bottom floor, and she was waiting for them to be available to dispense Dad's drink. A single bathroom, shared with four other families, was down the hall. Dad was heartbroken on top of heartbroken, and, having just had one home wiped out, he wearily began the process of figuring out a better living situation in Delhi. A new flat would need to be built, but it would take a couple of years. Until then, on our visits to Bhabi and Papaji, we'd all sleep together in that one room. Meanwhile, we heard that the house in Kashmir had been looted. Everything my parents had collected to furnish it with was gone. The next summer in Delhi felt almost luxurious, as the six of us expanded into a two-room rental. But if this was our new life in India, I fell asleep thinking, I didn't want to come back.

Matamaal cleared out in the same way, everyone moving to wherever they had the closest relatives. By 1992, when I was twelve, Nani and Nanaji—Mum's mother and father—had also ended up in Jammu, at the house of Nani's widowed sister-in-law, whom we called Mamiji. I loved Mamiji, a stately dowager with a plummy accent, serenely sitting under piles of knitting projects in her shaded garden. Her husband, Nani's brother, had worked at the UN, and their life had taken them all over the world. Her rambling house in Jammu reminded me of Matamaal, with its multiple living quarters. My grandparents lived in an apartment on the south end, facing a garden full of butterflies. They had found a tenant for Matamaal, which was still considered safe, for now. And it wasn't so bad in Jammu. Delhi had felt hostile, and even walking through its airport sent me into a spiral of despair, but Mamiji's house had enough familiar touches to remind me of our actual home. Even the patio, off of which my grandfather had a room of his own in which to read, watch movies, and have his nightly measure of Scotch after dinner. Evacuation may have been dramatic, but I took some comfort in the familiarity of Nanaji's daily routine.

But outside of Mamiji's house, nothing was the same. A horde of Kashmiri Hindus had moved to Jammu that year, after the troubles started, which gave us a sense of safety—there were people we knew around. But danger loomed there, too. One day, Mum and I had made plans to see a movie at the cinema, with her cousin—my Billie Masi. At the last minute, we decided to get ice cream instead, and heard that there had been a bomb blast that took out the entire section where we would have been sitting. *We were supposed to be safer here,* I remember thinking. But maybe I would never feel safe again.

Word continued to dribble in about what was happening to our house in Kashmir. It was still standing then, but after the looting, it had been gutted—every wire and fixture in the house gone, down to the kitchen sink. It was just an empty stack of bricks, with a roof over it—like the world's most expensive LEGO set—but we held out hope that we might be able to rebuild it on the same land, someday. I don't remember my feelings about this information. At twelve, I wasn't ready to process any of it yet. I took it in, numb, and grateful we had other places to go.

. . .

By our next trip to Jammu, in the summer of 1993, I was thirteen and hadn't seen the Natipora house in four years. Mum sensed my growing dissatisfaction with going to India—well, outside of Kashmir—and made an effort to get me to fall in love with it. She planned us a pilgrimage to Vaishno Devi, in nearby Katra, a shrine hidden at the top of the Trikuta hills. Photos showed me a small, whitewashed town nestled into a misty mountain landscape. Lured by the prospect of fresh air, an India I hadn't yet explored, and my mother's promises of its restorative qualities, I was on board. And I also felt a kinship to the manifestation of the Hindu mother goddess after which it was named.

Vaishno Devi, it was said, had come to earth to organize a festival, only to have some lust-addled man chase after her, up the hill. She managed to escape him by hiding for nine months in a cave, where he ultimately found her, but, taking the form of the goddess Kali, she beheaded him. His body, at the mouth of the cave, and his head, which landed farther along, became the sites of two of the temples in the Vaishno Devi complex. I loved this story. I related to Kali's bossiness, her anger, her hermit years, her desire to decapitate any man who looked at her funny. And to my mother, this all made sense. I was born . . . "a certain way," she said—and no wonder, for in the Kashmiri lunar calendar, Ma Kali and I share a birthday. I don't know if it's because of this, but when I see images of Ma Kali—dark blue, gaunt, with sunken eyes, wearing a tiger-skin sari and a garland of human heads—I feel calm, as one does regarding a kindred spirit. So does my mother, she says. The lengths to which the goddess will go—Destroyer of Evil, Protector of Innocence, Enemy of Fear—to take care of the people she loves, the terror she instills into the hearts of men who would try to harm them . . . Mum related as a mother, I as an enthusiastic sister and friend. It seemed like the perfect trip for us to pay our respects in person.

Our trek to Vaishno Devi started at the base camp of Katra, which was not much to look at, while being a lot to smell and hear. As at Lourdes, every storefront hawked religious souvenirs and trinkets for the hike up: flowers, coconuts, sugar cubes, and fruit to offer to the gods. The hawkers quieted down as we started the hike, a steep eight-mile zigzag up the side of a mountain. The path is a jumble of cobblestones, made slick with time, and we took off our slippery walking shoes to continue barefoot. We wound through a lush pine forest, dotted here and there with hardy salesmen and their three-wheeled food stalls. They sold steaming cups of tea and potato pakoras to a bunch of pilgrims, most of whom looked dazed by the exertion of so much walking. I loved it all—the warm, tired ache in my legs, my mother's smiling face, the scent of fresh snacks around the next curve of the climb. It was the first time I remember feeling truly happy in India after everyone left Kashmir. Here was beauty, humanity, a new trip I could look forward to every year, perhaps. Energized, we pushed forward.

The air got cold and misty as we ascended, and it felt familiar, almost like home. The altitude, probably. Six hours into our trek, the only light I could see was the single string of small round lightbulbs that illuminated the final curve around the mountain. Then, for the last couple of miles, everything was pitch black, except for handheld lanterns. The final bend goes around a hill and down into a valley, where out of the mist emerges a compact town of brilliant white. Such whiteness was jarring for me to see in India, where city air gave me the hacking cough of a two-pack-a-day smoker. But in the safety of a mountain's embrace, away from cars, the town looked pristine, breathtaking in the moonlight.

Vaishno Devi, at the time, felt like Capri stripped of its fancy awnings: isolated, intimate, quiet, lush, peaceful. Unlike Capri, though, the only things we could buy there were a vegetarian dinner and a night in a clean, spare room, lit by a fluorescent rod. The bed was as hard as a slab of wood, not that Mum and I noticed: we fell asleep immediately, satisfied and tired from the long walk.

A conch went off somewhere in the distance at sunrise. It was a surprisingly pleasant wake-up call—starting out slow and soothing, rising to sharp and urgent—before a rap at the door and the delivery of two hot, milky cups of strong black tea. Caffeine having jolted us properly awake, we hurried to line up at the mouth of the shrine. The cave entrance was tiny, maybe four feet wide, so we had to crawl in, propping our bodies between two slabs of rock, shuffling our feet along a narrow slab on the ground. Icy mountain water—reminiscent of our own Himalayan streams—ran over our bare feet. At the end of our forty-foot crawl was the shrine: a bedecked stone. After doing the thing, and kissing, and praying in its general direction, we were shuffled along to the exit, which, disappointingly, was a roomy, normal hallway to the left. The whole thing couldn't have taken more than ten minutes, and then we were out, blinking, in the early-morning sun once again.

We careened down the mountain, still barefoot—running because of the heat of the stones, but also because it was so steep that running kept us upright. We were punch-drunk, laughing. The visit had put some wind in our sails that had been sorely missing. The trip up had taken six hours; the trip down, one. We stopped only once on the way, to buy the village's famed paneer, slightly aged, with a tang I've unfortunately never been able to replicate since.

On the drive home, in the back seat of an Ambassador taxi, as soft as a plush sofa and smelling faintly of diesel, Mum and I napped on each other's shoulders. Nani greeted us at the gate in her familiar hand-wringing way, dabbing at the corners of her eyes with her sari, mumbling about how glad she was that we made it back safe. It was a reception I dismissed then—poor Nani—but I now recognize as the response of a woman who was trained to brace herself for more loss.

She had dinner made so that we could regain our strength, maintaining as she served it that I looked wan, pointing out imaginary bone contours where only teen softness existed. We sat down to an array of small stainless-steel bowls filled with the day's cooking, laid out on a plastic sheet on the floor. Rogan josh, kalia, winter squash in a yogurt sauce, kohlrabi, and sliced tomatoes and cucumbers. Ravenous, we positioned ourselves around the sheet, legs crossed, and dug in.

Nanaji joined us, as he always did, his magnificent hair a little mussed, one hand tucked into his wool pheran while he bore down with his spoon and gummed his food in grim silence. For an otherwise regimented man, he was an uncharacteristically messy eater: water and crumbs flew this way and that. As he left, rescuing his dentures from their water glass, it spilled, and a wet patch spread around his plate. Mum leaned back to take the pressure off her full belly. I uncrossed my legs and stretched them across the floor but realized that I could hardly move them because my muscles were so sore from our trip. Fed up with my whining about my stiff thighs, Mum said she'd take my plate into the kitchen and began to rise, only to find that she couldn't. Her back had given out. As she sat still at one end of the room, assessing correctly that she wouldn't be able to move for a few days, I registered that I couldn't even bend my knees to get up.

We sat six feet apart, working ourselves into hysterical laughter at each other's pathetic injuries. The phone rang in the hallway. Neither of us could get it, so Nani picked it up and brought it in to Mum. She sat, listening quietly, and her smile faded as she responded to whoever was on the other end. She hung up and looked over at me, unable to turn her body, and told me that the roof had been burned off the house in Kashmir. I began to cry, something I rarely did. I felt a terrible desolation inside. Everything hit me at once—the house, my grandparents' unsettled faces, my parents' grief, the random bomb blasts that had become a normal part of our lives. I had held on to a scrap of hope for four years, but it was like protecting a candle from a gale-force wind. When the roof finally burned off, I accepted that we were never going back.

But I couldn't move out of my sitting position with legs sticking straight out in front of me, and Mum couldn't move from where her back was to me, so we sat there, sort of reaching for each other, not quite touching, as every drop of fluid in my body seemed to drain out of my eyes. My delicious dinner turned in my stomach. My mother, in the spirit of Kali herself, had tried to protect me from pain. She had taught me I could thrive anywhere, find beauty in a hike in an unfamiliar land I didn't particularly want to like. She turned herself inside out to make me feel at home, no matter where I was. But even after this trip, which reinforced the string that's stretched between our hearts for a lifetime, there was nothing she could do. It had become the trip after which the house was gone, and it always would be.

. . .

I think of my mother, and that exact moment, twenty-four years later, as my son's small, round body shakes with laughter at the Kailua Public Library, on Oahu, Hawaii. He's pulled out a picture book called *Square* by Mac Barnett and Jon Klassen, and we both find it so funny we are repeating lines and wiping tears from our eyes. After a few progressively more deranged readings, trying out voices, noticing new details, we attract a crowd of children, who gather crisscross applesauce on the ground, wondering what is happening. They hear him gasping for air and come round to see why, so next I'm squashed into a tiny wooden chair, reading the book to a growing crowd. At one punch line—you just have to read it—he bursts into laughter again, and the only other kid who joins is a little girl, wild-haired, barefoot, probably a surfer since birth. They make eye contact and connect over shared joy while the others look around, puzzled, and wander away. As my son and this girl pore over the book, her mother approaches me. I know this dance well and am already pulling out my phone for an exchange of contact info when she asks: "Whereabouts do you live?"

I tell her Los Angeles, and she looks confused. "We're just on vacation."

We've had these meet-cutes all over the world: A little half-Danish boy at the Robot Park in Tokyo. The family of seven (!) in a small Tuscan town. Close friends we visit in France. Because we vacation hard, my family. Ideally three weeks, and always a home rental, never a hotel. We settle in like we own the place and have always owned the place. We start with a grocery store, a thrift shop for toys, a visit to the local library. We scope out playgrounds and children's classes, make some friends, set up playdates. The Google map I create during my research phase is color-coded and layered. We have set up temporary lives everywhere from Greece to Japan. On the aforementioned trip to Kailua, we did five grocery runs and nine loads of laundry and spent the rest of the time washing dishes. In the places we stay, there is no turndown service, often no air-conditioning, and the elevator always breaks on day two. The need to settle in immediately is pathological. Like my mother before me, channeling the spirit of Ma Kali, I am compelled to ensure that my children are protected from unease or confusion, that they feel safe and fed, wherever we are.

I originally thought my bone-deep aversion to hotels was born of all the moving. Since Kashmir, we have lived in so many places I have lost count. Stints in Britain, Saudi Arabia, New York, and then dragging a garbage bag full of clothes from a decrepit house to a more decrepit house as a student in Ann Arbor, plus some time in Italy, and now five addresses in Los Angeles. I have spent a formative amount of time in sterile extended-stay suites while these homes were found, furnished, or built. Hotels make me feel unmoored, worried, and now that I have two small children, the logistics are beyond me. How can so many people crammed into a room all manage to sleep? If you don't sleep, is it even a vacation? What happens when a growing boy needs breakfast at 5:00 a.m.?

But I have realized recently my "travel style" runs deeper: I don't have a home. Yes, I live in a house. But most people have somewhere to go home *to*. Even now, halfway through a lifetime of talking to my parents every day, I rarely ask for updates about Kashmir. I didn't want to know back then, and I don't want to talk about it now. I can hardly bear to hear the disappointment and grief in my mother's voice when she tells me that Matamaal is now a tech sales center. Even typing this out makes my heart clench, and I go back to the drawings in my head. Because I have mapped out Matamaal, room by room, obsessively, for the past thirty years. I have catalogued every beam and tile of the house in Natipora, so that I can remember them all. Because I can't (or won't?) revisit, this is my only way to access the happiness of those summers at home in Kashmir. It's why I make a home everywhere I go, and it's why I carry around a mental floorplan of every stupid apartment we've ever rented, along with the routes to their stupid broken elevators, corner shops, libraries, playgrounds. These facsimiles of home ground me. They make me feel the loss less.

We never moved back to Kashmir, because we couldn't. We just kept moving. But nothing else ever felt like home, and nothing still does. If you ask me where I'm from, it's easier to say "Michigan," which is where my parents live now. I don't want to tell anyone where I'm *from* from, because if they know anything about Kashmir, they might look at me funny, with soft eyes full of compassion, and not know what to say, and I'll rush to comfort them, for some reason, to reassure them that everything was fine and great. My family's fine, I've always had my needs—more than my needs—met. *I barely lived there! I didn't lose that much!* I'll clarify. I have everything. It was a blip. So many people suffered much more than we did. So many people are suffering right now. So many Kashmiris' grief and loss outweigh mine by a factor of thousands. Can we ever go back? Should we ever go back? I am neither historically nor politically fluent enough to unpack these answers.

And, to be honest, I've never wanted to. Indeed, I didn't write at all, about anything, for a long time. I didn't know I was allowed. Brown pain, I learned as a small child in Western libraries, was interesting. Brown joy, brown ennui, spunky brown girl detectives—nowhere to be found. So, even though I worshipped books, I thought writing them was for other people. Lofty types, or people who had truly suffered. I didn't want to write a treatise on the tangled sociopolitical situation in my homeland. I had no heartrending tale of persecution and woe to share. I just loved our home, and I missed it, and wanted to transcribe the stories of my family, before we all forgot them. If I could capture on the page how my mother's twinkling eyes or stern looks made me feel . . . how my father's steady energy was the ballast that carried us through stormy years . . . the small history of my loved ones . . . If anyone would let me get these stories out someday, I thought, I would cry with gratitude and disbelief. But Indian diaspora writers, whom I read again and again, shone a light brightly on the highbrow literary, the traumatic, the dark and complex. Writing wasn't for people like me, who didn't want to talk about our cultural burdens.

But holding it all in hasn't worked. Since that trip to Vaishno Devi, I connect stressful periods in my life with stomachaches. I can be calm on the surface, roiling in my digestive tract beneath. In times of epic stress, I have to take to my bed until the pain recedes. It's not an ideal way to live, and I'm afraid I've passed it all on. Because, out of nowhere, it seems, my young son, now nine, is scared of fire. First the oven: "Can we just cook stuff in the microwave?" he asks when I turn on the stove. Then he trembles in his seat, seeing a lit match. He won't go to a camp he used to love, because he overheard a fire advisory. He's being rational, but there's a terrified edge to his avoidance that sinks my heart.

At night, he asks me if the batteries in the smoke detectors are up to date. "What happens if we are sleeping and don't hear?" He saw I lit a candle earlier; did I remember to blow it out? I soothe him after I put him to bed. "Okay, just going down to lock up, just closing up the kitchen," I announce, hoping he'll sleep soundly. And he does, for a while. But he'll soothe himself in the car. "Nobody's house has ever burned down, though, right?" I bite my tongue, nausea curling up my throat. Does he know? I repeat that our house has safety measures in place. Still, he wakes up with nightmares, crawls into our bed. One day, I ask him to unload his worries, hoping he can get them all out before bedtime. He tells me it's knives now. What, specifically, about knives? "Them slicing me. Someone hurting me with one." I blanch, thinking of another family story, one I've buried even deeper. Where is all this coming from? The next night, in my bed, my own worries come bubbling up. Did I do this? Have I held so much fear in the center of my body for my whole life that I baked it into a baby? And if so, how do I spend the rest of his life undoing it?

He's too small to hear the truth yet, so I decide to write it all down, for a day when he is ready. It's like an exorcism, this writing, in that I feel less possessed as time goes on, but I'm a snarling, miserable beast in the process, snapping at anyone who asks how it's going. "Terribly," I say, rearranging my garland of human heads. It's going as well as one might expect, given that these are feelings I've ignored for thirty years. My stomachaches get worse, and crest, until they're chronic, until I don't know a day without excruciating pain. So I submit to a phalanx of doctors, a dietician, and—improbably—a hypnotherapist, who starts to sever the connection between my stress response and my churning belly. It's like a hurricane's passing; I wake up one day, after a yearlong stomachache, well enough to write again. But I find, in the writing, that I still don't like to talk about my cultural burden, because it separates me from the reader. It highlights that I'm not actually from here, that most people's insides feel connected to a place, and mine, though healing now, don't. I can only guess that this sense of place shoots out of everyone's feet like invisible lightning bolts that link them to something deep: The water table? The bedrock under the water table? It's a sense of belonging to a place that, no matter how much we travel, makes my husband mention how hard it would be to live in another country, because that would be "too far away." "Too far away from *what?*" I ask him. Every country exists within itself.

That said, I now look American, I sound American. There isn't a cultural reference I'd miss in any conversation. But my Americanness has always felt like a costume. A well-tailored costume, but still an overlay, covering up who I actually am and how I really feel. Rather, how I really *don't* feel. It's so strange and frustrating to miss a sense I don't even remember possessing: that of being "too far away" from somewhere. It's this streak of unease that makes me feel that my insides will never stop searching for purchase. Sometimes I think I've worn this overlay for too long, and an itchy discomfort sets in. It's a remnant of having moved so much that every location feels like quicksand after a while. *What's next, what's new?* I think, even after almost three decades in this country, including twenty years in Los Angeles, of all places. *What's new, what's next?* Then I settle in and remind myself: I live here now. Be grateful. Be still.

Such a Nice Face

"You have a mustache," said a Canadian named Paul when I was twelve.

"You have no chin," I told him. "So what?"

His lip wobbled. "It's my jaw. I don't have a well-defined jaw," he murmured.

When I got home from school, I reflected. Did I feel bad about what I'd said? I didn't. He shouldn't have been critiquing my face in the first place. My mother agreed.

"But you only get *one* face," she said, smearing a homemade honey mask on hers. I dodged her sticky hands as she reached for mine next. She sighed. "Just, please, take care of it."

I scowled. Ever since Brad F. had bullied me into shaving my legs that one time, beauty, for me, was something other people wanted me to perform. And because other people wanted me to do it, I had very little interest.

In my estimation, my mother was the most beautiful person I had ever known, and would ever know, and she seemed to get by with a good personality and some eyeliner. A trained botanist, she was forever treating her skin with a homemade potion: turmeric for redness, honey for breakouts, yogurt or fruit acid peels. But beyond simple upkeep there were assets—

things that made her stand out, beauty-wise—that I started to notice as I entered (yuck) womanhood. She was naturally hairless. I . . . was not. She loved to dress up for a party. I would much rather go to the dentist than wear buttons. And, absorbing this, she despaired. She had painstakingly hand-made clothes for me, her little doll, and dressed me up through infancy and toddlerhood. And then, one day, I decided I didn't want anyone to look at me, ever, so why should I draw attention to myself? "Boys don't have to do any of this nonsense," I growled. "Boys can just be. So why can't I?" My father peered over his tub of moisturizer, having completed his elaborate shaving ritual, and reached for his perfectly pressed shirt. "Because looking nice feels nice."

My parents seemed to enjoy upkeep. I found all of it inconvenient. Why couldn't I pee standing up, anywhere I wanted? I raged as a small child. Why did body hair matter, and why was I expected to take care of it? Why did I have to be saddled with a period, especially since I didn't want to have a baby for twenty more years? Why did my hair need to be brushed every single day? And though I understood the practical need to cover my body, why the heck was I required to have so many different *kinds* of clothes?

Furthermore, it felt unfair that I was expected to devote an entire section of my brain to things that boys didn't have to think about but somehow got to have opinions on. Periods and peeing were big ones, but I distinctly remember when my male peers started ascribing value to appearance. Each of us girls had a few data points, all different: Heather What's-her-name, who was nice enough but kind of boring, had a friendly smile and long blond hair. Meena's beautiful hair was tucked under a hijab, but she had dimples and huge boobs. Cindy Crawford was the celebrity gold standard. These were all things that boys seemed to approve of and find appealing: a sunny demeanor, a "good body." But all such assessments made me feel I was constantly being inspected, like poultry, like a heifer. Maybe it was a function of always being the new kid, or maybe I was born like this, but I would much rather observe than be observed. As a young girl, I felt eyes on me when I entered any space, and I hated when people noticed. Anything. When we lived in the Middle East and my abaya slipped at the souk—even sometimes when it didn't—men made kissing sounds at me. I wished the abaya could make me invisible. But it wasn't limited to creepy strangers. Everyone seemed to feel licensed to assess and comment on my looks. "Your hair is tied back!" said a well-meaning auntie. "Such a nice face, and now we can actually see it."

To the aunties, a nice face they could see was almost as important as good grades. And they, my mother's cohort, were all so attractive. It was a whole performance, desi dinner-party culture in the 1980s. The aunties would do their hair and makeup and wear elegant saris. They made each other laugh and trained their well-dressed children to make polite conversation. But I was unwilling to participate. Mum could throw a dress over me, but I growled in a corner with a book, hiding behind my hair. "She's a little grumpy today," Mum would say with a sigh. I was a little grumpy every day, because life felt like a constant pageant, and I wanted out.

Why weren't my insides enough? I was a smart, curious person, with a good heart. These traits would have rendered the boys in my class complete. But more was expected of girls. As I navigated middle school, I doubly resisted efforts to tame my hair, to be more feminine, until I grew into a high school woman who dressed like a neglected dude. I hid myself, slouching, wearing sweatpants and my dad's button-down shirts to high school. I "styled" my hair to cover half my face, and if you ever caught a proper glimpse of me, I was scowling. At the same time, I was setting up a sort of test. If anyone could get past my exterior, I thought—my nondescript, prickly exterior—they'd find a loving friend and a good hang. But woe betide you if you had anything, nice or mean, to say about my looks.

My parents—my stylish, attractive parents—groaned, hoping that I'd eventually grow out of it. "WHY?" I grumbled. So I didn't embarrass them? So I could snag a nice husband? I wasn't generous in my assessment back then, but they didn't know what it felt like when people looked in my direction. I felt strange eyes on my skin like fingers poking a bruise, like hot lasers pointed at me at all times. By the age of twenty, I could no longer ignore my looks, because young men wouldn't let me. "You have such a nice face," said a terrible boy in my study-abroad program, looking at me funny, and it felt even worse than the aunties. "If you lost some weight . . . it would really make a difference." That settled it, I thought, in a silent rage. I swore I would never buy a scale. If I ever lost weight, that jerk would win. I'd never even own a full-length mirror, just to spite him.

One would think moving to Los Angeles would get in the way of my pledge, but it took very little willpower on my part. Women swarmed the city in identical workout gear on their identical workout routes—a hike at Runyon Canyon, a smoothie at this new place, that exercise class. I felt surrounded by an army of toned, ponytailed automatons, driven by a fear that if they let their guard down for even one second, their looks might start to slip, followed by their value. I did not want my value to be determined by my looks. My one concession, though, was driven by my mother's voice echoing in my head, and I did miss my mother. "You only get one face," it said. So I found a facialist, and I dutifully took care of it—not that anyone could ever catch a glimpse.

But one can remain an overgrown ragamuffin for only so long as one starts to climb the corporate ladder and enter a more serious dating space. Now, instead of strangers, I was harangued by well-meaning loved ones.

My best friend, Jenny, always perfectly put together, had her own way of addressing the issue. "Just let me brush your hair," she'd wheedle every once in a while, wandering into my bathroom in the home we shared. "It could look so nice." To avoid that weirdness—she's goal-oriented—I started to brush it more often. And how I dressed had also become a problem by my late twenties.

At work, my boss, Sharon, looked at me like my mother used to, like she was holding herself back from pinning me down. I routinely lost my shoes at work—wandering away from them in my office or in a meeting—and she joked I shouldn't go back for them. "Good riddance," she'd say. "You can't dress like a child for much longer." Fortunately, I was good enough at the job, and surly enough when approached, that she didn't do anything about it. But she leveraged this wish when she was helping me get a new job. "You have to promise you'll dress up and wear real shoes every day," she warned. I got the job, and I dressed up, and I wore real shoes.

Real shoes sufficed for upkeep until I was about thirty,

when my hair mysteriously started to fall out, and I went to a doctor to find out why. An ultrasound revealed my ovaries sitting there like two juicy clumps of grapes. The doctor whistled. Significant polycystic ovarian syndrome, she said, and I needed to make some lifestyle changes. "You're insulin resistant, which leads to diabetes," she told me, after all the bloodwork. "Try not eating any grains for three weeks, and we'll see if that shifts anything." Three weeks later, I was twelve pounds lighter, but I was resentful about it. The doctor recommended I avoid starches and sweets, and buy a scale, because any sudden weight gain could indicate further hormonal problems. I was not happy about this at all. *I didn't do this for you!* I wanted to tell anyone who complimented me. In LA, talking about people's changing bodies sometimes passes for conversation. I shouldn't have had to change mine. But it happened, because my other option was, supposedly, diabetes.

Though I was certain I could never find happiness in anything having to do with my physical appearance, I was starting to find joy in making others happy—my proud boss, my roommate. I let my mother dress me for my wedding, to make up for all those years of not caring. She went shopping in India with my measurements in hand and picked out clothes for the entire eventful week. This wasn't so bad, I thought. It was a lot of work, but it felt kind of nice to put in an effort, if it made her this happy. And the photos turned out so well. My family was pleased, and that felt good.

Then, on vacation, my new husband tentatively asked if I had packed any dresses. I bristled, probably while handwashing the same five T-shirts and three pairs of shorts I brought along on every trip. "They don't take up a lot of room," he mentioned sensibly, and that old ire popped up. *I shouldn't have to make myself pretty for you!* I thought. But then I thought, *Why not?* We were going out to dinner, he had to look at me, and I did appreciate when he wore a nice shirt, demarcating that thrilling transition from a tiring travel day to a romantic night out. I started to find a little room in my suitcase for dresses, because it made me happy to make him happy. I still refused to buy that full-length mirror, but his sweet smile and appreciation when I made the most minor of efforts was mirror enough.

Then, before I turned forty, everything changed. I looked in the bathroom mirror one day—just my top half, let's not get carried away—and hated what I saw. I was hugely pregnant, with a four-year-old who wasn't sleeping, and had planned an ill-advised summer trip to Paris, not calculating that I couldn't really get around a city very well, especially with an energetic preschooler, when I was pregnant, roasting, and exhausted. So, as I washed my face one morning, I took in my sallow skin and my greasy shoulder-length hair. I examined the dress I had worn nonstop, with the hole in the armpit—the one I often fell asleep in—and I thought, *I cannot live like this anymore.* Or, rather, *I do have to live like this, and I would like to wash my face and not be startled by the pallid Victorian ghost that stares back.* So I searched "best haircuts in Paris" and made an appointment.

I should have suspected something when the salon was inside a fancy hotel, but I had looked up a price list and it seemed like a reasonable splurge. I was about to have a baby, I felt terrible, and I was going to spend money on a haircut, because I deserved it. It felt like an appropriate price to pay for a visionary life upgrade. And everyone was so nice to me when I got there. The two gorgeous shampoo assistants and then the hairdresser, David, himself. Australian, friendly. He took in my limp, ragged hair, and his kind face betrayed nothing. "Would you be okay with chopping it all off?" he asked gently. "It would be nice to give your roots a rest." I said I needed a change, so he could do whatever he wanted, and I walked out with a tidy little bob. When it came time to pay, though, I stifled a screech. It was double what I expected—I clearly hadn't looked at the right price list. I went home almost in tears, and my husband had to comfort me. "But you look great. And you never buy anything, so . . . ," he reasoned, smiling, always my mirror. *Still,* I thought.

But then I started to feel the shift. I woke up, haggard, after another terrible night of sleep, the baby kicking my cervix, to brush my teeth. I caught myself in the mirror and marveled. My haircut was so polished! So chic! Even though my insides felt like sawdust, my outside no longer reflected it. I could actually see my face, the entirety of it, for the first time in probably decades. I turned to look at angles I had never noticed before. Even my ragged old clothes looked better, fresher, against the new shape of my hair. And I felt different. *What was this witchery?* I thought. *What magic had this David wrought?* The compliments continued when I got home. "You were meant for this hair," gasped one otherwise rational friend over lunch. The attention felt ridiculous—it was just a haircut. But I couldn't deny the power it was giving me. I was a little more energized, less deflated by my reflection in the mirror.

I wondered why I didn't feel the need to hide behind a sheet of hair anymore. And I noticed that, while I had been busy working and gestating, the lasers I had always felt on my back, my face, my body—assessing and tut-tutting, and measuring, and dismissing—had mostly disappeared. The invisibility that came with getting older had brought me a growing comfort. My declining value in the marketplace of sexiness—meant to be sad, I suppose—was also a relief. And the trend has only continued in my favor. As I get older, as people stop looking directly at me, I stand a little taller. I'm not scrutinized and scanned in the same way when I enter the room. The relief even allows me to see—really see—that I actually do like my face, and I don't need to hide it from anyone, not least myself.

Now I might try a bold red lipstick. Now I might wear a flashy dress. I've even started hiking, although it's not at (yawn) Runyon Canyon. I've found a quiet, overlong set of stairs up a hillside where I walk, quietly, with my pals, even if they don't know they're my pals: a Mexican granddad before work, four noisy brown teenagers on their way to school. All moving for the joy of moving, not the fear of what we might lose if we don't. Now I participate in the pageant. But without the crushing weight of everyone's expectations, without the feeling that I'm being graded by everyone and somehow coming up short. Because now I get to do it for myself.

Dotted Lines

If India is a woman's body, her arms outstretched to hold her billion babies, Kashmir is the unruly forelock above her right temple. Or at least, that's what I thought as a child, when my Nanaji took out his historical maps, pre-Partition and post-, to show me how we had been carved up. Since then, since the internet, I've zoomed in on that northwestern border countless times, tracing my fingers over the mess of dotted lines that vaguely indicate where I was born. If you log in from Pakistan, the Kashmir region is labeled as disputed. From India, it is a solid line, appearing firmly under Indian control.

I wonder if this regional shape-shiftiness contributes to my geographic malaise. I've moved so much that I can feel comfortable in most places but always thrum with the sense that I'm supposed to be somewhere else. I love it here: I have built a family, found some peace. But I also hate it here sometimes and feel stifled by the sameness. What a crazy place America is, where you can drive for three straight days and everyone's still speaking English, and all were seemingly raised on the same episodes of eighties television. But they'll tell me, in a lather, that the barbecue is *dry* here, whereas in another place it's more . . . *wet*. I stare blankly, feeling like an alien that's landed on a well-meaning planet, one that believes that it is the beating heart of the universe.

My childhood may have been a little overstuffed, but I sometimes miss how exciting and surprising things used to be. I miss being thrilled and consumed by the strangeness of an entirely new thing. I feel fortunate to have made my way to stability, but it means an unsettling similarity of routine. Still, every once in a while, something does break through the comfortable monotony of my American life, and my body is restless: a Great Passion, something that possesses me, infecting my thoughts while I'm racing to meet a deadline or pretending to listen to my children.

This time, it's a song called "Pasoori," by Ali Sethi. It's recommended to me by the music app on my phone, and from the first note I feel like I've known it forever—a traditional raga laid over a beat that sounds South Asian, Middle Eastern, and . . . is that reggaeton, all at once? The anguish in Ali's rich voice is so stirring that even before I can make out all the words, I know what it's about: a longing for a love you can never really have. Ali belts out a line about drinking down a destructive love, like poison. Shae Gill, his raspy-voiced partner in this duet, hopes his love breaks his heart.

"It's my favorite genre," says my friend Iva. "A love song that sounds like a threat." The song reminds me of a former colleague who set fire to a Duraflame log and placed it in the back seat of her ex-boyfriend's car. She watched it from the opposite sidewalk, and it was said that she'd calmly smoked several cigarettes while it burned. I'm still dying to know what he did to deserve it, but "Pasoori" would have been the perfect soundtrack. I share and forward, share and forward, obsessively listening to it on loop, until I track down Ali in New York and ask if we can hop on a video WhatsApp—official communication tool of the global diaspora—to talk about it. I need to know more about the incubation and birth of the song, and I need to connect with the person who has made me feel this way.

Ali was born in Lahore—not two hundred miles from my Srinagar—in the 1980s, in a family of dissenting journalists and publishers. His parents' home was full of jail-going writers and activists. His mother played a lot of Sufi music to counteract interpretations of Islam that she felt were making the rounds at the time. A parent-pleasing, eldest-child overachiever, he sang traditional ghazals to impress his parents' friends and to "hypnotize [his] bullies at school." In his early teens, he decided he wanted to know more about how the music worked: how did the great qawwals go off on mesmerizing riffs, weaving perfectly pleasing, seemingly unplanned patterns of melody and rhythm? How could they be so wild and free (which he secretly wanted to be) while remaining rigorous and rule-bound, as society dictated? It was a paradox that held some kind of key for him, and, ever a model student, he spent the next fifteen years training with traditional singers to grasp it.

As we talk, we laugh at our instant intimacy—Ali mentions that we look related, and we really do; he shares pictures of an aunt who could have been one of mine. But the closer tie is that we both grew up as bookish older siblings who strove for one thing while wanting another. We may both have thought our relationship to art an intellectual pursuit—me questing to read every word that had been published, he studying centuries of music under the most traditional of tutors. It seems funny now that I once thought I'd grow up to be a pediatrician who owned a lot of books, and Ali also felt the pull of a conventional path as a student of South Asian studies at Harvard. But in our conversations, I recognize my own fire in him.

As a child, I found it exhausting, even sometimes embarrassing, being the most intense person in the room. I felt like I cared so much more than anyone else did, about everything. A book, a painting, a song, a meal. As I grew, I learned to hide about half of that intensity so that I didn't kill every conversation with the sparks shooting out of my eyes and ears. But when Ali and I speak, there's no small talk—only an obsessive compulsion and the sheer agony of caring.

Our first conversation is a deep, quick dive that feels familiar, and I'm overwhelmed with a sense of relief. A loneliness I've been holding on to for years fades as we connect over our tormented youthful desire to make our communities proud. But neither one of us could shake the impulse to create, albeit in a way our parents and their friends could digest. Like me, Ali was also an older sibling who grew up adjacent to political turmoil, so he turned to the creative because he wanted to dwell in those parts of himself that felt untouched by ideology—"the parts of me that are strange, tender, willful, horny," he says, laughing, and I relate. On some level, he also felt compelled to soothe strife and create a feeling of safety, not just for himself but for everyone who heard him—starting with his younger sister, his community, and now his audience. He's drawn to themes common in traditional desi music: distance, yearning, the quest for union with an elusive or unreachable beloved—the themes that speak to him most powerfully as a queer person and also as a South Asian migrant in America.

His songwriting process starts with the tune, he says. He'll make an elaborate melody with nonsense words and then rack his brain for lyrics that fit the mood. "Pasoori" percolated in his brain after he saw a version of the first lyric—*Agg lavaan majboori nu*, "set fire to your compulsions"—painted on the back of a truck in Pakistan. What compelled that driver to such a passion, he wondered, and where else could it go? "Pasoori," which translates roughly to "difficult mess," is a song about an age-old situation: two people who are prohibited from meeting each other. Illicit love, tortuous trysts—the whole song is written in the metaphors of a classical "courtesan song." Except what prompted it was a very modern problem: Ali was invited to work on a project in India, where he has many friends and fans, and then told he couldn't travel there because of a new ban on Pakistani artists. "So I did what desi bards have done for ages," he says. Wrote a joyous, dancey song with layers of meaning. As he was writing it, he knew he wanted to make a larger case for the free movement of peoples and ideas, but enacted through the Trojan horse of a South Asian song-and-dance routine. The ensuing duet blends genres in the service of something that feels ancient and modern and speaks to everyone it reaches.

"Pasoori" has been engulfed in a tsunami of love since its release. Eight weeks in, the video had sixty-five million views on YouTube, and climbing. People stream it in villages, in cities, in regions where they don't even speak the language but furiously feel the vibe. Ali has gotten love letters from every stripe of diaspora desi, including parents who play it to their children every day, the way he remembers his mother used to play her qawwali tapes for him. The most exhilarating response, though, has been that this song has brought people together across the usual lines of difference. It feels, to him, as though individual identity has dissolved for a moment and been "reframed through a campy collective burlesque," he says, again laughing. "I'm so happy I could fly!" He's executed his vision in every way, once again that little kid who had wanted everyone to get along.

The song has stirred up some dormant feelings in me, too, reawakening a memory of who I used to be. I've had too many years of sitting at my desk and then rushing to pick the kids up at school. I am desi, so I love to dance. I am hungry for more songs that connect me to home, to my own body, my own feelings. The song makes me feel like the main character in my own life, not, as I often do, some harried back-office engineer trying to keep a bunch of bumper cars on a train track. So I search for more desi music, and take up more space in my home, and I make everyone listen to me blather on about it. I ask online what people back home are dancing to. I add every suggestion to a playlist and flail around the house, dragging the kids out of their seats to spin around the living room with me. I remember what it feels like to pump my arms and legs, to shake off my overdeveloped sense of duty, to be my whole self.

Then a friend in India recommends another Pakistani song, "Joona," by a twenty-four-year-old singer-songwriter named Hasan Raheem. As I listened to the guitar kick in, and his smooth young voice, I had an unusual response. First, more wild dancing. And then the deep dive online. I was charmed by the video, in which Hasan boogies his way through a supermarket while shopping for groceries. I, an inveterate supermarket dancer, am sometimes dampened by my children's protestations, but will be no longer. "This is who I am," I tell them, pointing to the video. "I can't help it, either." As I listen to his entire catalogue—all catchy, thoughtful, delightful, romantic, playful—I feel a lightness I haven't felt in years. "Bring me this child," I announce, into an empty room. Bring me the joyful young person who wrote this bop! Where is he? How do I find him?

Another desi friend laughs. "Welcome to the Hasan Raheem fan club," she says. "There are a lot of thirsty young ladies in here." Though I'm old enough to be his teen mom, she still nudges me to look up Hasan's birthplace. So I do, and I gasp. Gilgit sits near Srinagar in that familiar forelock, a hundred and thirty miles from my birthplace. The photos—towering mountains, fresh rushing streams, country boys smiling on wooden bridges—remind me of Kashmir, and this knocks the wind out of me. I miss it violently. I can feel and taste the water, smell the air. I want to dive into these photos; I'm desperate to feel home again. But when I try to calculate driving directions between Gilgit and Srinagar, Google Maps won't let me. It tells me walking would take one hundred hours, over an elevation of thirteen thousand feet. Maybe a couple hundred miles isn't a large distance in the United States. It's a distance we cover in a morning, stopping for breakfast, and ending in another city that mostly echoes our own. On the subcontinent, though, a couple hundred miles can traverse worlds of thought, epochs of history, a hostility that looms taller than the mountains. The American in me feels like these guys are my neighbors from just down the street, while the Indian knows such a distance can prove insurmountable.

But we do have the internet on our side, so Ali puts me

in touch with Hasan, and we set up a time to speak. Shortly before that time arrives, Hasan sends a message asking if we can push the call twenty minutes, because he's on his way home from the hospital. It's 9:00 p.m. in Pakistan, and I fret briefly before realizing he's not sick; he's working: in addition to being an R&B artist, he's a medical doctor. "What are you going to do about that?" I ask him, on a video chat—his fresh little fame-ready face filling the top half of the screen—and he grins, used to it. He has no plans to leave medicine. He wants to open a clinic with his friends from medical school, and a label with friends from the music world, to mentor other independent musicians in Pakistan. He says all this so casually that I envy him his youth, with its distance from the rigid expectations that I felt when I was his age. Ali, also on the call, laughs at this—our creative work, compared with Hasan's, can be so torturous, so overwrought. We both felt in our early lives that it was only permissible to create art rooted in our own cultures, to labor under the weight of our massive histories, and here comes this guy, chill Dr. Pop Star, writing about the day he had, dancing around a supermarket, wrapping us around his little finger, wishing we could also feel a little lighter, a little more like him.

I envy Hasan's ability to elicit such a wide range of feelings—rapture, nostalgia, tenderness, regret—all in his very first songs. We didn't grow up like that, Ali and I. When things were hard, we felt we needed to be okay, for everyone around us. For our siblings, to keep them calm. For our parents, to reassure them that their choices hadn't been in vain. It took me thirty-five years to learn I felt anything other than "fine" or "mad," I joke. And Hasan's so young—I wonder how he's already so emotionally fluent. He thinks, warmly, of his close-knit family. "My house was the kind of place where everyone—all my aunts, uncles, cousins—knew they could come, get a good meal, stay for ten days if they needed to. I saw a lot of happiness there—but on the other side of a big happiness there's often a big sadness, so I saw a lot of that, too. Maybe most people lose their connection to the sadness, but I guess I never did."

"Joona," which has taken over my brain, as well as the brains of the entire subcontinent, came from that same community-building ethos that's going to build his clinic and his label. On December 28, 2021, thinking about New Year's Eve, Hasan sent the song to his producer, Abdullah Kasumbi, with a simple melody, just singing over an acoustic guitar, and said, "Let's make this something we can dance to." Abdullah—clearly a savant—sent it right back, and they knew. Hasan spent the rest of the night dancing around his room, thinking, "Well, if *we* like it this much—we who made this song—people out there are gonna love it."

It's this freshness and excitement that draws me in, I think: the idea that there might be a life to carve out beyond subcontinental politics. Our countries still bristle with tension—they might always—but I'm encouraged by evidence of this generation's desire to create. And it's not just in the work. Hasan's music has a buoyancy that comes across in conversation with him. I confidently guess he's a baby brother, and he tells me he's the oldest of five. Ali and I marvel. Can that be? What's it like to be the oldest sibling in a South Asian family and feel that you can write about the small moments, about your personal experience, instead of our collective, interminable historical burden? And Hasan's nod to his own culture—his mountain roots—seem rooted in joy rather than duty, to delightful effect. There's a small crumb in the middle of the song in the Shina language—as complex and obscure as Kashmiri, although somehow entirely unrelated—and I ask what it means. "I'm talking to myself there," he says. "I'm saying, 'How long will you be writing songs for girls, Hasan? You have to change your recipe.' Then I agree with myself—'Yes!'—but the irony is, I start talking about the girl again in the next verse." He gives this sweet little nod to his native tongue, his people back home, while remaining completely himself in this small moment. Later, I tell Ali that I feel lighter after speaking with Hasan, as though he's given me further permission to seek this kind of joy in my own work.

"We're just having a bit of fun," says Abdullah Kasumbi with a laugh, when I ask him what enchanted potions he's been drinking to churn out his hit parade. He credits the internet. He learned how to play everything from tabla to guitar on YouTube, learned how to produce in his home studio. He, like me, has the desi itch to dance, and he, like me, sought out dance music while trying to escape the duty he felt to pursue a practical profession. "Dance music saved my life," he says, and I feel chills, thinking of my own miserable time as a law student, how I escaped to warehouses and basements in Detroit to save my own life, often dancing eight, nine hours straight, to emerge reborn. He nods, knowing the feeling. I ask if he'd ever move abroad, and he shakes his head. "I have an opportunity to change the story here," he says. There's an outdated narrative of what it means to be a young Pakistani man, and he wants to update and reshape that tired old tale—to amplify the vibrant creative community he's found in Karachi, to follow the impulse to create, and the music is only a small part of it. He's in a streetwear collective, directs music videos, produces for other artists, and creates original music. He has a lot more to say and do as an artist; those avenues for a long time could only be followed via emigration, but he gets to change that narrative on his own soil now. I know how it feels to be tied to a story: to tell people I'm from Kashmir is to see them flip through their mental files to land on "beautiful" and "tragic" before sympathy sets in and they sigh, ready to hear my sad story. Fortunately, it seems that, although previous generations are still shaken by the echoes of Partition, this one, thanks to the internet, might be ready to break free.

Still, I'm over forty now, and it's harder for me to deprogram myself. In the spectrum of the diaspora, I fall neither here nor there. I didn't grow up in India, I present as American, and I don't exactly relate to either. This can be disorienting enough without the petulant urge to scream, *It wasn't supposed to be like this*. We were supposed to move back to Kashmir. I've been lucky enough to have a complex and meaningful life. I wouldn't change a single twist or turn that landed me the partner, the kids, the job I enjoy now. But even if we hadn't stayed in Srinagar, even if I had eventually left to pursue other opportunities, I still carry an anger and sorrow about having the choice taken away. *Look at these kids having fun,* I think, now obsessively scrolling through pop concerts in India and Pakistan. This is the music I wanted when I was growing up, and now I'm twenty years too late and in the wrong country. How dare these kids have that much fun, and why wasn't I there?

Trouble between Pakistan and India has bubbled, sometimes at a simmer, sometimes a rolling boil, since their birth.

To be Indian or Pakistani is to be told, over and over again, that the other country is trying to kill us. There's a lot of evidence to support this. A checkered past, rich with violent subterfuge. Errant missiles, sometimes. Terrifying edicts from all manner of leaders. Like Ali, I wish it could be different. I wish I could undo threads of history, at least undo having to leave. If Partition itself can't be undone without creating a chaotic black hole, I'd still like to wipe out horrors that have echoed loudly through generations since. Could there possibly be a time when I could intervene, I think, to undo all religious strife in South Asia? It would be a dream beyond the limits of speculative fiction.

I examine the map again, that firm line outlining India's definition of India, forelock intact. But people born inside the forelock are Pakistani citizens. In a world where facts seem to be increasingly relative, we were pioneers: agreeing to disagree on where one country ends and the other begins. Even if we can't actually cross each other's borders—India and Pakistan do not generally issue visas to each other's citizens—Pakistanis were raised on the same diet of Bollywood movies, and Indian households sit down to their favorite Pakistani soap operas nightly. Now, thanks to the internet, we are able to connect with each other's art, to cross borders online that we can't in real life.

I wake up to pictures from Mum, who is currently visiting Kashmir after many years away, and I call her to catch up. I was nervous about this trip: the last time she went to Srinagar, fifteen years ago, she returned with a broken heart for her ravaged city. But she looks happy now, and tears prick my eyes as she shows me the sparkling lights around Dal Lake, glimmering like a necklace in the distance. "Is it normal?" I ask, but I don't believe her when she says yes. "Does it feel safe?" My tears wind fat trails down my cheeks, confusing my children. "What are you crying about?" they ask; they've never seen me do it. And I mumble some words about where I'm from. I tell them these are happy tears, but they're all kinds. Tears of relief that Mum is happy, at home. Tears for a childhood I never got to have, because I was weighed down with the reality of how the world actually worked. Tears for the extra time we might have had with family members, if we had never had to leave. Tears for the sense of community I craved but never quite achieved. Tears for the harmony I remember in the valley before it all went to crap.

I can't believe she's just there. Like a tourist, having a nice time. Dressing for dinner. But Mum was an adult when she left, and I was a small child, with my shattered fairy-tale memories. Any glimpse of home takes me right back to the sobs I choked out when our house finally burned down. She's distressed by my tears, which are getting steadily more dramatic. My nose is running now. "Do you want to be here?" she asks, worried. "Should you come?" I tell her I will come, when I'm ready, but I'm not ready yet. I compose myself, and Mum, gently redirecting me, asks what I've been up to. I fill her in on Ali, and Hasan, and my discovery of the Gilgit link. Like all Partition babies, she feels a reflex to distrust, but it wrestles with her fondness for an adorable mountain boy, especially one from just around the corner. I share Hasan's music with her, and as she takes it in, I can hear the thought we're both formulating: if not for Partition, that little cutie would be ours.

A Remarkably Self-Assured Debut

◁ 1928–1996 ▷

The day my grandfather came home to find a python coiled atop his bedroom door, my grandmother and her first baby, my mum, were nursing within. He fetched his rifle, shot it down, and displayed the massive skin, bullet hole and all, on the wall of the study, where, as a professor of physics, he later held office hours.

"No, that's ridiculous," says Mum now. "It wasn't on the wall. It was rolled up in the cabinet, but whenever the story came up in conversation, he'd unroll it." It clearly came up often enough for me to think of it as a permanent fixture, but whatever the facts, I would rather remember him casually working through physics problem sets with students trembling underneath a massive snake he killed.

Nanaji cut a dashing figure: A voluminous crest of salt-and-pepper hair, parted down the middle like an old-timey aviator. A chin dimple, a substantial mustache he waxed and twirled, posture that made him appear twice as tall. His booming voice summoned the kids home for dinner from across the block when necessary. A cigarette, somewhere, always. He was who boys who read Hemingway wanted to be, and his resourcefulness and showstopping presence would be his genetic legacy.

I can't separate my earliest memories of Kashmir from my memories of Nanaji's house. Nanaji and his younger siblings, whom I called Chhota ("Little") Nanaji and Auntieji, built my Matamaal, my mother's ancestral home, on a shared plot of family land in Karan Nagar, then a peaceful Srinagar suburb. Their father had dreamed of using it as a post-retirement yoga-and-meditation retreat for himself. An early demise cut that dream short, but the siblings built two stone structures—one large, four stories tall, for the brothers and their rowdy families, and a smaller second house, separate, for their sister, the more private, introverted Auntieji, and her quieter kids. In this solid joint-family compound they raised eleven solid children, nine girls and two boys. Mum was the oldest of the cousins, molded in her father's image, and relished her camp-counselor girlhood. "We had a new baby every other year!" she remembers with glee. She rattles off the nineteen-year spread: In her immediate family were Baby (my mother), Muni, Babbu, and Asha. Upstairs were Billie, Pinky, Daisy, Cherry, and Simi, and Raju and Nymphaea lived next door. She glows, remembering the parade of children. "It was so much fun!"

"What would you say Nanaji taught you?" I ask Mum, with a recording device at the ready, and she pauses. You have to understand, she said, that parenting was different then. Adults weren't really around much. The adults in her house, specifically, were vastly outnumbered by the children, and if the kids weren't at school, they were up to something, somewhere in the house, unsupervised. Adults only appeared at meals, and Nanaji brought down the wrath of Zeus when someone was in trouble, but that was about it for active parenting. His rulebook for the household, if you had to assemble one, consisted of three nonnegotiable pillars: study, don't lie, and don't embarrass the family.

A fourth pillar—a pillar of omission, I guess—was that Nanaji didn't want the girls to cook. Well, other than snacks sometimes, or tea. He didn't want them to clean, either, or do anything else considered "ladies'" work. The only useful pursuits for a young woman, he said, were those of the mind. And he enforced this in his distinctive way. After visiting a craft-loving cousin as a teen, my mother remembers settling into a corner with some borrowed knitting needles and yarn. No sooner had she started than his shadow loomed over her. "What are you doing?" he asked, knowing full well what she was doing. "I'm . . . knitting a sweater," she said. "Why?" he asked, that one word telegraphing the weight of his disapproval. "Did all the stores burn down?" She put the needles away and slunk off to fix a broken fuse—the general working of things was a permissible interest.

But Nanaji's choices were deliberate. My mother, and the women who followed her, grew up without the time suck of household duties, working instead on their minds, familiarizing themselves with the mechanics of the world at large in addition to the mechanics of the bulb that kept going out in one damp bathroom. "When you know how things work," my mother told me once, parroting him, "and you can use your knowledge to earn a living, nothing is scary." He was a blazing progressive for his day, and the upshot of all this was that Matamaal turned out an army of pathologically assertive women. The Kaul girls—doctors, engineers, professors, and some now grandmothers—have no patience for wallflowers or fools. They enter every unfamiliar room as though they own it.

Greet each stranger as though they've been reading up. Every summer night I slept there, I closed my eyes, happy and spent, listening to my Masis' heavy footfalls, their peals of raucous laughter at all hours of the night. Long, shiny braids swinging as they ran up and down the warren of stairs. Quick-talking voices that carried through layers of stone. I'm not sure anyone on that side of my family knows how to whisper, and I'm happier for it.

It was quite a soup to grow up in, and perhaps an unusual model of womanhood for the time—outspoken and uproarious. A quiet, thinky child, I wasn't sure I'd ever be as loud or confident. But it helped that I was loved so heartily. Imagine an empty cup under a gushing faucet. It fills up, it tips over, the faucet keeps gushing, and the cup thinks, *I really don't need any more water, but, okay, this feels nice.* That's the adoration I felt from my family. Their love, over time, made me feel invincible. And what Nanaji really taught the girls, what was baked into them forever, was to like themselves. He taught Mum that being smart and interesting was worthy of pride. That what anyone else thought or valued was irrelevant: strong minds and character were their greatest assets. "No one can take your mind away from you," he said sternly to his daughters and nieces and, eventually, to me.

The women of my family took that edict and ran with it. They are paragons of presence and poise, and, I soon learned, entirely unflappable. I remember waking up on the floor once, after falling asleep on the bed—and the adults chuckled at my scared little face. "Just a rumble in the ground," said my Cherry Masi, dismissing the earthquake that had tumbled me off the bed. "Nothing to worry about." She shushed me back to sleep.

Mum and I walked by a house that had been abandoned for a while, and Mum mentioned that it might have been "since the first air war. Maybe the second? Or that thing with China." The grown-ups were so casual about what seemed like really big deals, and I soon understood that we Kashmiris weren't supposed to be rattled by any disaster, natural or man-made.

Their attitude makes sense when you dive into the history of Kashmir, a place of staggering natural bounty that has been pillaged and fought over by gangs of marauders since time began. In addition to the thoroughly catalogued series of invasions and wars, Srinagar itself was prone to large-scale tragedy. The 1911 *Encyclopædia Britannica* runs almost incredulously through Kashmir's natural calamities up to the turn of the century: Srinagar burned down eighteen times, suffered ten major floods, eleven massive earthquakes—and all this before the Raj and bands of militants finished the job. Kashmiris are survivors a thousand times over, wired to anticipate and navigate eventful lives. And my grandfather symbolized everything I love about my people: fortitude, curiosity, bursts of drama, and the overwhelming sense that if countless bouts of cholera and frequent invasions didn't get us, nothing could.

On top of the cultural wiring, though, the Kashmiris I know tend to live plot-heavy lives. So many stories in our family start with an amusing little detail my mother remembers: The strange flap of skin on the back of my great-grandmother's head, like a warm little pocket the kids were allowed to stick their hands into if they were cold. The way she tucked back her bright-red braids and, in a whisper, asked her grandkids to sneak cigarettes from Nanaji's stash, after he made her retire her hookah. My non-Kashmiri husband stops me at these times. "Why is every story you tell me a folktale?" he asks, certain I must be making parts of it up. But it's all I know of our history. With nothing written down, I tell stories the same way my own mother told them to me. After a charming start, one must brace for calamity, because all Kashmiri stories, big and small, are rife with it. There's always something, and it's always sad.

It was always something, and mostly sad, for Nanaji as well. His father was an administrator in the police department, and, having been the first in the family to earn a college degree, he saw how it elevated his station, especially during the Raj. His education got him a stable job and allowed him to start a side business: buying a bus with two friends and hiring a driver who ran the route from Srinagar to Muzaffarabad (now in Pakistan). Charaghdin and Sons Transportation Company was the only link between the two cities at the time and kept Nanaji and his friends financially secure. Thanks to an ancient practice of tenant farming, the family also owned a parcel of land in the country, so seasonal deliveries of produce lined the halls: sacks of walnuts, almonds, and rice, so that even in cash-lean times they had food. The food, the land, the luck—it could all dry up, Nanaji's father often told him. But no one could take away an education.

His father died when Nanaji was fourteen, making him the man of the house. He had promised his dying father that no matter what, even if they had to beg, they'd get their little sister educated, and Auntieji ultimately became a professor of botany. Nanaji was on his way to a degree in physics when he married a young woman, who died a year later from complications of pregnancy. The year after his heart cracked came Partition, so sudden and bloody that their meal ticket, the Muzaffarabad bus driver, showed up one day without the bus, having left it in now-Pakistan during a raid. The bus was torched, and the driver had barely hung on to his life. The family business was done, and at nineteen, with two younger siblings and a mother to support, Nanaji started teaching physics.

A couple of years into his teaching career, he was nudged into remarrying, which is when my sweet grandmother, Nani, entered the picture. As with most arranged marriages of the day, it's hard to pinpoint if they had anything in common. But, if nothing else, Indians are great at staying married, and that's what they did. The food still came in, and with the addition of Nani to the household came her family ties to mustard fields, more rice—Kashmiris eat a lot of rice—and lentils. His marriage to Nani, though born of tragedy, ushered in a period of stability for Nanaji. Their first baby, my mother, showed up, and he liked her very much. Then the other three babies came along, and he took pride and satisfaction in what the family had built and who the children became.

Eventually, I was the house's new baby. Two weeks after I was born, Mum dropped me off at Matamaal so she could get back to the lab where she was wrapping up her PhD. Then the real fun began. With me, his first grandchild, my sharpshooting Nanaji softened. He loved to button up my fussy shoes, and doubled his commute to drop me off at nursery school, where he would linger at the gate to make sure I snagged a tricycle in the play yard. In the first years of my life, my dad was working in England, to lay the foundation for our eventual move. Without Dad's calming presence nearby, and with her own mother prone to tears, Mum leaned on Nanaji's iron spine. He held me as I got my first shots while she hid in the hallway, covering her ears. But my tears rattled even Nanaji. "You have to do that next time!" he said to Mum as I bawled into his shoulder. "She's going to hate me!" But he kept doing it, and I kept loving him.

What wasn't to love? It was like being the main attraction in a commune of sixteen acolytes. My youngest fan was Simi Masi, only ten years older than me, and the oldest was my devoted grandfather. They all took turns holding, feeding, and entertaining me. Simi Masi remembers when I started walking and Mum bought me a little pair of shoes that squeaked with every step. She would have been about eleven then, and the last two periods of her school day felt impossible as she counted down the minutes until she could come home and play with me and my noisy shoes. Daisy Masi says I would come sit with her as she got ready for university, and describes a ritual where I'd open up her jewelry box, take everything out, try it all on, and put it back before she had to leave.

I was the center of their universe, and I knew it, too. The house itself was a child's dream, a flap book come to life: Freely wandering up and down stairs, I found clusters of Masis, studying, or brushing their lustrous hair, or, more often, making one another giggle in a pile of colorful handmade quilts on the floor. One day we'd make flowers out of scrap paper, another day I'd be handed a small mortar and pestle to crush cardamom and almonds for kheer, Indian rice pudding. Pinky Masi helped me add the fragrant powder to warm milk, Chhoti Nani (Chhota Nanaji's wife) added sugar and rice, and we watched it simmer.

Inevitably, I ate too much kheer and needed to lie down, so I climbed the spiral metal staircase tucked away in the back of the upstairs kitchen. Perched atop the house was a room made entirely of glass, like a tiny greenhouse, in which we stored our winter linens. I could sit there with whatever books I was into at the time—mythology-heavy *Chandamama* comics in early days, Pippi Longstocking later—and snack for hours. The sun burned hot, hot, hotter, until I felt it singe the fine hairs on my forearms. Then I opened the door, which led directly to a tin roof, and peered out at the neighborhood, pretending I was the captain of a large metal boat: the SS *Villa Villekulla*.

Unlike my idol Pippi, I had an army of adults catering to my every wish. Ever hungry, I could go have dinner in Auntieji's orderly kitchen, where she would first help me change into Japanese wooden sandals; the clack of them on her stone floor was often the only noise in the house. While waiting to be fed, I could wander around upstairs, where the main bedroom hid a closet with a false back. Nymphaea Masi helped me climb into a dark pile of pashmina shawls wrapped with mothballs and cedar, and tumble out in the guest room, my own little Narnia. Raju Mamu might take me for a quick ice cream run in his red Maruti hatchback—naturally, I sat in the trunk—and after a peaceful chat with Auntieji, soothed by her quiet, calm manner, I could return to the chaotic main house, claim not to have eaten, and have everyone shower me with snacks anew.

My earliest memories of Nanaji are impressionistic, but I remember sensing that he liked all the things I liked about myself, and I liked all the things he liked about himself. He loved me most of all the children (this is fact); he liked that I was dead stubborn and a little strange. He liked that I didn't like the bathroom—a damp concrete box with a bare bulb and bars on the windows—so Nani hosed me down on a tiny folding chair in the front yard whenever I was due for a bath. I'm not sure where I peed, but I don't remember outside being a big deal. He liked that I told people what I thought, to their faces. "Why does her voice sound like she has a cold in her nose?" I asked of one gossipy neighbor on the way to school, at full volume, and even though he shushed me, I knew he enjoyed it. He wasn't one to express affection through language, but I knew at an early age that he respected me. He liked my mind; he liked how it worked. He taught me that being difficult was fine—preferred, even—if it was an expression of my true self. As I grew older, my true self—sometimes prickly and asocial—created a distance between me and my peers. Whenever the distance felt like too much, I returned to this feeling—*Nanaji loves me*—and stayed the course.

Nanaji loved things besides me as well. He loved his Royal Enfield motorcycle, which Nani made him retire after he took her to the market on it and the engine ripped off her sari. He loved drinking his tea with lemon and honey, anathema in our milk-and-sugar culture. He loved holding court on the porch, smacking his flyswatter down with a vigor that broke off its head, then soldering it back together with his cigarette lighter. Although we ate all our meals with our hands, Nanaji loved eating with a spoon, one edge of which he had sharpened for cutting meat. He loved dunking his fake teeth in a tall glass of water after dinner, cackling at everyone's horrified faces.

An otherwise serious man, he had a passion for Hindi film, most of all the musical aspect, and specifically the actress Jaya Prada. He called me into his room more than once to pop in a VHS and show me her dancing. "You see that?" he said. "That's training. Classical training, not like these other actresses, just wiggling about." I could never tell the difference, but his fervent attitude that One Must Have Standards never left me. He taught me that our worth lay in who we *were*, in who and what we loved, not in what we had done. He valued interesting, good, and true over nice, conventional, and pleasant.

He only ever disapproved of three things I did.

One was the whistling. For all his insistence on raising strong women, he thought anyone who whistled was rude. I told him I enjoyed it, and the compromise was I'd only do it out of earshot.

And then, in the summer of 1988, the ChapStick Incident. My parents and I were living in Saudi Arabia at the time, although we always came home for the summer. I'm not sure what it was about that year that smudged my normal sense of self, but, out of nowhere, I started to care about what other girls were doing—and other girls at the American International School in Riyadh were hoarding jelly bracelets and Lip Smackers. "So important," said Ayesha on the bus, reaching for her raspberry tube. "The desert air, you know."

I definitely did not know, but I wanted to. I begged my mum to buy me some ChapStick and took a three-count with me to Kashmir that summer. In retrospect, I must have known it would enrage Nanaji, my sudden vanity, but, like him, I wanted to see what would happen if I poked a bear. "Who are you copying?" he asked suspiciously as I smeared a greasy circle around my mouth, multiple times a day. "Nobody!" I insisted. "My mouth is VERY DRY." I overheard him arguing about it with Mum. "It's not right for her to be concerned with her looks," he said. "Next she'll be on to makeup." "She'll outgrow it," said Mum, but in that moment I doubled down. "When can I wear real lipstick?" I asked Mum, who sighed and told me, as she did for everything else, "When you're fourteen." When I reached fourteen, Nanaji's voice echoing in my head, I couldn't think of anything less important.

The last time was about his cigarettes. One middle school summer, self-righteously inflamed by anti-smoking adverts, I flushed his newest carton down the toilet one by one, and he came roaring for me. "I'm just going to buy more!" he yelled. "I'll flush those down, too!" I screamed right back. He started to hide them—in utility closets, in his study, once in between a pillowcase and a pillow in his room—but I found them there as well. Though he was furious, he seemed to recognize his own iron will in me. I never got him to quit, but, again thanks to him, it was never in my constitution to stop trying.

When political unrest came to Kashmir in the 1990s, and the Hindu families left, Nanaji and Nani moved to nearby Jammu, and eventually to a high-rise tower apartment in Delhi. They were safe, but I could see his discomfort at being exiled from his element, a discomfort that radiated out to the rest of us. Even though our extended family members had all landed else-where by this point, our center of gravity had shifted, become diffuse and confusing.

Nanaji had raised a magical family, in a magical place, at a magical time, and leaving that place unmoored us all. The sprawl and congestion of Delhi wore on him, and summer vis-its to India lacked the joy of our stays in Kashmir. They became check-ins, just making sure everyone was okay, was hanging in, had enough to do, enough financial and emotional support to get by. But Nanaji needed long walks and fresh air. He needed a job where he felt like he was making a difference. And we all needed him to have that, because our sense of security lay in his. Though he was still the same person, it was hard to see those avenues of joy and enrichment cut off for him. Hard to see him outside the role of earthy patriarch. He had been the sun that made us all feel safe and warm in the solar system of our Matamaal, and now, with his previous life gone, he was an emperor in exile, his light and warmth diminished.

In the summer of 1996, before my senior year of high school, we received a call in the middle of the night, which always meant bad news from back home. When Mum got off the phone, she was in tears. Nanaji was in the hospital. He'd been on his scooter and had been sideswiped by a bus. My mother flew to Delhi to be with him as he spent a month in the ICU. She flew back after being told he was on the mend. His lungs gave out a week after she got back. He was sixty-eight. I don't know if he could have held on if I had convinced him to quit smoking. But even as Kashmir was fading slowly from our lives, each building from our memories literally going up in smoke, Nanaji suddenly ceased to be, and I never got to say goodbye to him.

But, as with my memory of his menacing snakeskin, I've created a tableau of his last moments of health, as clear as if I had witnessed them. I close my eyes and see him perched on a wobbly scooter in a jam-packed Delhi rush hour. It's dusk, and he's weaving in and out of traffic. In my mind, he is wearing a white kurta tunic and matching pajama bottoms that glow against the murky air. He raises a handkerchief to his runny nose to shield it from exhaust, loses his balance and, in a slow-motion blur of clanging, his life.

The bus floored him when he was headed off in an ill-timed effort to pay his electric bill. He was whisked away to the hospital, and the medical staff might have been able to piece him back together, if not for his lungs. He was gone too soon, everyone says. I said it, too. But I wonder now whether it would have crushed us all to see his slow and steady decline, whether he was always meant to exit our world as powerfully and dramatically as we remember him in it. He was never meant to be frail, forgetful, or human. Not like the rest of us.

Nanaji didn't leave us with many physical objects, just a handful of well-trodden memories, stories I beg my mother to repeat, and the single photo album my grandmother brought with her when she finally immigrated to Toronto in the late 1990s. And my cousins are so much younger than me that they never experienced Nanaji in full effect, in his seat of power. But he's all around them, I say. He's in my mother's knack for reducing a crowd of children to fits of giggles, but also in the way she glowers at misbehavior and has them stand to attention. He's in my utter inability to be anything but my true self, even if others sometimes find that self rude. He's in how we all navigate the world: with openness and a comfort about our place in it. We may have lost our Matamaal, but we carry it, and him, with us.

To that end, I've covered my own children with the same blanket of adoration that swaddled me, in hopes they'll slowly gain an armor of unshakable confidence. My nine-year-old is eternally skeptical. "Don't all parents tell their kids they're the best?" he asks, eyebrow raised. "Yes, but they're all wrong, because mine are," I say, as my mother said aloud to me, as Nanaji implied to both of us. I'm hoping eventually he'll stop questioning it, and my outer voice will become his inner one. But our little girl is already wading in the deep end of her self-assuredness. She treats labels—animal names, colors—as inconveniences; if she feels that a shirt is blue one day and pink the next, who is anyone to argue? She, like my Masis, walks into every room as though she built it with her bare hands and she's proud of her work. She's only four, and she loves herself. And, as I learned from Nanaji, my job is to enjoy her company, cuddle her when she's in pain, support her education, and mostly stay out of the way. Nanaji taught us that who we are is worth celebrating. And though it was never expressed in so many words, I know, when I look at my babies, what Nanaji felt when he first saw my mother, or me: I'm so proud of them, and they haven't even done anything yet.

On Language

Anyone can say "I love you." Not everyone can say the things my mother does, not even I. *"Myon zuv!"* ("My life!") she squeals to my children in Kashmiri, as she did to me. *"Shoosh myon, redhu myon, poot myon!"* ("My lungs, my heart, my teeny-tiny baby chick!") She would cut her organs to bits for them, she says. Smother them under her bosom. Put them in her pocket and carry them around all day. Turn into a teeny-tiny bird and watch them sleeping from their windowsills. "Love" is laughable. It can hardly compete.

This is how I was accustomed to being addressed when we arrived to live full-time in Britain from India, when I was almost three. I was bundled off to nursery school in the warm, aggressive embrace of Mum's words, not speaking one crumb of English, and that first, mute week was a bust. My teachers radiated sweetness, but that wasn't enough to surmount the fact that we couldn't connect over language. I couldn't be comforted by their words in this new place. But I took it all in, and my little brain did what little brains do. Mum says I was quiet and dispirited until that Friday, when she asked how my day was, hoping for something better than a shrug. I looked at her askance and supposedly said, in English, "Oh? You no speak English?"

I learned quickly that I didn't need much to express myself—just a small collection of essential words: "please," "thank you," "sorry," "yes," "no," colors, numbers, "I want ___," "where is ___," "help," and some foods. Exaggerated facial expressions and hand motions filled in the gaps as my vocabulary expanded. Between the onslaught from school and cartoons, my third language was soon far more comfortable than the two we spoke at home. I don't think it was English itself that I loved—I wasn't especially drawn to the sound of it—but I took growing satisfaction in having clusters of new words start to make sense. Competence turned into a love of the language once I started reading, and I learned to take deep pleasure in expressing myself in my adopted tongue.

As I grew, surrounded by immigrants of all backgrounds, I became more and more attuned to scraps of language in general. I was drawn to the calming "zh-zh-zh" of Serbo-Croatian, which felt like having my head scratched as I fell asleep on someone's lap. I traced the shapes of Khmer lettering, lined up like a row of elegant, dancing birds. I taught myself the Cyrillic alphabet one summer. *"Mockba,"* I muttered to remind myself, laboriously writing out "Moscow." I loved existing on that precipice I first encountered in nursery school—just before the tipping point where cacophony starts to make sense. I took French in school and Italian in college. I've started to study Spanish many times, forever chasing the high of that original linguistic click. But my favorite language in the world will always be the one I left behind.

Kashmiri is a magnificent tongue twister of a language. It's such a reflection of the core values of my people—so sharp, funny, and specific—that I end up reaching for it in situations I can't describe in English. I'll call our toddler a *"khin-metz,"* a snot-smeared, wild-eyed child. "This has neither neck nor tail" *("Na ho't kun, te na lo't")* might sprout out of my mouth when I'm confused, or, my favorite, "I hate it with both my eyes!" *("Don ech'hin chhum kharan!")* The language, like my family, is wildly affectionate but also highly dramatic: If a cousin didn't feel like studying, my Muni Masi might say, *"Accha, tel'i dimmuv kitaa'bun naar?"* or "Great, so should we set the books on fire?" A messy teen, I was daily awarded a "gold medal" in *"tsot vahravun,"* or "carelessly tossing garbage about," and I remember Mum's friend Nirja Auntie wrangling her son Vikrom to tidy up: "If anyone broke into the house, they'd think someone's been here already."

On our most maddening days, we (still) might hear *"khash kar'ai,"* a thrashing that literally means "I'll cut you." It's much cuter and less homicidal in person, and no one ever lifted a finger against us. But with that kind of imagery, they didn't have to. In my own parenting, I admit that my native tone can sometimes scare the children, and other parents. "If you turn that corner, you'll get kidnapped," I toss out, casually, to the alarm of passersby. "What? That's terrifying!" screams my son, screeching his new bike to a halt. Is it? Not to a woman raised with threats of flaming textbooks, used to the threat of a parental knifing.

But still, I relish a good English sentence, spoken or written. I highlight books and write down overheard bits of dialogue. I remember first reading Elif Batuman's *The Possessed,* a memoir of her time in a graduate student program in Comparative Literature. I must have underlined close to one-third of the book, cackling as she described a colleague as "average in both appearance and demeanor, like some kind of composite sketch."

But beyond its being funny on its face, I loved her shorthand for the cultures she travels through—always in the context of language. Of her ancestral home, Turkey, she writes, "Most people just weren't into novels at all. They liked funny short stories, funny fables, serious fables, essays, letters, short poems, long poems, newspapers, crossword puzzles—they liked practically any kind of printed matter better than novels. Even in 1997, of course, there was already Orhan Pamuk, already writing novels . . . and you could see how miserable he was about it." And on Russian, her chosen field: "When the Russian Academy of Sciences puts together an author's *Collected Works,* they aren't aiming for something you can put in a suitcase and run away with."

She ultimately spends some time in Samarkand, finding that "Old Uzbek had words for wanting to cry and not being able to, for being caused to sob by something, for loudly crying like thunder in the clouds, for crying in gasps, for weeping inwardly or secretly, for crying ceaselessly in a high voice, for crying in hiccups, and for crying while uttering the sound *hay hay.*" The observation offers insight into a specific culture while also making me think of the endless variation on organs my mother would have sacrificed for me. But, like my mother, Batuman also made me laugh, ending this passage: "What did you know about Uzbekistan once you learned that Old Uzbek had a hundred different words for crying? I wasn't sure, but it didn't seem to bode well for my summer vacation."

Reading her memoir was the first time a book in English made me feel the same way that being immersed in Kashmiri does—like wandering through a garden maze of linguistic left turns. Sentences bursting with hyperbole. Unusual combinations of simple words that could reduce me to giggles. An almost Dada approach to metaphor: "Comparing Tolstoy's *Works* to Babel's is like comparing a long road to a pocket watch," she writes, making as much and as little sense as our Kashmiri proverbs. Her work made me feel less alone, for I had found another bookish woman who had gotten lost in the shrubbery of words and never wanted to leave. Here was someone else who saw that language was a landscape and offered a key to the psyche of its people. And whatever fortuitous combination of traits led to the way her words tickled me, thirteen years and as least as many reads later, I own three dog-eared copies of her book, in case I lose two.

But with all my enthusiasm for perfect English sentences, they still pale against a perfect Kashmiri one. "I'd remove your thorns with my eyelashes" was a new one from Mum last week—*"Ech'er valuv seeth kadey kend."* It hurts me to receive those feelings but not be able to give them back to her, because I'm ashamed to say I don't really *speak* much Kashmiri. I understand it completely, but once I learned English, it stuck. It was faster, and easier, for me to integrate if I spoke in the language of my thoughts. "What language do you dream in?" I've been asked, when people learn that English isn't technically my first. English, I say, always English. But I wish it wasn't. I dream *of* speaking in Kashmiri, because English never feels enough, somehow. How are the kids going to feel the depth of my love, I think, if I'm limited by tidy English phrases? And will I ever be as funny to them as my mother, who has the wildness and intensity of our native tongue at her disposal?

I think about this often under my mountain of cultural guilt. Because of our scattered, shrinking community, I was raised with a stronger-than-usual emphasis on preserving the culture, the food, the language. This extended to marrying within the community, and I tried to meet a nice Kashmiri boy, I really did. Strangely, it wasn't that easy to find one, working in entertainment in LA in the early aughts. So I met and married a wonderful guy from New York, who doesn't speak one word of Kashmiri (although he'd probably love to), and we speak English together.

There's a tired trope in immigrant-themed movies: "Mom, Dad, I'm American now!" the protagonist shouts, and the parents begrudgingly accept it. *This is how we do things in America* is the gist, and immigrant parents had better get in line. But it's a false argument, as anyone who's been through the process can tell you. The fight has never been with my parents; it's with myself. Building a life outside our tight-knit community meant the closing of a door and the grief that came with that. I wasn't necessarily ready to assimilate, because that meant leaving behind a piece of the culture I was raised with, in a way that can't be easily replicated. I hear no Kashmiri in my day-to-day life unless I'm talking with my parents, and to practice it, all alone in my home, would feel isolating. Everyone is full of advice about this. To raise kids as bilingual, they say, each parent should talk to the children in their native tongue. But this is unworkable for me. My husband wouldn't understand what I was saying to them, so how could we all laugh at the same thing?

The joy of raising dual-culture children, for us, was going to be about passing down the best of both worlds. My husband is Jewish, so, when the kids are of age, they'll start taking steps toward bar and bat mitzvahs, a proper training in their Jewish heritage. I do my part—I cook Kashmiri food, we celebrate our holidays, we have our attire on lock. But I wring my hands about the language and wonder how to build the children a bridge. They're starting to be old enough to spend some of their summer vacation with my parents, who can (and will) immerse them in our language. But in the meantime, I've been watching closely, collecting scraps of evidence that an inherent love of words will blossom in both. Any words, even if they're not in Kashmiri yet.

I seem to be in luck. "A spectacular baby," our son called our daughter when he was four. He tears through his chapter books, bursting in, bushy hair on end, to ask for definitions: "Perplexed"! "Secretary"! "Brassiere"! We give him most, and fumfer around others, especially when he gets into the newspaper. He does that thing all voracious readers do, where he knows how to read a word, and what it means, but not how to pronounce it ("BRACE-ee-uhr!"). He notices my delight at his verbal curiosity and plays around with it.

"I need to tell you something the baby does when you're not around," he said to me, solemnly, when she was one. "She makes up long words and says them in a clear voice." He knew nothing would make me happier, or more frustrated. There's the sharp, funny, and specific that I love.

He also may have willed something into being, because the toddler wasn't far behind. She showed a strong preference for the more chewy parts of the dictionary. The standard "Hi!" and

"Dada" quickly gave way to "octopus" ("oppodippo"), "helicopter" ("hakaliko"), and "jalapeño" ("jalapeño"). She'd roll a new word around in her mouth, use it in a brief, take-charge sentence ("Oppodippo, sit, watch me eat oatmeal"), and then practice it in her crib until she fell asleep. Her bravery in the face of consonant clusters will serve her well, if and when she ever picks up Kashmiri.

The way the children use words together is playful and joyous, sating the same hunger that conversations with my parents always have. In these moments, seeing them delight in language, I do feel some inner peace, knowing for sure that I'm raising Kashmiri kids after all. They may not understand the language yet, but there's still time for grandparent lessons, or textbooks. And we cherish moments like the time when, as we put the baby to bed, she smiled up at Dada and said, clear as a bell, "Dishwasher." Intention set, she cuddled in with her loveys to practice her new favorite word. An affectionate, ridiculous chatterbox, Kashmiri through and through. *Myon redhu, myon shoosh, myon zuv.*

My heart, my lungs, my life.

You Are My Life

The only grudge I ever held was in nursery school, thanks to a tiny witch named Christina. I couldn't have been more than three years old. Mum had just dropped me off, given me a big smooch, and left me alone near the books before the pressure of morning song circle. Then this mean little girl sidled up to me and said "EWWWWW!" in my ear. "EW WHAT?" I asked, and she said, "Why does your mother kiss you on the mouth? That's disgusting." I didn't get into an argument about it, not right away, but I narrowed my eyes as she ran off. I didn't care what she said about me. But my mother? The center of the cosmos, my best friend? I filed away that outrage for later use.

Mum and I spent a lot of time together when I was a baby, which I guess is standard, but I mean more than most. Dad had left for the UK, to sort out a life for us, and we stayed back in Kashmir as Mum wrapped up her PhD thesis. On days when she had to run to the lab, she dropped me off at Matamaal so Nani could take care of me, but other than those brief separations, I was somewhere on or near Mum's body: we ate and slept together. With Dad thousands of miles away, his only presence the frequent letters I couldn't read yet, Mum and I became an inseparable unit.

On our first trip to visit Dad, I was a toddler, and England felt daunting to Mum. She remembers a time when we ran errands all day and, exhausted, stopped to get something to eat. Mum splurged—two pounds!—on a few hot dogs for us to share, and it wasn't until two bites in that she understood they were beef, which we didn't eat. She tried to wrestle mine away from me, but I had it firmly gripped in my chubby hands and managed to stuff the remainder into my mouth before she could get at it. She threw hers away, stared sadly at the garbage can, and wiped the ketchup off my face, feeling dismal about having wasted food and money, and failing to feed her child properly. Shortly thereafter, Mum and I returned to India. She planned for us to travel back and forth, because she wasn't entirely ready for a move.

By the time I was two and a half, she felt more prepared, and we shifted from Srinagar to England. At the time, it was a thirteen-hour flight with five stops: Delhi—Karachi—Dubai—Frankfurt—London. This sounds horrible, I know, but flying felt so different then. Seats were bigger, entire rows empty, so Mum could put up the armrests and we'd pretend we were in a long, skinny bed. Cheerful Gulf Air flight attendants checked on me the entire time, and I got a little box of toys when I boarded to keep me busy. I loved it all, and international travel felt as glamorous and welcoming as my mother had always hoped it would be.

Less welcoming was my attitude toward Dad, after almost a year apart. "What's this uncle doing in our room?" I said on our first night together again. "Is he going to sleep here?" I looked him up and down, skeptical, and parked myself right in the middle of the bed. And that was our life for a while.

Dad worked the hours of a young doctor on call, and though my parents were grateful to be in the same place, it felt like the beginning of an arduous journey for Mum, even with me, her tiny teammate. It must have been difficult not to have any family or friends in the area, and she did try leaving me with a babysitter one time, a West Indian woman who ran a small day care out of her home. That didn't work so well. "Your daughter says 'what' instead of 'pardon,'" she said, stern, at pickup. "She needs to learn some manners." Mum silently got my things, lips pursed, jaw clenched against starting a fight, and we both knew we were never doing that again.

So, she decided the team would remain just the two of us. Mum knew, when we moved, that she only ever wanted one child. Her pregnancy with me had been difficult, nine straight months of nausea, and the birth had been a nightmare: a ragged C-section that gave her a four-pound baby. Then her husband had to leave for an entirely different continent, after which she had to get upright and finish her doctorate before joining him. She wasn't riding high on working motherhood, didn't foresee adding another kid to the mix, but no matter. She was going to pour all her energy into me and making a home for us in England.

She remembers the initial thrill of exploring freely—no family members keeping tabs on where she went, or with whom, entire days to spend as she pleased. She had felt safe in the small-town comfort of Srinagar, where everyone knew her family, but tired of what she calls "the gossip hotline." If she did anything out of the ordinary—talked to a shopkeeper, had an unscheduled ice cream, whatever—by the time she got back home, everybody knew about it. As a married woman with a young child, and her in-laws' family and hers watching her every move, it must have felt stifling. So in London, free from that, she began to build days around her own curiosity. When I was tiny, before I started school, she created a routine for us familiar to parents around the world: a walk along the high street, a stop by the grocers' to collect provisions for dinner, and a visit to the library. I fell in love with a yellow teapot in the window at Argos, she says, and I made her walk by every day so I could check on it. It couldn't have cost more than nine or ten pounds, she said, but that was too much for us then. It made her happy enough just to watch me stare at it.

Her wobbly immigrant legs led to some memorable missteps, like an attempt to buy oranges from a greengrocer who told her "fifty p a pound, love." Mum froze, and scurried home, almost in tears. She didn't know what she had done to make the grocer fall in love with her, but she was never going back to him again. It took her a few months to register that he called everyone that, and that *everyone* called everyone that. Mum went slightly farther afield from there, trying new grocers, seeking out other vegetables that reminded her of home, but she stayed within a safe, walkable radius while she got used to her big new life.

For maybe the first time, the outside world seemed as vast and exciting as her imagination. She'd grown up surrounded by master storytellers at Matamaal. If Raju Mamu wasn't eating, for example, Auntieji might make up a fable about a little mouse whose wife ate his dinner. If one of the kids was dawdling, they were chastened by an impromptu, grave story about a rabbit who missed all the fun the other rabbits were having. And she continued weaving these tales with me. Her blurry lines between fact and fiction mirrored a child's, which held me, an actual child, in thrall. Her passion for elaborate story-telling added an enchanting layer to our otherwise ordinary life. One time, she pulled me aside to whisper about some-thing she had just read in the newspaper. "There was a special doll," she told me, like it was a secret, "that was taken care of so well by her owner, who carefully brushed her doll's hair every night, that over time it started to grow, like real hair." My eyes widened, and I ran upstairs to pull my lone doll out from wher-ever it was, probably in a drawer. After a week with no visible change, I marched up to her, furious. I asked if she'd made it up, to make me play with the thing. She remained mysterious. "Maybe it doesn't work for all of them," she said. I couldn't even get mad at her, because I recognized it was a good story, and an even better trick.

Once I started nursery school, I had my own, separate world to map out. I had had such an entertaining, competent companion in Mum that no one else was up to snuff—I didn't express a lot of interest in other kids. Maybe I'm understat-ing this. I asked recently, and I thought jokingly, what my chal-lenges had been as a small child, and Mum quickly answered, "No interest whatsoever in social interaction, and an aversion to crowds." I did love my teachers, and started a lifelong habit of sitting right up front, under their noses, hand up high. They had so much to offer—their smiles warming me like the sun, their patient answers to my endless questions. The other kids? They were just stumbling around, taking up space.

While I was at school, Mum started venturing around Lon-don in earnest, her nerves about the big, labyrinthine city outmatched only by her curiosity. She knew that she had to venture outside the neighborhood, so, one day, she rode a bus to the end of the street, or at least the last part that she recognized seeing on foot. The next day, she took that bus an extra stop. The day after that, two extra stops. She made her way to the end of the line, and the day after that, transferred. Eventually, she had mapped out a large enough radius from our flat so that she felt powerful enough to try the underground.

And what did she find on her explorations? The clean roads of multiple high streets. Sainsbury's supermarkets, with their organized rows of anything she might need and tons of things she didn't. Woolworths, where she purchased her first household possessions—pans, knitting needles, yarn—so many starter items that, a million lifetimes later, when she heard it was going out of business, she cried a little. She made her way to Elephant and Castle, then a few streets over to the open market. Another day, she peeked into a fabric store near the open market, and started to pick up odds and ends to make some clothes and decorate the house.

After her daily outing, she'd come pick me up from school; we'd swing by the library and hurry home before cartoons started. "I hadn't seen anything!" she says, and she wanted to catch up on it all. So, in those early days, before I could read, we settled in to *Tom and Jerry, Sesame Street*—whatever was on, it was all wildly entertaining for both of us. After I went to bed, her attention turned to (more) television, and specifically the screen adaptations of the books she had read and reread. Like every other woman in the world at the time, she was riveted by Richard Chamberlain's tormented priest in *The Thorn Birds*. Jeffrey Archer's page-turner *Kane and Abel* became a three-part miniseries starring Sam Neill. A miniseries about

JFK's presidency called *Kennedy*. And, of course, the 1977 BBC adaptation of her favorite book, *Anna Karenina*.

Mum was settling into contentment. But the distance from home ached, until her sole friend in England, sweet Auntie Razdan, tipped her to Southall. "It was like being able to go to India every month!" she says. And once she found a good butcher in Green Street, who would cut the lamb exactly like they would at home, she didn't miss a thing. Any vegetables she needed, any spices, anything from home—it was all there, in a biweekly visit to Ambala Sweets.

Meanwhile, at school, I persisted in my unmatched ability not to need or make friends. One November day, we were all locked outside the building for playtime, and I didn't understand why. It's not that I had a problem with rules; I just wanted them to make sense, and being outside in the cold was irrational to me. I surveyed my options.

In one corner of the drizzly, gray, cold playground was a little folding table where two local mums sold Hula Hoops, a circular potato snack that fit snugly on chubby little fingers, for fifty pence a bag. I had already had one of those. Off to my left were the bathrooms, with little boys and girls darting in and out. Actually, it looked like the girls were darting in and out while the boys waited excitedly at the entrance, breathing heavy plumes into the frigid air. I tugged on the warm coat of the playground matron near me, who was whispering schoolmarm secrets to another teacher.

"Excuse me, miss. Can we go inside?"

"Not until playtime is over, pet," she responded, and went back to her gossip.

"But it's cold," I pointed out.

"Run in a circle." She gestured to a group of girls who were doing exactly that, in a never-ending game of tag. I didn't want to join in, really, but anything was worth a try. I lasted about a minute and then huffed and puffed my way back.

"It's still cold, miss!" I pointed out, hoping to convince her to unlock the door and let us into the cozy warmth of the radiator-lined building.

"Run faster, then!"

Giving up on my ability to persuade this one particular adult, I walked purposefully toward the bathroom, which was at least shelter, and possibly warmer than the wet London fall. The same two girls, blond curls flying, kept running in and out. It wasn't until I got closer that I understood what they were doing: taunting the boys at the entrance with glimpses of their flesh. Sweaters tied at their waists, both girls had their shirts unbuttoned and knotted over their flat chests, in naughty beachwear style. My sudden appearance didn't deter them in the least, or tear the five-year-old oglers away. Rather, Christina, for she was one of them, grabbed my arm, dragged me inside to the safety of the stalls, and said, "You should do it, too!"

"Do what?" I asked.

"Unbutton your shirt and tie it up. The boys are going bonkers!"

"Why do you want to drive them bonkers?"

She thought about this for a second too long, and decided, "The attention is nice?" before running off to get some more.

Well, that was that. I didn't need attention. I got lots of attention, maybe too much. ("GET A LIFE!" I would later yell, as a closely monitored teen. "YOU ARE MY LIFE," came the response from Mum.) But as I looked around the bathroom, I appreciated that it *was* a little warmer than the open air. I was just wishing I had brought a book when the bell clanged and we all went back into the building, where our principal/music teacher, Martin, taught us the words to "Yellow Submarine."

Kids aside, I now felt so close to my teachers, Penny and Gail, that I asked if we could have them over for tea. I give full credit to my mother for not thinking that was weird. So we did have them over, like a civilized playdate for me and two women in their thirties. At tea, Mum and my teachers also struck up enough of a friendship that we went over to Penny's next. There, Mum fell in love with her Minton tea set, a Haddon Hall microfloral pattern. She maybe hadn't spent a lot of time in an English home before, but the place settings, full china service with matching plates and napkins, must have reminded her of the fantasy she'd had as a student in India. She was going to come home after a long day of lecturing, she thought, and be served a full tea in the garden, dressed in a freshly starched and laundered sari. "A colonial fantasy," she says with a laugh. Life in England was a bit more DIY, a bit grimier than expected, but Mum could at least obtain a china set, which she started collecting immediately, piece by piece, especially once she found a Minton "seconds and remainders" shop just off Regent Street. I scoured the shelves with her, excited, looking for a missing Haddon Hall cup, an upgrade from the coveted yellow teapot at last.

Then, when I was four, almost five, my parents started hinting they might be ready to have another kid around. I ask Mum now what finally changed her mind about having a second. She says my yearslong campaign wore her down, and that she could see me loving a sibling with the same companionable, protective love she and I had shared. She saw that I was thoughtful, and loyal, and didn't suffer fools, all great traits for a big sister. "Plus, you had no friends," she jokes. "I thought, Oh God, if anything happens to us, she'll be alone forever." I laugh along with her, but I don't think it's a coincidence that she felt ready to have another baby once she had built a life with reliable, non-romantic grocers and a complete tea set.

As my mother came into her own, so did I, in a way. Many months later, just around the birth of my brother, my parents had asked Christina's mother to walk me home after school. When she arrived to pick us up, I thought it over, and I pretended I didn't know anything about the arrangement. I was still grumpy about being teased for kissing Mum and saw my chance for payback. Christina had to wait around, increasingly frustrated, as I shrugged and told everyone I wouldn't leave without my dad. The adults stood around me, bristling with impatience, arguing amongst themselves—could I be released into another adult's care if I refused to go? Why hadn't the request been made in writing? As it became a proper Incident, we littles stood there, in limbo. Christina was losing her five-year-old mind, while I stared ahead, stoic, satisfied. A small part of me worried I might be inconveniencing my own parents, but I was intrigued by how it upset Christina.

I saw that I, a small child, was holding the strings to how this scenario would unfold, and I felt the first stirrings of my own power. I could keep them here for hours. Or we could all be home in fifteen minutes. Everything, for once, depended on me, the tiny master of this specific domain. But I soon felt a growing sense of discomfort. How little it had taken to turn this girl's life upside down, like she did mine that morning after Mum's kiss. But, unlike me, she seemed openly distressed, and no matter the disdain I felt for her in general, I liked the sensation of influencing a situation but also knew I had a choice to make. Did I *want* Christina to feel bad? As bad as she had made me feel? Probably not, but I'd have to think some more about it later. I feigned remembrance. The teachers let me leave. Christina, her mother, and I walked home in silence, past my friend Amit's dad's corner shop, the theater, the hospital, until we got to my building. I ran up the stairs two at a time, impatient to get away from her and back to my mum.

Sibling Revelry

In the photos of my baby brother's homecoming, first I lurk in the background, five and a half years old, and seething with rage. This isn't because of the competition. It's because I'm irate that my parents promised me a baby, and now they won't give him to me. I then reach for him again and again; finally, they sit behind me, encircling my body, supporting his neck. It dawns on me, in this array of photos, that I'll have to share him.

By the time Punit was born, I was a fully formed, fully bored person who wanted a baby in the house. But my campaign for a younger sibling had begun when I was around three, when my nursery school peers in England started bringing by baby sisters and brothers. I was otherwise occupied by my books and my blossoming friendships with my teachers, but a baby seemed like the best sort of companion—a pet, an acolyte, and an outlet for my desire to be in charge, all in one. My mother claims not to remember the details of this, but my recollection is that the baby was my idea, that my parents had him for me, and that when he was born I gratefully took him off their hands, keeping him company, packing his lunch, and making his afternoon snack, until I went to college.

Every morning, on waking up, I'd go give Punit a cuddle.

When he was nine months old, we left England for Saudi Arabia, and my caretaking moved with us. Every afternoon, I came home and prepared us a meal, as my mother had done for me. And Punit was so easy to love. He was born with a serene smile on his face, game for whatever I wanted to play. He never gave us a day of trouble. As Dad sometimes says, "He raised himself," and he must have been a vacation to raise, after me, the questioner. I was a dissatisfied child, always ready for the next thing, not quite happy with how classes were being taught or how tags felt in my clothes. I was so sensitive to the world; everything was too bright, or loud, or slow, or just *wrong*, somehow. But Punit ate anything, did anything the family asked him to do, with not so much as a peep of complaint. And always, always, his peaceful smile.

I had all these . . . I guess we call them "leadership qualities" now, and no boardroom to use them in. So I did everything for that sweet boy. The night before his first day of kindergarten, I couldn't sleep. A die-hard school enthusiast, now entering fifth grade, I had talked it up like the moon landing. I vibrated with the anticipation of walking him to the playground, showing him where to line up his backpack, helping work the water fountains. His first day would be flawless, I would make certain. I was too excited to sleep, so I waited all night, wiggling in my bed, until I couldn't any longer. I tiptoed into his room and shook the little guy awake. "Wakey, wakey!" I whispered. He groaned, stumbled to the bathroom, and swayed, eyes closed, as I brushed his teeth, scrubbed his face, combed his hair and then my own.

His voice croaked, "Didi, I don't know if I can do this every day!"

"The more you do it, the more you get used to it, I promise," I said.

I got him back into his bedroom, into the clothes I had picked out, and put on his backpack, after which he crawled back into bed, fully dressed. I heard my mother at his door and turned around, beaming. I was ready, as usual, for her to commend what a good Didi—big sister—I had been. But wait. She was bleary-eyed, in her nightgown. "It's four in the morning," she said. "Everyone back to bed."

Other than that blip, my parents marveled at my caretaking—in hindsight, even cultivated it—and I guzzled up their praise like a mouse in a puddle of syrup. I had taken over so much of Punit's daily schedule that my role echoed a parent's. In making sure he felt happy and taken care of, I was happy. We polished up that morning routine, eventually, and created new ones after school. I made him ramen or toaster pizza after we got home. I packed his lunches, and I remember a day in middle school when I panicked, realizing I had given him my turkey sandwich and I had his peanut butter one (no jelly). I raced across to the elementary school to switch out the lunches and made it there before he could be disappointed. For my dedicated service, he repaid me in adoration. "I can always tell when Mum makes the lunch," he whispered to me once. "It doesn't taste as good." For this, I would have made his lunch for the rest of his life.

Still, there were times when my self-appointed responsibility weighed heavily. During his fourth-birthday party, when I was nine, I felt suffocated and overwhelmed, surrounded by screaming kids while I hovered, trying to make sure he was having a good time. I slipped out into the courtyard of our apartment complex and sat for a moment by myself at the edge of the fountain. Mesmerized by the water, grateful for the peace and quiet, I stood up and walked around the rim, a thin balance beam, in my party shoes and party dress—cream silk with thin diagonal chocolate stripes. I made it halfway around before I slipped and fell in, then had to scramble to get out, totally drenched. It was a warm, sunny day in Riyadh—most days were warm and sunny in Riyadh—so I took off the dress, laid it out in the sun, and hid behind a bush until it dried. I felt guilty for slipping away—I felt like I was being punished. *Well, this is what happens when I take my eye off the ball,* I thought. And then that worry blossomed: *Thank goodness it wasn't him on the edge of the fountain. If he ever fell in, with no one around . . .* I thought . . . and I then couldn't think about it anymore. With the dress dry, I slipped back in. I wondered if anyone had noticed I was gone.

My world was starting to feel fragile that following year. It was the same year everyone left Kashmir, but I was too small to do anything about politics, so I poured my uneasy feelings into controlling what I could: my life with my baby brother. And as my responsibilities with him grew, so did my worries about them. When I was ten, my parents once went for a walk around the block while we were watching cartoons. They weren't going to be gone more than a few minutes, but, out of nowhere, Punit got a stomachache. I panicked, and went looking for my parents, screaming down the stairs of the apartment building, and into the neighborhood. They were just outside on the front step, getting a little air, and I collapsed in tears of relief. I don't remember how this stomach episode resolved itself—it may just have taken a comically long fart—but it redoubled my vigilance. My parents couldn't understand why I had been crying hysterically about something so small, but I felt that we had lost enough. I wasn't going to let anything happen to him, too.

Every August, I tie a rakhi, a symbolic red thread, around Punit's wrist, and he gives me money or a present. It's my favorite Hindu holiday, Raksha Bandhan—a celebration of the special relationship between brothers and sisters. Like many of our holidays, it's celebrated differently by each region, and even each home. I'm not sure how other families do it—maybe they include sweets or prayers—but for us, it's always been the thread and the gift, little bribes stipulated by my parents. It's a small ritual meant to symbolize the bond of protection between brother and sister, and, unlike Holi or Diwali, it's never had a cinematic musical extravaganza built around it that I'm aware of. But nothing in our family of four is more sacred.

I treasured Punit so, and he was so sweet, that we never fought. Except for once, when I was thirteen and he was eight. He wrestled the remote control out of my hand; I punched him in the leg. He screamed and developed a bruise but moved on, while I cried about it for two days. I still bring it up and apologize, thirty years hence. But other than that, nothing. We never argued over resources (except that TV remote), because we never needed the same thing. We had both felt the full glow of our parents' attention: me for five years solo, and my brother for much of his early life as I grew into my own. During our shared childhood, we often found ourselves in new neighborhoods and schools, where we didn't know any other kids. Raksha Bandhan was our yearly reminder that we'd never be alone as long as we had each other.

I can't speak for every Indian, but a survey of my extended family points to the potential of a larger cultural norm: that the sibling relationship is understood as a gift, to be celebrated rather than navigated. I asked my cousins' text group whether they felt any sibling rivalry growing up. Of the eight of us, now living in five different countries, I got the same response from six: nope. "Only American kids fight," joked one Toronto cousin. The only two who reported any conflict growing up were also the only pair of the same gender (boys). They were born just two years apart, whereas the others had four to eight years between them. Maybe they fought because they didn't celebrate Raksha Bandhan? There doesn't seem to be any sort of celebration for siblings of the same gender. My cousins all laughed at me. Okay, maybe the holiday was only big in my family.

As we grew up together, I remained perhaps overly involved, until Punit came to visit, well after we were both working adults, and asked if we had anything to eat. I was running out the door for an appointment, and it was the first time I had ever told him to feed himself. I felt like I was doing something wrong. My roommate, Jenny, looked at me askance. "He's in his twenties, he knows how to make a sandwich," she pointed out. *But it doesn't taste as good,* I thought. Since then, I've made a conscious effort to let go—I can't help looking at him and seeing a five-year-old with a little scar near his eyebrow from falling off his bike, or the knockoff Members Only jacket he insisted on wearing every day for a month when he was seven. I have to shake off those visions to see the man he's become. We live in the same city and work in the same industry now, and I love when people make the connection. They call me right after, thrilled. "I just met your brother!" they say. "He's the best! Why didn't you tell me?" *Because I desperately wanted to,* I think, *but he's his own person now.*

When I was married, and then pregnant with my first child, a son, Punit was happy. So happy. But I saw a touch of sadness in him around the baby shower, and he told me it was strange to feel a sense of loss, knowing I would be less available. I felt it, too. I was nauseated for eight straight months during that pregnancy. What strange, uncomfortable surprises would actual parenthood bring? I was terrified. "I was the practice baby," says my brother, smiling. "You did everything right. This kid will be fine." But raising my own kids has been nothing like that time with Punit. I was, all of a sudden, in charge, all the time. Just like I always wanted. And, technically, I'm great at being in charge. I can cook and organize. I have systems, I have ideas. I telegraph confidence and safety. I can sell a rowdy group on almost any series of activities. But the responsibility for a human life is overwhelming. If I messed up, I thought, staring at our newborn, no one could fix it. "You're not alone," repeats my husband, puzzled, every time I get like this. He's here right alongside me, also parenting. But in moments of crisis, I'm a little girl, the baby has a stomachache, and I'm terrified I'm going to lose him.

And the clench in my chest when I leave—on a work trip, for example. I feel like something will happen if I abandon my post. It's important to get alone time, everyone says, but I try and mostly fail to enjoy it. I'm at the fountain again, waiting for my dress to dry. Worried that I'll be punished somehow if I leave.

Some of the terror faded as our baby grew less fragile, but

I was soon worried about having another child. Apart from the whole childbirth and postpartum situation, what if they fought? If all American kids fight, and these kids were definitely going to be American, was my fate sealed? His dad and I were in no rush to decide, but history repeated itself when our son's biological clock kicked in when he was two, just like the baby boom I lived through at Snowsfields Primary School: baby brothers and sisters started showing up in his preschool's Yellow Room, and our son wanted one, too. If he heard the word "baby," he'd shout, even to strangers and empty rooms, "*I'd* like to have a baby!" For almost two years straight, he told his entire school, "We're going to have a baby soon, because Mama and Dada are working on it" (untrue). Eventually, though, his lobbying for a sibling somehow worked on us. By the time he was about three and a half, we felt ready to try it all again. Ten weeks into the new pregnancy, my husband and I found out it was a girl, and the next time our son brought up the Baby Issue, we were ready to lay some groundwork.

"We'll see what we can do," we said, as did my pregnant mother before me. "But if we decide to have a baby, do you think you want a brother or a sister?" We were prepared to nudge him in the right direction if necessary, but he was immediately set on having a sister. "Like Baby Margaret," on his favorite cartoon, *Daniel Tiger's Neighborhood.* After I started showing, we told him we had, indeed, arranged for a baby sister, and he couldn't believe his good luck. "Like I've always wanted!" he said. After her birth, I was nervous about what this would look like in practice, but, other than some impatience at my inability to do everything at the same time, and hiccups resolved by the book *Siblings Without Rivalry,* he's besotted with his sister, whom he refers to as "my little sissy" or "the little missy."

My mother came to visit after the birth of Baby Two, when I kind of knew what I was doing, and she was immediately restless. Did I need her to clean or cook? No, there was food in the fridge, and the cleaning lady had just come, I reminded her. She sat on her hands, fidgeting. "Why am I here, if you don't even need me?" she murmured. And I laughed, thinking of myself shoving sandwiches at my brother when he could easily make his own. "I just need you to be here," I told her. I could see she didn't exactly know what to do with that information, but, honestly, I wouldn't have, either. So she went through the pantry instead, throwing out dusty old spices, replacing them with fresh, buying specific storage containers for cinnamon bark, that kind of thing. "That's so helpful," I told her, and she beamed.

That baby is a preschooler now, and as I watch both kids, wrestling on the couch like kittens, I wonder what I'll do if their fights get real. "We never fought," I tell my husband. "How do I make sure they don't?" He's skeptical, asks if things were really that rosy, and I insist they were. "If you thought everything was so great," he jokes, "maybe you were the mean one." It makes me think. I call my brother. "Are you sure?" I ask. "You would tell me if you were mad about stuff, right? There must have been something I've forgotten," I poke. He claims not to remember, and then starts, delicately: "You had no filter," he says. "You could be very blunt. And sometimes, when people thought you were rude, I felt like I had to clean up the mess. Remember when you didn't like that book, and you announced that anyone who did was probably an idiot?" I don't remember this at all. "Well," he says. "It was embarrassing."

I can see how I was a little embarrassing. He never was. I wasn't exactly resentful of the ease with which he moved through the world, but I was envious of the response he elicited. We could go to a party and he'd sit in the corner smiling quietly, and then, afterward, everyone would say, "That guy's the best!" "He didn't even say anything," I'd grumble, even while agreeing that he really was the best. But, in his own way, he was taking care of me—he knew that there was a big squishy heart under the prickles, and he wished everyone could experience it. As we grew older, he took care of me in other ways, too. When I worked in a Hollywood mail room, always broke, he'd take me out to lunch; his grad-student stipend was more than my income. When the mail room turned into a "real" job, he treated me to dinners, because his engineering pay was almost double mine.

He's also modeled the most wonderful relationship with our parents. I've always known every up and down of their emotional maps. Maybe it's being the firstborn. I witnessed major changes in their lives before they became the self-assured parents Punit encountered. "What are you doing?" I'll ask when he's visiting them. "Oh, we're at the grocery store; maybe we'll watch a movie," he says, easy-breezy. This is never my experience with my parents. Any time with them involves massive character development, usually for all of us. We absolutely must get into an argument about why it's not okay to say everything's okay, I decide, and then we have to work through that for a whole weekend. Or we'll unspool a psychosocial history of the entire family tree. Or discuss the ripple effects of a strange choice some neighbor made, thirty years and seven thousand miles ago. I live for a difficult conversation with my parents, and my brother never has them. It's like we exist in different universes, and mine is one where we pull our hair out a lot more. But I could learn from him, to have a nice, easy time. To go to the grocery store, maybe watch a movie. Not that I ever do learn. But I aspire to, someday.

During my current parenting challenges, it helps to think of his serene face. When my parents nagged me about school, I responded by doubling down on my studies. But not my brother. I think of him evading my mother's pleas for him to practice his phonics, when he was seven or so. "When I'm fourteen, I'll know how to read," he told her calmly, and she couldn't argue with that. It's a mantra I use with my own kids. *When they're thirty-five, they won't leave pee on the floor,* I think. *When they're twenty, they will probably sleep. When they're fourteen, they'll know how to read.*

And, frankly, most of my parenting challenges are internal. When I'm with my kids, the drive to be the old me is strong— the unsmiling little girl who needs to cook every meal, and panics over every ouchie, and micromanages everything in between. That's how I am coded to love, I think. But it doesn't seem to work the way it did with my brother. My son seems frustrated with me: I don't understand; I don't love him, he says. But look at everything I *do* for you, I want to scream. His feet grow a millimeter, new shoes appear. The weekends are packed with enriching activities. I home-cook almost every meal he eats. He admits, begrudgingly, that he likes the food, but most of the stuff I'm doing for him doesn't seem to make a dent, emotionally. I fret. How much more can I give? I already feel, like most working parents, that I'm being squeezed dry.

Until I have an awakening, with my husband. We have a tiff about something minor—one of those logistical "It's in the calendar!" arguments that I assume all busy parents have, except this time he's mad at me all day. That's unusual for him, and I ask what's really going on. "It's nice that you feed us . . . ," he starts. But he wouldn't care if we ordered in every meal or just ate toast. He'd take more hugs, instead. So I give him some hugs, and he's way happier. Like my own mother, trying to feed me after the babies were born, like myself trying to feed my fully grown brother, I realize I've been giving my loved ones meals when all they want is me. So we order more takeout. And I give my son company, and hugs. He feels understood, I think. He feels loved. I can tell.

"Can you believe this wondrous child was in your belly?" our son said once, when his sister was still a baby. He was marveling at her as she ripped apart a toy box. She roared like a bodybuilder as he cheered her on. "She was just a tiny little thing, and now she's cooler than I ever imagined!" They're small yet, so we know that this could be a brief window of peace, and that the kids might spend the rest of their lives trying to punch each other in the face. Who knows? But Raksha Bandhan comes every summer, and I always have solid plans to overdo it. Snacks, desserts, special toys, a new piggy bank. Because bribing us to like each other worked for my parents, and I'm not about to abandon our cultural heritage.

Sixteen Kitchens

◁ 1986 ▷

Mum can't be around real knives, because she'll drop one right through her foot. I've seen it happen myself, twice. I also saw her slice her hand open when the glass she was washing cracked in half. And one time, she was watering the plants and looked down to see a trail of blood around the house—she had bumped into a dining chair and almost ripped her toe clean off. Fortunately, we lived close enough to the hospital so that they sewed it right back on. My point is, domestic accidents find her. So the sharpest thing in her kitchen is her kitchen shears, which she uses to break down most things, from woody herbs to entire chickens.

But, like any smart cook, she's developed workarounds, mostly in the form of single-use gadgets for finer handiwork. Like her garlic slicer and green-onion slicer. The garlic slicer, which looks like a miniature egg slicer, obviously slices garlic cloves, and the green-onion slicer makes those curly ribbons for garnish. Then a bean julienner, which she bought in England to cut her beans into the perfect width for a particular Indian dish she likes to cook. Since then she has acquired a food processor and pre-julienned green beans, but this contraption stubbornly remains in the rotation—probably for nostalgic reasons, but also because it's the least useful specimen in her museum. The egg cuber is a good one, too. "Tired of bumpy sandwiches?" reads one ad for this item, a mold that forms a cube out of the standard ovoid so that we can cut perfectly square slices to fill our perfectly squared sandwich corners. I don't recall having any egg-related challenges growing up (or since?), but Mum says she bought this because it was "so cute." As good a reason as any, and technically a space saver if you need to stack a thousand boiled eggs in the fridge.

Mum trained in botany and limnology—specifically the study of inland aquatic ecosystems—and spent much of her youth in a lab, sketching cell walls while stationed next to a microscope. When she left India, the lab disappeared, but her experimental energy took hold in the kitchen. In England, she started to cook in earnest. She hadn't cooked much as a child, and as a newlywed she shared kitchen duties with her mother-in-law, so London was the first time she was on her own. Still, she was busy with me, my brother, and an eventual research job, so her culinary aspirations lay dormant until we moved to Saudi Arabia.

We landed in Riyadh when I was almost six and Punit still a baby. Our family was escorted through a gold-plated airport lobby into the dry, silent air. Nothing in sight besides palm trees, highways that looked like they had been freshly laid on the ground for our arrival, and low airport walls the same color as the sand, which stretched in every direction under an even, clear blue sky. I hadn't been to a desert before, and it felt like being warmed up in a low oven. After the wet of England, where I was always slightly cold, I loved the feeling of being only just too hot.

Dad had been recruited by a Saudi health attaché in London to start the Kingdom's first pediatric dialysis program. It was an intriguing clinical challenge, which also turned out to be a great research opportunity. And good money for a young family, especially one that dreamed of building a house and a hospital back home sometime soon. The Kingdom took care of its expats, and Dad's contract came with housing, tuitions, travel expenses all covered, to offset the difficulties of a transition to a mysterious land. Like most foreigners, we lived in a compound: a walled-off neighborhood with supermarkets, and rec centers, and Olympic-sized swimming pools, outfitted so that we wouldn't miss home too much. In the country just outside the walls, we would have been monitored by the religious police, but inside we could wear whatever we wanted, and freely mix with the opposite sex.

A gleaming white town car showed up at the airport to take us to our new home, and I noticed that most cars we passed were also white. To reflect the sun, explained Dad, and to hide the dust. A bell dinged throughout the entire ride, because the airport driver did not want to wear a seat belt. I started to feel ill, because the ride was almost too smooth, like driving on glass. Uncomfortable, and looking around at the unfamiliar surroundings from our car, I saw a Tesco sign and sighed with relief. My parents had joked, in London, that it was near impossible to get me to leave the house unless I was promised a grocery run, so at least we had that here, I thought. But as we neared this Tesco, I deflated, noticing that it was just a hardware store. One that clearly scoffed at trademark laws.

Our actual apartment wasn't quite ready on that first day, so we were taken to an extended-stay place in a squat brown seventies sandstone building in a nondescript part of town. This wasn't the poolside life we were expecting. The temporary housing was drab: wall-to-wall beige shag, mud-brown kitchen, two boxy bedrooms. Factory-made art and wicker baskets were arranged around the apartment to make it feel less bare, but as the sun set, the haphazard staging of it all started to depress me. I walked with Dad across the street to a fast-food restaurant, Herfy. This is before there was much fast food in the Kingdom—it was a major event when we got our first McDonald's, eight years later—and we ordered two lamb burgers and a plate of chicken. I don't know if we were expecting the pace of a fish-and-chips place, but we stood under those buzzing fluorescent lights for an eon. My father smiled at me. "I guess they're still out catching the birds," he said, hopeful, tired, and ready with a dad joke.

Back at the apartment, tummies full, I pulled out the books I had stowed in our checked bags. *The Secret Garden* probably, which I had read until pages fell out. But I didn't get too far in before I passed out in a twin bed across from Punit, who snored gently. I tried to ignore my discomfort at being in this new place. I had liked England, I thought. But I could like this, too, maybe. I was told there was a swimming pool at the end of it, and a school I would like. I could make this work, eventually. Even if tonight I felt like I was falling asleep on the moon.

In the morning, I woke up to the sounds of Mum flipping through the TV channels. Not that there was much flipping to do. Saudi TV in 1986 had two channels: Channel 1 was in Arabic, and 2 was in English, but everything was heavily censored, down to hugs between the sexes. She beamed at me from the next room, and I ran in to see what she was looking at. *Sesame*

Street, my old favorite. I snuggled up to her and Punit on the couch, and we watched Snuffleupagus and Big Bird have a conversation I'd already seen. But I felt the glow of immersing myself in the comfort of one small familiar thing.

A few weeks later, we moved into our real apartment, and I got that neighborhood swimming pool. Directly downstairs from us lived Miryam, who was about my age: an adorable girl with a curtain of shiny black hair and a sweet, constant smile. In a stroke of luck, she was also Kashmiri and had also just moved from the UK, and I gained an instant best friend. When we weren't physically together—swimming, riding bikes, idyllic little-kid things—we set up a basket on a string tied to both of our balconies so we could send messages up and down. My parents enrolled me in the same school as her—the American International School in Riyadh. It was a sleek campus filled with expats from every country, "a place where people really seemed to care about learning," I, a hopeless dork, told my mother, who nodded, solemn. She must have been wondering what she was going to do to keep herself busy in her new, slower-paced stay-at-home lifestyle. She had been working in research in England and needed somewhere to put all that energy, so the kitchen became her new lab, and I her assistant and guinea pig. She started collecting ingredients. Saudi supermarkets were stocked to cater to expats, so Indian spices were easy to find, but so were foods from all over the world—Pocky and Yan Yan from Japan. Shrimp crisps. Laksa-flavored ramen noodles from Malaysia. Chewy Haribo Coke bottles. And the equipment! Saudi, with its endless souks, is where my mother fell in love with her single-use gadgets, a love that endures to this day.

My mother, used to burning off miles of energy all over London, had to pivot. Women couldn't drive in the Kingdom back then, and public transport was rudimentary at best. But one bus that stopped nearby went to the souk, and she started bringing home new, intriguing foods. Basbousa, a golden semolina cake drenched in syrup. Knafeh, a lattice bird's nest filled with a sweet, fresh cheese and drizzled with honey. Shawarmas, the fattiness of the meat cut by a sharp, crunchy sliver of pickle. In Batha, the old city, we discovered a charbroiled chicken that was so spicy it hurt our mouths and made our eyes water; its accompanying flatbread was flaky, buttery, and studded with sesame seeds. But because it wasn't so easy for a woman to get around Riyadh, Mum had to figure out how she could re-create these foods at home. After mastering them, she fell in with a bunch of other parents on the compound and started in on the cookbooks. A wok appeared, and we ate Chinese food for months. A bag of yeast, and every Friday became a pizza party. And it was the 1980s, and my parents were friendly, so we had party snacks galore: puff pastry vol-au-vents stuffed with mushrooms cooked in cream and tarragon; tea sandwiches, all sorts; mini-samosas. All of this before our homemade Indian buffet. And dessert: date-and-walnut loaves, honey cake, chocolate cookies, gingersnaps, trifle. We ate so well there.

Any laboratory has its spectacular failures, and we still talk about the chocolate yogurt. One of Mum's early gadgets was her yogurt maker, an incubator with seven small glass jars, which are ubiquitous now but were futuristic then. We started with plain, then fruit on the bottom, then a few savory versions, full- or low-fat, depending on health trends. And then, one day, I suggested chocolate yogurt. "We should try it," she said, and I made a jug of chocolate milk, poured it into the machine, and left it to sit. I cracked it open the next morning, and I can tell you that I've never quite shaken the taste of it—imagine a rancid Jell-O pudding—but Mum shrugged it off. "And now we know," she said. When I asked if I could turn our potato chips green with food coloring, she said, "Why not?" So I did. "Is there any distinct improvement in taste?" she asked, her apron standing in for a lab coat. "Not really," I admitted. She thought more. "Does the green make them more appealing to eat?" Not that, either. Hypothesis rejected.

But all those experiments also led to wonderful innovations. A soy-marinated, rice-flour-dusted crispy fish. A warm chicken salad with grilled pineapple. Perfect little flower-shaped vegan tea cookies that tasted faintly, pleasantly, of buttered popcorn. And our shared pride in answering, when asked for the recipe, "Oh, it's just something we made up." It was a small choice, my mother's willingness to let me run rampant with her in the kitchen. But during what could have been an uncomfortable move, she taught me to embrace the discomfort, to funnel my busy hands and busier mind into something I could control and enjoy. I learned that achieving competence in anything meant making plenty of mistakes, and that it was worth it to try, because on the other side of a chocolate yogurt I would eventually invent a blissful custard instead. "Now we know what doesn't work," I can still hear her say briskly, wiping her hands on a tea towel. "What do you think we should do differently next time?"

It was a small room, that kitchen in Riyadh—just a galley, all shoved together, but I wonder if it wasn't the foundation for everything that came after, because I took those lessons out into the real world and launched myself into mistakes like I was inventing a cake. Some decisions burned to a crisp, others soured on the tongue, but each one gave me the confidence of knowing I was a step closer to figuring things out.

But even my mother had her limits. Dad came home once with a job offer somewhere near . . . Newcastle, I think it was. "Should we move again?" he wondered, and Mum threw up her hands. "I've packed and unpacked sixteen kitchens," she said, cross. "And I'm not going to do it again."

But of course they did it again, many more times. Ever that young couple that had fallen for each other's wanderlust, they couldn't help themselves. And through all the moves, the things that have endured aren't childhood art projects, which were photographed in batches and thrown away. It wasn't furniture, all donated or left behind. And it certainly wasn't, God forbid, any mementos of us as children. No, still intact is my mother's cabinet of curiosities, her single-use gadgets: symbols of her whimsy, and her refusal to back down in the face of a challenge.

Mum's collection has only grown, with each kitchen she adds. Recently, she brought me a folding platform that allows me to microwave two plates at once. I rolled my eyes at her, but now I use it every day. She came home once from her happy place, the Japanese dollar store, with a "snack bag sealer," which looks like a toy stapler, but two AA batteries heat up the metal surfaces enough to seal your plastic bags. Though it was better in concept than in execution, I'm sure that, if we left her alone with goggles and a few stray wires, she'd figure out a way to make it useful.

But utility isn't the only criterion by which she curates

this collection, because some items exist for pure emotional impact. Like the I Love You toast stamp, a letterpress she used to smush into our bread when we were kids. After a couple of minutes in the toaster, it pops out reading, "I love you," with a big heart in place of the word "love." My brother adored it back then, and I thought it was ridiculous. But how lucky I was, I know, to be able to take my mother's love for granted. For all the plot that was packed into our early lives, her love for us spilled out of her heart in a cascade she could barely contain, one we could barely accept. We were smothered in hugs, in food, in loving words, in heart-shaped toast stamps. As I raise my two children, absolutely sickening them with my own uncontrollable love, I think of her, busy raising a young family in a country where she couldn't work much outside the home, and I think about that toast stamper—a cheap plastic investment, a simple tool that could represent the entirety of her devotion.

I'll Show You

"You're so nice," Nani's older sister often told her. "But your children, well . . ."

She'd disagree, halfhearted and loyal, but her sister wasn't wrong. Nani was the sweetest person I have ever known. I used to joke that she was the only nice person in our entire family. If you met the Kaul girls, you'd understand. They're all brilliant and hilarious. But nice? Even the word is confusing. In a culture and family that value presence in our women, "nice" can imply a toothlessness, or gullibility. It is the limpest noodle of compliments, and it's still impossible to call someone nice in front of my mother without her reflexive addendum: "poor thing." In cataloguing Kashmiri compliments for women, I grew up hoping to be *tez* (sharp), *thrat hish* (like a thunderclap), *zahar hish* (like poison), *toofan hish* (like a storm), an overall *patakuh* (firecracker). Even my great-grandmother valued a woman's "indy-pindy" above all. Nary a mention of nice, gentle, or kind. Those traits were not necessary for survival.

Our tumultuous history selected for tough cookies, and the Kashmiri feminine ideal was codified in the fourteenth century by our renowned poet Lal Ded. She was a mystic prone to running off on her own, and it doesn't take a deep read to figure out what kind of lady she was. In my favorite *vakh,* 127, she says:

I can scatter the battalions of southern clouds,
Dry the ocean, play physician
to the most lingering fever and cure it.
But I can't knock sense into a fool.

As the French have Marianne, their symbol of liberty, equality, and fraternity, Kashmiris have our beloved Lalla, patroness of self-sufficiency, skepticism, and a powerful side-eye.

The irony, then, of my Nani Lalita, or "Lalla Bahen" to her friends and family, sharing a name with her polar opposite! Unlike her namesake, Nani floated around Srinagar like Amelia Bedelia in a sari. One time, she went for a walk, stopped at a friend's, and absentmindedly came back wearing one of the wrong shoes. Only one, but with a heel, and the other one was flat. "Oh, Nani!" we said, even as children. We worried about her. Not sharp, not poisonous, she was more gentle mist than thunderclap. This time it was a shoe, we murmured. What would it be next time? Her wallet? Her jewelry? I was glad she had us, her wary phalanx. Silly, sweet Nani, the softest, whitest sheep, bobbing solitary in our sea of darkness.

Nani's agreeable nature was especially unexpected after the life she had lived. Through the tragic deaths of siblings, a perfunctory marriage, the eventual devolution of her homeland, Nani still laughed like a child: her helpless peal so loud and clear she'd have to lean to one side and wipe her eyes, her whole body shaking, whether it was the first time she heard a joke or the hundredth. Though she was quieter than her rowdy brood of children, her voice cut through their noise, a warble powered by surprise and delight. So much about the world surprised and delighted Nani, not least her own name. "Lalita?" people remarked her whole life. "That's such a beautiful name." She'd light up like it was the first time she'd ever heard that and agree.

Nani, unlike her daughters, did a lot of "ladies' work," partly in keeping with generational gender roles, but also because marrying and rearing children in her early twenties didn't leave much time for higher education. She devoted herself to the domestic sphere, and some of her pursuits were more successful than others. I think it's okay to share now that she was a dreadful cook, who never met a foodstuff she didn't boil to an unseasoned mush. I caught a rare glimpse of disgust on her sweet face once, and it was directed at a plate of salad. "Those vegetables are just *looking* at me," she said, and shuddered. Even when I was well into my thirties, she would groan with despair if she heard I'd skipped a meal. When I visited her from college, she microwaved my orange juice for ten seconds so I wouldn't catch a cold. Oh, Nani. She'd startle my uncle, mid-nap on the couch, to insist he'd be more comfortable in bed. And everything made Nani cry—from watching TV commercials to hearing thirdhand about a stranger's recent illness. Her heart was as soft as her tear-filled eyes.

However, Nani shone with a needle. She loved to crochet, and spent the months of my mother's first pregnancy whipping up billowy matching baby sets for me. During my first year, when Mum was dropping me off at Matamaal to finish her thesis, Nani memorialized each handmade outfit with a run to the photo studio down the street. After we left India, and Mum was away from her mother for the first time, she taught herself the crafts she had been denied in her student days, and I grew up surrounded by her handiwork: whimsical sweaters, crocheted hats, and, for a notable period in the 1980s, macramé plant hangers. It was part need—as recent immigrants, why would we buy something we could make?—but also a connection to Nani, and meditative, too. Mum knit sweater after sweater to combat the British damp, while I read next to her, with a bowl of custard, under the one window in our London apartment that let in enough sun.

The summer when I was five, Mum took me to our library in London to pick out books for our summer trip to Kashmir. I lugged over a pile of books, and she plucked out the one on teaching yourself to crochet. It wasn't like her to tell me I wasn't ready to learn something—I wonder now if this related to her father's edict about ladies' work—but she says I was too small to mess with needles on my own. Somehow, I managed to check it out anyway and keep it hidden.

Mum dropped me off at Matamaal in that summer of 1985 with no crochet hooks but that book tucked away in my backpack. Nani was soft, and I already knew it. By the time Mum was back a week later, I wandered in nonchalantly, holding my favorite doll, who usually wore a green gingham A-line dress but was now drowning in an outfit I had made her, with materials from Nani. My intention had been to crochet a pair of overalls, but after mastering the simple stitches needed for straps and pinafore, I became drunk with ambition. I ended the whole thing in kind of a tiered meringue-looking skirt, all lemon yellow. My mother looked at me holding that poor doll—plumber on top, flamenco on the bottom—sighed, and bought me my own hook.

Lalla the poet would have been proud. She beat a constant drum for autodidacts, as in *vakh* 13:

> *Love-mad, I, Lalla, started out, spent days and nights*
>   *on the trail.*
> *Circling back, I found the teacher in my old house.*
> *What brilliant luck, I said, and hugged him.*

On being self-taught, and only on this point, she and Nani agreed.

But why did I love crochet? Who knows. It's only two motions, looping yarn around a hook, pulling it through another loop. I liked the simplicity of the materials, just a ball of yarn and one needle. As a small child, I liked the sureness of the hook, wary of knitting's slippery pokiness. Eventually, I taught myself how to knit, and sew, and macramé, and felt, and découpage, and who knows what else, but I always came back to crochet. The possibilities of crochet are endless. A blanket? A hat? A jacket? Try *knitting* a tablecloth and see how far you get.

Also, the repetitive, small motions calmed me. I noticed early that the world was sometimes too much. Mum says she'd "never known a toddler to need so much space." Loud noises, multiple people talking at the same time, long social interactions wore me out. And today, still, when my brain feels curdled, after I've spent too much time with the memes, and the news, and the agitation of people shouting at one another on the internet, I feel in freefall, and I reach for the needle. I don't know any better reset than that endless loop and pull. As I sit here, currently working on a rainbow blanket that will never end, because I've sized it impossibly large, it connects the invisible dots. I'm under a warm window in London with my mother, beneath an open shutter with my Nani, in Kashmir. Peace and quiet, yes. But it also reminds me of loving, and being loved.

It took us a long time to notice that Nani was forgetting more and more, because she was absentminded to begin with. But her absentmindedness gently blossomed into the most pleasant dementia. Dementia through a Vaseline lens. While we thought it would defeat her, she proved us wrong again and again. Nani rode out Alzheimer's in the best possible way, in a state of constant delight at how much her grandchildren had accomplished. I'd call, and she'd remember me, ask how school was. Every time, I had the pleasure of telling her I'd finished law school, gotten a job, and gotten married. With each revelation, I'd hear the joy notch higher and higher, until the climactic reveal, my two children, and she'd coo and giggle, ecstatic on the phone.

Years back, when she moved to Toronto after Nanaji passed, we worried she would take her sweetness, her naïveté, out into this unfamiliar world, and it would eat her up. Those mismatched shoes were still fresh in our minds. But she found her rituals and her people. On her daily walk to the mall, she stopped at the smoothie stand to haggle the price of bananas, as though in a bazaar. Oh, Nani. We cringed, assuming she'd be discouraged and confused. But they started selling her the bananas and then just kept giving them to her. The unfamiliar world was kind to Nani, because it saw her kindness and reflected it back.

A few years ago, I learned that dementia will come for me, too. It's written in my genes. My doctor claims there are ways to keep it at bay. Crossword puzzles, busy hands, and, says cutting-edge research, a fasting diet. Under her care, I go sixteen hours between dinner and breakfast, to prevent the cobwebs from settling in. But, still, every time I forget anything, I wonder, and I panic a little. Is that one sticky strand of plaque calcifying? Or did I just not sleep enough? The blurring of my sharp edges is my worst fear, as Lalla laid out in *vakh* 12:

> *My willow bow was bent to shoot, but my arrow was*
> *   only grass.*
> *A klutz of a carpenter botched the palace job I got him.*
> *In the crowded marketplace, my shop stands unlocked.*
> *Holy water hasn't touched my skin. I've lost the plot.*

But Nani walked right into that fate, into losing the plot, with an open heart. I've come to realize that, during all those years we spent worrying about Nani, she did everything right. She left us with a road map for a slow exit. She showed us how it pays to be kind, to laugh, to make things. To tell people she was forty-eight, forever. When my mind goes, which I assume it will, I hope my decline is something like my grandmother's: peaceful and constantly reinvigorated with wonderful news. Maybe you've seen those dementia internet videos: A creaky ballerina remembering the choreography to *Swan Lake*. A quiet retiree claiming never to have seen a piano, then breaking into Chopin. They tell us that, even though our memories might fade, our muscles can hold on to the familiar movements of a craft. Like Nani, I don't know if I'll remember a face when I'm ninety. But hand me a hook and I'm sure I can keep you warm, even when everything else has faded away. I hope I meet that fade with the same serenity and grace that my Nani did.

Nani passed away a few years ago, after a stroke. It wasn't a surprise. Nor was the immediate response I felt in my hands. I went rummaging through the crafts cupboard for something to do with my sadness. I couldn't find any yarn that was worthy, but I did find a cross-stitch kit. The pattern was nothing involved, just flowers in a jar, but I felt that connection to her: guiding my hands through new stitches, unraveling mistakes, urging me to take breaks when I got impatient. It doesn't matter how long it takes, she had told me, as I raced to make my doll's lemon-meringue dress in time for Mum's arrival. It just matters that every stitch is one closer to finished.

The funeral was thronged with friends we didn't even know she had—kids of other patients at the nursing home, staff, friends of friends, distant family of those friends. People I had never met sobbed in my direction. And back at my uncle's house, we felt the full weight of what Nani had given us. We looked through old photos, and laughed, ordering Indian take-out and watching the littlest kids wrestle one another to the floor. We hadn't gathered in the same place since my wedding, probably, and I glanced around happily at the family that had sprouted from Nani's body. I passed out paper plates to her children, grandchildren, and great-grandchildren, and composed a heaping plate of my own. I dug in, delighted to find that, in the perfect tribute to my sweet, silly Nani, and her slapdash cooking, the paneer was woefully underseasoned.

A Good Match

My parents are soulmates—not that they'd ever admit it.

On their last visit, Mum brought a sheaf of tiny black-and-white wedding photos to show the kids. My dad, skinny and dapper in a checked suit. My mother, drowning in her embroidered sari. Both of them a young twenty-two, sitting cross-legged on the floor outside Matamaal, following the priest's directions next to a small, smoky pyre. I spread out the photos on our dining table so our son could get a better look.

"Aw, so sweet," he said, already a romantic. "Did you love each other so much?"

"God, no!" said my mother.

"I didn't even know her!" added my dad.

"We like each other now, though . . . ," he continued, to my son's confused face, as he looked to me for an explanation.

The story in my head has always been this: my parents met at a community event and chatted a little bit; then Dad went home and asked his own father if he knew hers; a year later, they were married. These were the facts fed to me, laying the groundwork so I'd be open to an eventual arranged marriage. "But yours wasn't arranged," I kept pointing out, more aggressively, as I grew older, and as I picked up more details.

They relented slightly over time, joked that it was, perhaps, "assisted." Whatever the circumstances, said Mum, it was a good match. They were from the same community, shared values, an education level. Like all decisions, the one for a life partner should be made from the head, say my people, because feelings cloud judgment.

My parents weren't in love, they say—we don't even have the words to express such a thing in Kashmiri—but they made an excellent choice and, forty-nine years in, consider their marriage an exemplar of smart life decisions. But I've watched them closely for my whole life, and I'm not buying it. There's so much more to their pairing than "an excellent choice." They sparkle together—the kind of couple who elicit bright smiles when they walk into a party. They amuse each other in a million shared, secret ways. Even when they bicker, which all Kashmiris do, their fondness is so obvious to me. This is not the kind of pairing that just happens, and I know that the universe worked its machinations to get them together. There's a romantic story there, and I decide I'm going to extract it.

Dad grew up in Habba Kadal, in Srinagar, Kashmir, in what he terms an average, middle-class family home. Three narrow wooden stories, clay floors, windows open onto the busy street below. Habba Kadal was the nerve center of Srinagar, a warren of streets on the east bank of the Jhelum River. "I would never have said we were poor . . . ," says Dad, but I've seen his elementary school. On a visit when I was about eight, he took me there to give me some perspective. I saw a gaggle of dusty boys gathered on a threadbare carpet. In a room with no electricity, they learned on individual chalkboards, grasping their one stick of chalk each. Even by 1988, not much had changed, he noticed. While technically wanting for nothing—he was surrounded by love—he thirsted for more in life.

Dad's father, Papaji, was a clerk at the Indo-Kashmir Carpet Factory, a high-end showroom for Kashmiri crafts. Foreign dignitaries came in and out of the factory, and my Papaji, an affable man, gradually became an outward-facing part of the office. Despite their relative lack of money, perhaps being around it, and around such fine things, instilled in him an eye for quality handiwork. I can still see how Papaji would examine a rug, picking his glasses off the bridge of his nose, stroking the pile with one thumb, turning it over to grade the knots. From him, I learned about the relative price points of a rug that was wool-on-wool (cheapest) versus silk-on-silk (most expensive), the amount of time and effort that went into a tightly woven rug, the interplay between knots per square centimeter, quality of materials, and the brilliance of the design, which, taken all together, established the price of the piece.

My grandmother Bhabi was a quieter, more serious type but ended up with the partner she needed. Although it was arranged when they were teenagers, they had an unusual union for the time. Most couples of their age seemed to be just getting on with it, but they actually enjoyed each other's company. Papaji made Bhabi laugh, her green eyes, more common in Kashmiris of old, crinkling at the corners as she swatted at her silly, cheerful husband. She raised three kids with him, my father the oldest, and his two younger sisters. She was so young when she had Dad, and Dad was such an old soul, that he still speaks about her as less a mom than a sister. Bhabi, thin as a reed, never stopped moving—a carbon copy of her mother, Kakni, my irrepressible great-grandmother, who lived slightly outside of downtown Srinagar, in a stone house built into a hill-side, with a terraced garden out back where she grew squash, corn, and runner beans, which we would clean on sunny summer days before she cooked them for our lunch.

I don't remember Papaji as ever less than beautifully dressed. Not expensively, but in well-made clothing—I have mental images of him in a heather-gray Nehru suit, tailored just so, or carefully examining an arm seam on a sweater that felt like a cloud. His morning and evening routines were sacred. When I stayed with them, I'd wake up to a low humming as he ended his morning prayers and transitioned into a close shave, moisturizing and powdering; his cheeks were as supple and sweet-smelling as a perfect leather jacket. He was a happy-go-lucky man with a childlike energy that never quite left him. I was probably his most dour grandchild, but he had ways of softening me up, always sneaking me a chocolate bar or improvising a nonsense song ("When Does the Grandfather European the Lady," for one). Papaji was immensely proud of his son, who would grow up with Bhabi's more serious demeanor but also with his father's love of cutting a fine figure.

"All the girls teased your dad," says Mum, not one to give him an inch publicly. He paid a lot of attention to his clothes—nothing flashy, but quality, stylish, worn well, she says. His calm temperament and studious, quiet ambition gave him the air of a much older person, so the women at medical school all called him "Daddyji" behind his back. My parents hadn't encountered each other, which was strange in the small community, until a family *mekhal,* sort of a Hindu bar mitzvah, to which they were both invited. By her early twenties, my mother had perfected a frown for any man who looked her way. Her glare could—and still can—shrivel a guy's confidence at a hundred feet. But she attended the *mekhal* with her outgoing, impish cousin Nirja, who pointed Dad out from across the room. "He seems so pleasant, don't you think?" said Nirja Masi. "Pleasant personality, pleasant looks," she continued. Mum thought about it.

Mum hadn't yet decided what she wanted in a partner. It was still early to think about that kind of thing—she was just starting a PhD program, and in her family, a girl didn't even think about marriage until her (extensive) education was complete. Still, she longed for one thing. Some cousins and her Indra Auntie had wandered abroad, bringing back gifts and stories that made her yearn for adventure. So she stopped at the Ganesha temple on her way home from the lab every day, with the same silent prayer: "Please, God, let me travel."

No part of her wanted to leave Kashmir permanently, because nobody ever wanted to leave Kashmir. In addition to the presence of her family, and the region's incomparable natural beauty, Kashmir was an international tourist destination. With all manners of rock stars and matinee idols traipsing through its gorgeous hotels and gardens, it was easy to stay put and have a lovely, sophisticated life there. Living elsewhere was as unfathomable to her as the von Trapps' willing departure from Salzburg, but she wanted to be with someone who had the same sweeping vision for a life. She dreamed of being a respected university lecturer—like Nanaji and his sister—and during school breaks, she thought, she would travel far and wide with her family. So she prayed at the temple, and once even consulted a palm reader at college, who after telling all her friends that they would travel, pronounced that she was destined to stay. This made her sad.

Thrumming just under her practical shell was the heart of a girl who loved Russian novels and whatever was playing at the local movie theater, especially if it made her cry. She was drawn to tragic stories about women who wanted more than an unfair world could give them. *Anna Karenina,* for example, or the Hindi movie *Sangam,* about a woman torn between two loves, one of whom she had presumed dead. Mum and her cousins went to the movies en masse, as a family activity, and there's something so sweet to me to think of this ritual bathing in melodrama. Living an otherwise cerebral life, celebrating common sense, studying hard, she must have found it a relief to be able to load all her knotty feelings into the tears streaming down her cheeks in a dark movie hall. She demurs when I bring it up, but I suspect that these movies and films, with their portrayals of big, international lives, were integral to the formation of her romantic blueprint. In mentally conjuring up a partner, she claims to have had no reference points. But when I asked, she said her childhood celebrity crush was the megastar Raj Kapoor, who established his own film studio at twenty-four, who telegraphed reliability, and thoughtfulness, and had kind eyes.

Enter Dad. Reliable, thoughtful, kind-eyed Dad. When I make the connection to her screen crush, Mum looks at me like I pulled a quarter out of her ear, and then brushes it off. But they were looking for each other, even if they don't know it. Dad, too, thought he was too young to get married. He was just wrapping up medical school, and thinking about starting a pediatric practice. Ever a planner, he thought he might work abroad for a time, training in England, say, and then bring his knowledge back home. Like Mum, he wanted to see the world but not to leave permanently. I ask where his desire to go abroad came from, and he says opportunities for further training were limited in Kashmir, but then he brings up the family astrologer. Though they were as firmly grounded in reality as the rest of their community, my paternal grandparents could be quite superstitious. And, like many families, they consulted a trusted astrologer, one Madh Kak, when Dad was quite young, to ask for a sense of how his life would go. One prediction was that Dad wouldn't have to worry about money. This must have been a relief. Another was that he would travel abroad. Dad gives me the small, sideways smile that peeks out whenever he's telling me about something not entirely fact-based. "I don't know if he planted a seed, or saw my future, but he wasn't wrong about that part."

At twenty-two, knowing he would probably leave the country soon, Dad didn't want to set out on that voyage without a partner. He hadn't much thought about it before then—I've already established that my parents were real bookworms—but he had one touchpoint for a feminine ideal: the actress Dimple Kapadia. Though many were prettier, she came across as a woman with intelligence, a center of gravity, a sense of humor, and a great head of hair. A woman with "presence"—high praise from Dad. And it didn't hurt that she looked terrific in a sari. So he went to this family event, and who should be there but an intriguing woman, one he had never seen, wearing a sari. He still has trouble articulating why he felt drawn to Mum. "Well, she has a beautiful face, but there were plenty of nice faces in Kashmir," he says, hedging. But my dad, with his eye for style, thought she looked "elegant" and wanted to know more. Neither remembers what they talked about, neither can recall a specific takeaway, but Mum got a sense that he wanted to travel, and he got a sense she was the one to pursue.

Back in Srinagar, Dad called her a few times on the Matamaal phone—I don't even recall there being one, but Mum says it was upstairs, in the front room, where Nanaji wouldn't hear it. They made arrangements to meet up at the medical school, a short walk from her home, a few times.

"I can't believe Nanaji allowed that!" I scream, and, once again, Mum looks at me like my brain is gone.

"Oh God, no, nobody knew about it. He would have killed me."

"That sounds romantic!" I squeal. "Can you admit that sneaking around was a little romantic?"

She sighs. "It was the dumbest thing I've ever done."

If that isn't the very definition of romance.

But Mum, true to form, wiggles out of the precision of "love." "He's a good man," she says about Dad. A man of character. "I didn't like spoiled boys, throwing around their parents' money." He was much more understated, and hardworking. He came across as a grown-up. "And very tidy," she adds, approving. That's less romantic to me, but to each her own.

Supposedly, neither of them recalls the subjects they discussed during these clandestine walks—they guard them with all the privacy of merger talks—but here's where I like to point out that their courtship took place in Srinagar, iconic honeymoon destination and film backdrop. With its soaring peaks and Mughal gardens, Srinagar was built for romantic walks. Its cozy cafés, delicious ice cream, benches placed along the glittering lake begged couples to share a moment and stare into each other's eyes. How was it possible for my parents to be so anti-romance when surrounded by a literal film set? Well, probably because so many significant films of the time reinforced the futility of romantic love. The heroine in *Sangam* is reunited with her true love only after her husband kills himself. Then there's the actress who ruins two men's lives in Dad's favorite, *Guide*. Love stories, though entertaining on-screen, were for suckers.

And Kashmiri culture reinforced this. Our wildly unpredictable history, just coming out from under the shadow of the Raj, featured planners, workers, people who could keep their heads on straight during challenging times. Alliances from friendship to marriage were coordinated with the same sort of practicality. There was no room for flights of fancy, for the druggy highs of romance, in the world that raised my parents. "Love marriage," one initiated by the actual participants, was for dreamers, not for the good, grounded citizens of a newly independent India. But that's why they had the movies, and why the movies were so thick with drama, serving as a vessel for every emotion that a new nation was yearning to express but didn't know how to. There's more variety now, but every plot of every movie of my childhood, whether a gangster film, or a mystery, or a biopic, felt exactly the same: two young people fell in love; the world had other plans. My parents would have never done something so foolish.

Nani and Nanaji were married out of necessity—the need to pair up and procreate—and, even as unlikely partners, they built a family unit my mother treasured. In its own way, it was a testament to the possibilities of a traditional arrangement. The only example of a "love marriage" my mother had ever seen was her cousin Reena, who "wasn't made for school," says Mum. Although she was my mother's age, she had failed each grade a few times, and by the time Mum was getting her master's degree, Reena had fallen ten years behind. She found her purpose when she met a handsome fellow who had dropped out of high school in order to work for her family's company. After hearing of their dalliance, her parents forbade her from meeting up with an employee and allowed her out of the house only to go to school and back, furious when the Srinagar newswire got word to them that she had been talking in public to the boy. The young lovers devised a method of communication that involved cracking the shells of walnuts, removing the nuts within, stuffing small folded-up notes into the empty shells, gluing them back together, and then rolling them out the kitchen drain so that they could be collected from the street.

One normal day, the two left their houses as if going to school but instead found a justice of the peace and married. His family was horrified, for reasons twofold. First, in those old, mean days, they had hoped for a daughter-in-law who could bring a substantial dowry, and, second, he brought her home immediately after school to move in, per Indian tradition. After a month or so of misery for both families, they settled into an odd, if loving routine, with few glitches.

The first significant speed bump they hit was in the late 1960s, when her husband, having grown fed up with the overdone beehive that Reena wore, went on a hunger strike and stayed in bed until she reassessed her hairstyle. His boycott lasted a week, and she finally relented. Second, in a supposed fit of boredom she joined the army in a clerkship position and convinced him to do so as well. They moved to a base in Dehra Dun and built a house in the foothills of the Himalayas. Their picturesque, eccentric life was steeped in tragedy, as their attempts at childbearing ended in miscarriage after miscarriage. But, in a show of solidarity with her, one day he finally disappeared and came back to announce he had had a vasectomy, and they've remained happily married in the decades since.

Though Mum grew up fascinated by this story, it had as much relevance to her as Humpty Dumpty, so my parents completed talks and decided to get married, in August 1975. My single favorite thing about their wedding photos is how miserable my mother looks. In most of them, she's barely holding back tears, her mouth and eyes downcast. In one, she glares at a guest. In another, she's kind of smiling—maybe she was told to—and then we come to a series of outright sobs as she leaves the family home. Tradition dictated that a newlywed daughter exit the house from a window, to symbolize that the door is always open for her to return, and you can see she's heaving with tears as a group of men help her onto the ground and into the car that would take her away. "Why were you so unhappy?" I ask her. "I didn't want to move out!" she says. "I liked my life. I liked our home." I nod. It was a really good home. "It all happened so fast," says my dad. And when my brother points out that of course it did, marriage was the only way a respectable young man got to take a respectable young woman home, Dad coughs.

Because they were stretched for time and money, they took

a one-night honeymoon, in the mountain resort town of Gul-marg, an occasion Dad is glad they celebrated properly. "No particular moment in your life comes back," he likes to say, in lesson mode. My dad, a pediatrician and educator, does this thing. He pulls me aside for serious talks, ones that require his full attention, and mine. He slowly, deliberately, walks me through a concise lesson, a bullet point that he wants me to internalize. "I want to talk to you about something impor-tant," he'll say, and I know he's about to tackle an item on his child-rearing checklist. "It wasn't perfect, it wasn't the honey-moon of anyone's dreams, but if you wait for everything to be perfect, the moment can pass. You still have to commemorate it." He lets this sink in. "It was terrible timing," he says, laugh-ing, about so many events in his life. "But there's never a good time for anything." After a pause to make sure I'm listening, he smiles his crooked little smile. "I'm glad we went."

Terrible timing would be a hallmark of their early years together. Dad heard about an opportunity to go to England while my mother was pregnant with me. They decided he should grab it, and Mum would join him when he had settled and she had finished her PhD. In one sense, it was the perfect setup, because right after she had me she could head back to the lab, dropping me off with Nani and Nanaji for the day. But his life in England was grueling. For a paragon of orderli-ness and stability, crashing on friends' couches, moving from home to home within his small Indian network in the UK, was discouraging. In the weeks before Dad left, he remem-bers wondering if he was making a huge mistake, leaving his growing practice, wife, and tiny baby. But he hoped it would allow for a bigger life for us. Meanwhile, the photographs of

Mum's PhD ceremony show she was sullen again. "Why were
you sad this time?" I ask. Again, she looks at me like I'm nuts.
"I was getting my doctorate, I had a new baby, and your father
lived thousands of miles away," she says. "So you missed him,"
I coach her, "because you loved him." Right? "Because I was
lonely," she says.

"Young people mistake infatuation for love" was another
speech of my dad's, often, as I was growing up. "Infatuation is
chemical—but, like all chemical reactions, it burns out. Real
love grows over time." Again he would pause to let it sink in.
That's maybe the biggest part of his rhetorical style, letting
things sink in. "Do you understand, my child?" I didn't, at the
time. I found it profoundly anti-romantic. Even less romantic was his idea that marriage should be structured as "eight-
year options—because, you see, you've committed for a while,
but you can't back out until eight years are up. And then you
decided to reenlist, but it has to be for another eight years."
As a teenager buried under a pile of Gothic romances, I rolled
my eyes. But as I grew older, I thought it charming that they
seemed to like each other more as each eight-year increment
passed.

Though it's hard to get them to talk about warm fuzzies,
I've been watching my parents for my whole life, and to me,
they're a perfect match. For evidence of the romantic trope
"opposites attract," we'll start in Dad's closet. It's a tidy, compact walk-in, organized by season, wherein each item is ritu-
ally examined for wear and tear, refreshed, and rotated as the
weather changes. The shoe-closet annex, downstairs, is where
he polishes his large collection of small shoes—we are a family
of dainty feet—to a sheen, by hand. Every article of clothing,

every glistening oxford is a thoughtful purchase, and understated, designed to last, each item tended to like an heirloom.
He showed up a few months ago wearing a maroon cardigan,
which I complimented. "Mongolian wool," he murmured, por-
ing over some work before setting his reading aside to tell me
about the particularly fine qualities of the sheep whence it
came.

Mum's closet couldn't be more different. She has her
antique shawls, saris, jewelry, but loves a sparkly fast-fashion
shoe, some costume earrings, a pair of brightly colored capris.
Her closet is a riotous jumble, ten feet but worlds apart from
Dad's. She teases him about his fastidiousness, jokes about the
days when he'll quietly wander off for hours, to return with one
perfect pair of socks. But he's a creature who finds peace in
systems, eating the same sack lunch at the office for forty-odd
years now: a turkey sandwich, a yogurt, an apple, and a cup of
tea. Mum laughs when the turkey runs out and he's unnerved
by having a substitution—ham, say, or even cheese.

But, ultimately, like a jigsaw piece looking for its perfect
fit, his reliable, thoughtful nature is what she sought out in
him. My mother appreciates my father's steadiness and moral
compass. My father appreciates my mother's lightning-fast
mind, her resourcefulness through a lifetime of befuddling
situations, her exceptional hands-on parenting when he was
unavailable. My father is deliberate. About everything. Work,
rest, vacation, naps. Reading every word of the Sunday paper.
My mother moves haphazardly, full of surprises. She'll call
to say she's retiled the bathroom, for example, or to share
her detailed opinions on which *SNL* sketches aren't working
and why. I can't predict with any accuracy what she'll want to

talk about. Dad teases her with a diagnosis. "It could be adult ADHD," he says. Or she could just be curious and fun, right? "Yeah, well." He smiles. "She's a lot of fun, I won't argue with that."

But they still won't speak of romance, not that I'll ever stop noting evidence of it. I've seen Dad bringing home Pond's cold cream and English tea biscuits—traditional courtship gifts—for Mum on their anniversary. I see how content they are when they travel together, how they settle in when a train is delayed, to chat for an hour, or a day, doesn't matter. How they've shared the ritual of a small fries and coffee at a McDonald's in every country they've visited together. They'll call from a place they love, be it Portland or New Zealand, and claim they're building a new life there and never coming back, that I should send the children in the mail. In these moments, I see the adventurous kids they must have seen in each other, when they decided to join lives in a place where no one ever left.

And Dad didn't even want to get married when they met, as I remind him. I keep teasing it out: "She must have been something special for you to change your plans, no?"

"Well, look at her," my dad says, grinning. "Look at that face." And her hold over him endures, even if the decades since have made them grumpy. Once, when he was mad at her, my brother asked if Dad didn't find her behavior kind of—well—annoying. "The truth is, a man will tolerate a lot for a woman he finds attractive," he said with a sigh, and went back to his newspaper. And Mum lets her propriety slip from time to time as well, like when I asked her what drew her to him when they met and she, distracted, said, "His chest hair." She denies now ever saying this, but it's obviously seared into my brain, because it supports my theory that their relationship was born of something other than just common sense.

I know how much they love each other but have made it a personal goal to get them to acknowledge it, probably because they're so reticent—I want to strip them of the cultural wiring that allows them to discuss only facts, not feelings. I see the magic of what they've found in each other, and I push them to notice it as well. As I've become more fluent in talking about my emotions ("so sentimental," according to them), I fantasize about dragging some out of them, too. "You're always arguing with them," my brother once said, nearing the end of his infinite rope. "Could you just relax?" But I like to think I embrace the difficult conversations that bring us closer. I hope we get even more close as we get older, and sense that it will be easier to unpack their happy feelings before we get to the tricky ones. So I tell them that just because they don't talk about their love doesn't mean it's not there. They wave me off like the gnat I probably am. I pepper them, always, with leading questions, in some mad Sisyphean desire to have them collapse in a declaration of love in front of me. "Did she always own every room?" I asked Dad recently, and a smile slipped out. "She definitely had presence. From the beginning." He thought some more. "And you know what else? I liked her walk," he said. "You did???" I leaned in, excited about this new crumb. "I did," he said. "She had a sexy gait."

"He said WHAT?" screeched my mother into the phone, then burst into laughter. "Oh, I don't like that word! I always hated 'sexy.'" This could only come from a woman who takes it for granted, because she's been called it an incomprehensible number of times. A friend of mine once said he finds it difficult to maintain eye contact with her, and I understand why. Glare aside, she's magnetic—total strangers seek her smile and her approval. It's part of her magic, her hold over people. She grumbles on: "I've always hated it, like sexiness is something to aspire to, like that's all a woman has to offer." She heads down a winding feminist road before I remind her that no one who spends more than a minute with her would say she's anything less than a brilliant mind as well.

A brilliant mind in which the left brain always wins. As does Dad's, although he's trying. Surely there was something to their union beyond a pretty face, a sari, and an education, I tell Dad, still digging, at the end of a ninety-minute video call. It's a solid checklist, but he's describing half the women he grew up with. His brow knits as he mines his neatly filed memories. "Did she make you laugh?" I ask, and he says he didn't know she was funny until after the wedding, that the laughter has been a wonderful bonus. "Then what *was* it?" I ask, frustrated, and we sit, both irritable, for a while. He looks down, seeming for all the world like he's solving a problem set, attempting to unpack a lifetime of feeling, after seventy-odd years of mostly thinking. After a long silence, he looks back up and finally gives me the words I've always wanted. "Well, I suppose you'd call it love at first sight," he says. "Because I certainly didn't have any other basis for my decision." He lets it sink in, this time for both of us. "Yes. You can call it that, if you'd like."

Basherte

◁ 2011 ▷

". . . It's unfortunate, because the symbol has been used for millennia in the Hindu tradition," said my dad, doodling on a cocktail napkin. My Jewish fiancé paused. "But the thing is, Dr. Mattoo, the Nazis really made it their own." Dad nodded, and it was decided: no swastikas on our wedding programs.

To knit together our backgrounds in a more . . . culturally accommodating way, we recruited a friend to design all our wedding stationery, and she came up with a fun play on an Indian mandala, made up, if you looked closely, of little six-pointed stars. The motif was tasteful inclusive, which is what we hoped our wedding could be. Both sets of parents oohed and aahed.

I had never thought about my own wedding, growing up, but I did know how I thought weddings should *feel*. I ached for the intangibles of the Kashmiri summer weddings I'd attended as a child—vats of steaming food that never ran out, my family's rollicking laughter at all hours of the night. Jobs for everyone, even me, the tiniest guest: sometimes decorating the front steps with chalk, or carrying an important garment from here to there, in a mess of color and movement. The farther we moved away from home, the less likely a traditional Kashmiri wedding seemed, but I still held on to the vague hope that I might attend another one, someday. I supposed it would have to be mine.

But first I had to check everything else off my list. When my family moved to the United States, I was a teenager, and we had a plan for me: valedictorian, medical school, residency, marrying a nice Kashmiri boy. This plan was our armor against the great unknown. Coming from a relatively sheltered background, we didn't really know what distractions awaited us. America had wonderful things to offer, yes, but also a foreign parent's worst fears: sex, drugs, "hanging out." My life plan, unlike that of a lot of Indian kids who grew up here, wasn't really forced upon me. It was certainly supported, but I was an intense child, a "type A+," according to one history teacher. I didn't understand a lot of things when I first moved to the United States—social cues, jokes, or plotlines from everyone's favorite TV shows and movies. But as long as I could perform the valedictorian / medical school / marriage triathlon, I thought, I didn't have to. My immigrant soul craved stability, both professional and romantic. If I had my degrees in hand, and basic life needs under control, everything would fall into place, I thought.

My parents were good at marriage. I saw them cycle through hardship and stress, conflict and repair, and consistently come back to a foundation of mutual respect and affection. I also knew our community was small and scattered, so meeting someone from the same background would take some research and preparation. Still, thanks to the internet, and a fierce loyalty to one another, we Kashmiris are a tight-knit group, and for a long time, I couldn't imagine seeking a partner outside of it. I had wanted to give my parents this gift, after all their losses, and I believed in it for myself. I wanted a close-knit double-Kashmiri family. I saw it as an act of love for my culture. So I did everything on the expectations checklist: I got the grades and the scores, got a scholarship to college, pursued a second degree after that, and eventually figured out a stable job. And then came their gentle questions about settling down.

If arranged marriage is a spectrum, each unmarried Indian's experience—at least in my generation—was unique, like a fingerprint. I was on the fortunate end of that spectrum, because, in my case, no professional was consulted. There were no dramatic blood-pressure readings or preemptive wedding dates thrown around. My parents asked my permission to set me up with a few people and permission to put the word out that I was open to setups. It all seemed reasonable, and I wasn't exactly meeting strong candidates on my own. But demographics make marrying within our community statistically improbable, at best. Because there are about four hundred Kashmiri Pandit families in the United States, I was looking at a pool of maybe twenty single, age-appropriate men in the entire country. And I already knew most of them.

On the sliding scale of romantic to skeptical, I certainly didn't think I could settle down with just anyone, but I didn't believe in soulmates, for I am my parents' too-rational child. My longtime belief was that there were multiple people in the world I could probably make a life with, and who exactly I ended up with was a matter of geography and circumstance. I had a type, in my dating life: good, kind men, who were close to their families and had seen through my prickles. I loved them dearly and am fond of them still. Everyone I seriously dated is now happily married with two kids. But none of those keepers were right for me, and I had shied away from defining why. I hid behind the Kashmiri thing. It was probably the cultural stuff, I thought. So I kept my dating life hidden from my parents—I didn't need to burden them with information that wasn't going to lead to any major life changes.

"I need someone who makes me laugh," I told my parents, over and over again. A funny, kind guy with a nice family. One who wanted kids. But this was a goal they didn't know how to achieve. Traditional Indian matchmaking starts with who we are on paper. How were they going to quantify which of the résumés they collected were funny? Maybe a personal essay, I suggested, and my mother sighed. "Funny's not important!" she said. "Who's funny?" "Well, you are," I pointed out, and she used it against me: "See, you already have me to make you laugh."

I was good on paper, too—I had a bunch of degrees and interests, and our family was well liked—but that meant nothing when men met me, because I had visible trouble mustering up any enthusiasm for anyone who wasn't an immediate fit. I was set up with one guy whom I then tried to set up with another friend. His mother called mine to complain. Another guy was fun (and almost funny), but we didn't click in that way. "What's wrong with him?" asked my parents, who apparently would have married him in a second. But I couldn't explain the lack of chemistry, a factor they found totally irrelevant. "He . . . ummm . . . drank a lot," I lied, grasping at straws, and though I still feel terrible for slandering him in that way, at least it crossed him off their list.

Mum finally got frustrated about my "pickiness." "What do

you even want?" she said at a family wedding in India, as my adorable cousin Aditi—far too young and chill to be harangued about marriage—floated nearby, laughing at my mother's comment. "Show me one man here who you might talk to." I pointed to a guy across the way—in a linen kurta, with his friends laughing at something he'd just said. "That guy's cute," I told her, and Mum's face fell. "Oh God. Don't marry a writer type," she said, and walked away, complaining about rumpled clothes and cigarette smoke.

But meeting all these men was making me question myself. *Was* I being too picky? What if I never felt a spark, or recognized that I wanted to be with someone forever?

I've since used the word "pressure" to describe how I felt painted into a corner by these setups, but it wasn't necessarily just external. As I started meeting these guys, the hardest part was feeling like I was disappointing people I loved so much. The hope in my parents' voices when they'd bring up a young man, the confusion and negotiation in response to my "we just don't click." My far-flung aunties' disappointment when they felt I had rejected their sons. I didn't have much experience at letting so many people down at once. I had been a gold-star Kashmiri kid! But now my star was imploding, dashing hopes and bruising feelings left and right. An invested, optimistic audience was watching my every move as we worked our way down a short, intertwined list. With every failed match, the hope of re-creating the community we had lost dimmed, and it all started to feel suffocating and hopeless. Rather than share all these feelings with my parents, feelings I can only now articulate with the benefit of time and distance, I silently spiraled down, far away and lonely in Los Angeles.

Dating in LA was unsatisfying. I met men when I traveled, probably because I was happiest somewhere else, and it felt friendly and low-stakes. But in Los Angeles, where we all worked obsessive, stressful seventy-hour weeks, I shuddered to think I might pair up with another Hollywood type. People were starting to take internet dating seriously, so I made a Match.com profile and flagged a cute guy who had recently moved to the city. By the time I got back to my laptop to run him by my roommate, Jenny, his profile was unavailable. We joked that we should screen guys at the airport, holding signs. And our only social life was work events, which were never fun, because our bosses hovered nearby, and you couldn't have real fun in front of the clients. One notable exception was the premiere of a forgotten movie called *Fred Claus*, which I remember as a peak Hollywood experience—some pals and I scraped together tickets from a kindly exec and just plain looted the party. There was a bouncy slide, an ice-skating rink, many drinks, and Larry David yelled at us about leaving a mess at one of the booths. After a last-minute stop at the picked-over Build-A-Bear station, I fell into a cab with a teddy bear wearing a yarmulke, tighty-whities, and a beard. *This life isn't so bad,* I thought. *Maybe it's okay to be alone. Better than just settling.*

Then a visit home. "I don't know why it's so hard for you to meet someone," Mum mentioned, breezy. "I've met lots."

I normally would have tuned this out, but I could tell she had more to say. "Where have you met them?" I asked.

"Shaadi.com"—the Indian matrimonial site.

I yelped.

"Not under your real name!" she assured me.

I looked at the profile, which was basically a catfishing

setup, and "my" overflowing inbox. This is when I threw a tantrum, and distanced myself from them a bit.

I was disgruntled and homesick the following week, when I walked into another premiere—this was right around the time when I started to realize maybe I shouldn't be a Hollywood agent. I stood there, miserable, in flip-flops and an army surplus jacket, surveying a terrace-full of people I mostly wanted to avoid, and I made a beeline for the closest friendly faces I saw, even though I didn't know them at all. Joan and Howard were in from New York, visiting their son, who usually worked as a writer but had produced the movie. I loved them instantly. They were so proud, their beaming, open faces had drawn me from across the room. We chitchatted for maybe ten minutes, and I remember feeling comfortable and safe. It felt like hanging out with my own parents, but without all the stressful marriage talk. A few minutes in, a young man walked up with a drink for his mother, and that is how I met my husband, Rodney.

As it happened, I had read a book he'd written—a memoir about living in a retirement community in Florida in his late twenties—and it was definitely funny. I remembered him describing a high-end retirement home as "designed to make a retired fabric wholesaler feel like the CEO of Fiat." But I also found it sweet and thoughtful. I remembered that he dated here and there in the book, but the woman he found the most enchanting was a sultry retiree named Vivian, who'd lived a big life. I found that charming. I had jokingly asked my mother for personal essays, and here I had access to an entire memoir.

We didn't date right away. He was working out of town for a little while, and I had moved to a new job. I was too preoccupied to close the gap between us, but I remembered his smile, and his nice family. I also remember, very clearly, thinking, *I'm dating the wrong kind of guy. I should date someone like Rodney.*

When he got back home a few weeks after we met, he was drawn to a Facebook comment I left on a mutual friend's wall. He liked my photo—I have it somewhere, an off-kilter, blurry party-girl shot, with which I may have sold myself as more fun than I am (too late now!)—and sent me a message. The nice thing about messaging with a comedy writer was, he was good at banter. The terrible thing about messaging with a comedy writer was that it went on forever. By day three, I had had enough. "Are you going to ask me out?" I finally said. It was before we LOLed with impunity, but he responded with a string of exclamation marks, a time, and a place. I asked around for friends who knew him and had opinions. "With Rodney, what you see is what you get," said one mutual friend, and that was the most appealing review of an adult man I had heard in a long while.

We had drinks at the Prince in Koreatown, a dimly lit basement bar with red leather booths. I mentioned that I had read his book. "Really?" he asked, eyebrows shooting up his forehead. "Not for this *date*," I told him. "Just because I *read.*" He had also written for a show I liked called *Undeclared,* and I mentioned I loved the episode where Jason Segel's character falls asleep crying, clutching a pillow on which he's printed his girlfriend's face. "I wrote that!" he said, genuinely excited that I liked it. I texted my brother this information while Rodney was in the restroom. "MARRY HIM," said Punit. I quickly put my phone away before Rodney got back. At the end of our drinks—I don't even remember what we talked about, just that it was a fast four hours—he said he wanted to see me again. I asked when, and he said tomorrow. "I'm not seeing anyone else," he started. "I would really . . . like it if you didn't see anyone else, either." "Sure," I said, tickled that he thought I had a bench of suitors to disappoint. On our third date, to another work party, he started to introduce me as his serious girlfriend, seeing if I'd blink. I did not.

The first time I went over to Rodney's house, a cozy little bungalow tucked away on a hillside, he roasted some salmon on a cedar plank. While he wrapped things up in the kitchen, I looked over his bookshelves. I already sensed we'd have all the same books, and we did. I smiled at a memory of my most recent ex, who had been a kind man and terrific boyfriend but not a book person. Still, I'd been reluctant to break up, and as we were negotiating the inevitable but sad reality that we'd need to, he sighed and said, "Don't you want to be with someone who reads?" I'm not proud to say my infatuated response was "I read enough for both of us!" But now, as I moved along, reading the titles of the books, I knew I definitely wanted to be with someone who read.

And in addition to the books . . . well, there's no cool way to get into this, but I love dioramas. Maybe it's because they exist at the intersection of storytelling and crafts. Rodney had a large, intricate wooden one on his shelf that drew me in: a crowd of busy people in a workshop. I asked what it was, and he poked his head out. "It's a diorama of people making dioramas," he said. I absorbed that for a second. It seemed like an important sign, and I couldn't stop the words that next popped out of my mouth: "We could have a nice life together." He didn't hear me clearly from the kitchen, and asked me to repeat myself. "WE COULD HAVE A NICE LIFE TOGETHER," I shouted. He sort of scratched his beard, nodded, and finished cooking the fish.

I called my mother to say I had met someone, and it had the potential to be serious. I took a deep breath. "He's not Indian," I continued, and she sat in silence for a while. I thought I would be terrified—I had never really shared news of a relationship before—but something about this one made me feel brave enough, and she could tell. "Let me know when it's real" was her reply.

"If he's not going to be Indian, he should at least be exceptional," I'd later learn my dad had said as they lay awake at night, worried about my future. And Rodney was exceptional—exceptionally sweet, and, yes, funny, with a beautiful brain that surprises and delights me still. I wasn't sure what my dad would think, but I knew my parents well enough, and I had a hunch. My father's voice echoed in my head as our relationship deepened: "You'll know real, lasting love, because it grows over time," he always said. And the more time I spent with my new beau, the more I liked him. I had also spent a little more time with his family, who were still lovely. Joan and Howard were just as supportive and patient as they had been that first time we met. His twin sister, Samantha, was a dream, with two adorable kids and the sweetest husband. Just seeing the way they all talked to each other reminded me of my own home. And I found it soothing, in the early days of our dating, that I already knew that his family was objectively not crazy.

Rodney's book spends a whole chapter on *basherte,* the idea that every Jewish person meets up with the other half of their soul. He had done a lot of thinking about this in his twenties.

"Your *basherte* can be non-Jewish. But she has to convert to Judaism. Her soul is already Jewish, even if she isn't," said one of his octogenarian pals, in the book.

"I think my *basherte* is one of the non-Jewish ones," says Rodney carefully.

"Too many exotic girls will make your putz fall off," warns his other friend Arthur.

I didn't have a lot of people to talk to about the cultural implications of my relationship, but my brother met and liked Rodney. Still, when I mentioned he had dated a few brown girls, Punit asked how many: "Two times is a coincidence, three times is a fetish," he said.

On the anniversary of our first date, we went to Santa Barbara for the weekend. He casually asked, while pouring a glass of wine, "Can kids have bar mitzvahs if their moms aren't Jewish?" My heart sank. Here came the religious thing, where we'd have to part ways. We'd had a nice run, but I was never going to convert. But he wasn't asking me to convert, it turned out. He really was just wondering. So we looked it up on the laptop right there, and learned that they absolutely could, and then we sat there quietly for a bit, thinking that things seemed pretty serious. But then he wanted to meet my parents, and I warned him against it. "The wedding clock will start ticking immediately," I told him. There was no dating with my people, or so I thought, before I realized my parents were liars. "It's just gonna be 'Okay, when's the wedding?' every week until there's a wedding." He insisted that he wanted to meet them, that he understood what he was getting into and was up for the challenge.

The next time my parents visited, we all had dinner at a Middle Eastern restaurant, because everyone involved loves hummus. My father was in professor mode, assessing Rodney as though he were defending a dissertation. Mum was unusually quiet, just listening and waiting for my dad's lead—and at some point, Dad pushed his chair back and said, "So you're a funny writer, but does that mean you're a funny *person?*" Rodney hesitated, and I had to jump in to defend his honor. "He's very funny, Dad!" I said. And I met my mother's eyes. She knew this meant a lot to me. We rode home in silence—me, my mother, and my dad. I could see his wheels turning, and fifteen minutes in, he spoke up. "He must have worked very hard to accomplish what he's accomplished," said my father slowly. "Hardworking" is his highest compliment. I smiled into the dark.

And then came the questions. My parents really hadn't had any experience with the idea of Western dating, so any conversations about my relationship were executed in a tone of pure sociological, data-gathering curiosity.

"If this doesn't work out, do you have a backup plan?" asked Dad, almost two years into my relationship with Rodney. I asked him to clarify. "For an engagement," he said.

"Are you asking if I have a second boyfriend, with whom I'm also so serious that marriage is an option?"

He considered this for an unreasonably long time.

"Yes," he said.

I did not.

The unrelenting barrage of questions confirmed that my

parents loved my boyfriend—not that they'd ever say the word "boyfriend." They'd rather he was my fiancé.

"Can you . . . not ruin this?" asked Rodney, irritable over brunch one March, when I shared that my parents had indeed been following up on our engagement plans every weekend. I reminded him that I had warned of this, and now he had to share the burden. I wasn't necessarily in a rush, but I did want all the noise to stop. "Tell them we'll be engaged by summer," he said, going back to his eggs. "But, please, ask them not to take the fun out of it for us." I told my parents we'd be engaged by summer, and they immediately dropped the subject.

By May, Rodney had been in Las Vegas for work and we hadn't seen much of each other for a while, so we planned a weekend trip to Big Sur. It was as magnificent and serene as everyone said it was, but I was nervous about the lack of cell phone reception. Though my mother kept trying me—I had somehow missed her thirteen times in a row—I wasn't able to pick up or reach her. Rodney encouraged me to ignore it, saying that we could wait until we got back. I sat, uneasily, with the idea that I might be missing an emergency. He pointed out that she would have texted, which eased my mind. But I found a large rock I could stand on and get a little reception. The phone finally connected, and she picked up. I was relieved to hear her voice. "Is everything okay?" I asked.

"Yeah, I was just calling to catch up," she said, relaxed. I told Rodney this, and he shook his head.

That night, he woke me up with a plan to see the Milky Way. We wrapped ourselves in plush hotel robes, and as we entered the chill of night, I put my hands in my pockets, finding a scrap of paper in one of them.

"Someone left trash in the robes!" I said, and then I looked closely at the paper under the moonlight. It was the stub of a boarding pass. "To where?" he asked, nonchalant.

I squinted—the lack of light pollution was not helping. "From Las Vegas to Detroit. How weird! I wonder who went to Detroit!"

"I did," he said.

I hmm'd, still squinting at the paper, trying to make out more information.

"I did, to see your father." He was louder this time.

Then I noticed he was down on one knee, and I screeched. "Who knew? My parents knew? Jenny? Did anyone else know?"

"Are you gonna say yes?" he asked, and I did, and he slid the ring on my finger. It glittered in the light, a round rose-cut diamond surrounded by a ring of smaller gems. I had never thought about an engagement ring in my life, but I was instantly in love with this one, which felt streamlined and modern, but looked Indian, somehow. I found out he had asked our friend Irene to design the ring, with the guideline "It has to be something her mother will like."

It meant so much to me that he had known that this would be important, that my parents were fully invested. I would have said yes anyway, but it double-confirmed our choice. We drove home the next day, giddy, and blew a tire just outside Santa Barbara. The tow-truck driver who picked us up had a white handlebar mustache and a matching mullet. He teared up when we told him we were newly engaged. "I love love, man," he said as he dropped us off at the tire place.

My mother squealed on the phone, beside herself. She had known the plan and had barely been able to sleep since I left

LA. Now all those missed calls made a lot more sense. "It happened at dinner, right?" she said, glossing over the facts. This was an easier story to retell to her friends and family, instead of a sleepover before marriage. "Congratulations," said my dad on the phone. "Excellent progress. And you're not going to move in together—that won't fly." I laughed.

The two sets of parents were nervous about meeting each other, but I wasn't at all. I was on weekly catch-ups with both sets by that point, and the calls were generally the same. Costco, errands, seeing some friends, maybe "a nice walk." They could have been buddies already. By sheer coincidence, Rodney's parents were in Michigan for a wedding a couple of weeks after we got engaged, and they went over to my parents' for the big summit. My mother sounded nervous on the phone, but afterward they all chatted about one another like they were old pals. As I knew they would.

And then wedding planning kicked in, in earnest. My only touchstone for weddings I liked were the family pile-ups from home, so we got married in Michigan, near my parents' house. We both wanted a big fun party, and, because we were both marrying outside of our own cultures, wanted both families to feel included and involved. Rodney and I picked the venue and DJ and arranged for a constant open bar. Everything else was delegated to our parents, and both sets got to work, elated.

The day I landed in Michigan, a week before the ceremony, I tried on everything my mother had bought in India and had to negotiate down the jewels. She would have had me laden like Nefertiti, and I hadn't considered how heavy the embroidery and beadwork would be on my body, forget the pounds of gold on my head. We arrived at a compromise of heavy necklaces and light earrings. I allowed one delicate thing in my hair, but it had to be pinned down—we couldn't rely on my posture. Enough bangles to jangle but not to restrict my movement. She was happy with her Kashmiri bride, and so was I.

Twenty-nine members of our extended family slept at my parents' house. We do not have close to twenty-nine bedrooms, as you can imagine, so people were piled up in sleeping bags and blankets in every spare inch. But it felt like the Kashmiri summer weddings we had loved: everyone up all night, falling asleep late to music and raucous laughter wafting up from downstairs; when I woke up in the morning, I stepped over snoring bodies to find my way to the kitchen, where one or two early risers were making a gigantic cauldron of tea. We were a long way from Srinagar, but it felt like home just the same.

I was so happy to be making everyone happy that I also submitted to a full henna application, which was, strangely, when things started to unravel for me. The artist arrived at 7:00 a.m. to start the process, which took four hours to do my arms, from hands to elbows, and legs, feet to knees, followed by eight hours of just sitting there as the henna set and dried. I stayed on the couch, watching DVDs and not moving, while people wandered in and out. By hour six, I was bored to tears, everyone was gone, and the DVD player was stuck on the pilot episode of *Arrested Development,* which played on loop. I leaned back on the couch to try to nap, but couldn't find a position that wouldn't smudge my hands.

I started to crack in hour seven, when my cousin Aditi had come back and was assembling the gift bags I wasn't allowed to touch. We found that the decorative stickers with the wedding motif on them were printed off-center. Aditi, almost fifteen years younger than me but twice as calm, volunteered to trim them properly, but watching her do it drove me into a tizzy. I was starting to get anxious about everyone's arriving and having a good time, and the stickers were the unfortunate recipient of my growing agita. "Why are there corners on them?" I grumbled. "Circles aren't supposed to have corners." "I'm doing the best I can," she murmured, "and no one's gonna notice." Finally, after hours of this, my head about to burst, my henna starting to flake off, I lunged for her and tried to fix them myself, only to find that the scissors I had given her were left-handed—and neither of us is. She's never let me forget it.

The day of the wedding, I woke up bleary-eyed from the welcome drinks of the night before. But makeup started at eight o'clock, and dressing soon thereafter, so there was no time to recover. Around lunch, my friend Ali helpfully gave me a five-hour energy drink—my first ever—which made my heart race and my nerves jangle. There were so many guests, I gasped, and everyone was going to be looking at me in my . . . *costume*. I had been so focused on the big happy multicultural wedding—on making sure our families were satisfied, on giving them everything they had ever wanted in a wedding—that I had forgotten I'd be at the center of it. I knew how it all looked, from the outside: Is there anything more symbolic of good fortune than a lively Indian wedding? But my lifelong fear of attention and scrutiny picked an inconvenient time to bubble over.

When I thought of all the eyes that would be trained on me, the breath nearly left my body. My stomach dropped, and I broke into a full sweat. "Find Rodney and tell him I want to get married in the parking lot," I told my cousin Preeti. Was it too late to elope? By the time I was supposed to be walking in,

I was breathing into a paper bag while Jenny—now my maid of honor—tried to calm me down. I hyperventilated for half an hour. I'm so rarely late to anything that Rodney started to think I had run away, and mentally prepared remarks about it for the assembled crowd. *How am I going to explain that Pri has left me at the altar?* he thought. *What words am I going to use?* I finally got it together enough to let my parents walk me down the aisle—I was so nervous that it felt like they were carrying me. But I grasped Rodney's hands at the end of the aisle and held on tight. Fortunately, the endless double ceremony— with the open bar we had negotiated—did its job, and my agita passed. I got used to standing up there, in pounds of finery, with everyone looking at me while I looked only at Rodney. And when I finally calmed down enough to take in the guests, my heart swelled at the sight of our sprawling families, all beaming, all together.

It was always going to be books that brought me my husband, and it's only fitting that I stepped right into the one he wrote: many of the characters from Rodney's memoir were guests at our wedding and are now some of my closest friends. The book is a beautiful artifact to have, and as I reread it, I think about how lonely he was when he wrote it, how he also wondered if there was anyone out there with whom he could build a life. I love the chapter about his sexy elderly friend Vivian, in which they have a conversation where she keeps referring to the actor Christopher Reeve as "Reeves," and he's tried to correct her a few times, in vain. "I look at Vivian for a few seconds, and then I understand that she is a woman who has never lost an argument in her life, even when she was wrong," he wrote.

This dynamic sounds awfully familiar to me: Rodney often marvels at my breathtaking record for presenting conjecture as fact. I text him to ask if I'm Vivian. "Vivian-adjacent," comes the quick reply.

"It's like I set out a piece of bait for the family I wanted to start one day," he says now, about his memoir. "Well, I tasted a crumb, and went looking for the whole loaf," I joke. And it wasn't just him sending out flares to the universe. When we finally moved in together, a full three months after we got married, Rodney helped me move out of the house I shared with Jenny. In the back of a hall closet he found the Build-A-Bear I tipsily made a year before I met him, and silently took in its kippah, its shaggy beard, its tighty-whities. And here's where I have to reveal that Rodney often walks around the house in his undies, because he was immediately startled that I had created a semi-naked bearded Jewish teddy bear, for no discernible reason. "Did you magick me into being?" he asked, dead serious, and it seems like I did. "It was the underwear that tipped you off, right?" I say, and he laughs. "No, Pri. It was the yarmulke."

Fifteen years after we met, we have two kids, whom I birthed in my mid- and late thirties—"Excellent progress," said Dad, when I told him, both times. And . . . marriage is marriage. We love each other deeply, and also we make each other nuts in a way that was previously incomprehensible. We hobble through hard times and emerge stronger and ever more grateful to have each other. We hurt each other's feelings, we get cranky about schedules and kids and I-thought-it-was-your-turn and all that kind of normal stuff. I still cringe a little at the word "soulmate," which diminishes the depth and breadth of the journey we're on. But he's the only guy I was ever meant to take it with.

And we have lots of company. Both sets of parents are about to fly out for our daughter's birthday, and tasks are carved up among them: balloons, cupcakes, goody bags, decorations, chauffeuring. A full-family group project, like we're re-creating a mini-wedding every time. And I'm chatting on the phone, mid-belly-laugh, when my husband walks in and asks who I'm talking to. I used to feel a little funny when I said "your parents," but he's used to it now. "Can I say hi?" he half jokes, and I, magnanimous, allow it. I've only recently learned that not everyone calls their in-laws that often, but Joan and Howard are not everyone's in-laws.

I have created the most conventional of Kashmiri lives for myself, if you overlook my technically non-Kashmiri husband, with the warm double family I always wanted. And my parents love it all, too, not that they'd ever say it in those words. "That *SNL* sketch reminds me of you and Rodney," teases my mother. I wait for what's next. "It's called 'Two A-Holes,'" she says, referring to Kristen Wiig's and Jason Sudeikis's gum-smacking narcissists, and I cackle. She pretends she doesn't know she's being funny. "What? They call each other 'babe' a lot. You guys do that." Okay, fair.

"A relationship with a non-Jewish woman is like a vacation. It's short, it's exciting, it's different, and if I want I can go home afterward," wrote Rodney when he was twenty-eight, and I will never let him forget it. But I can't blame him for that, because it's exactly how I felt. And I guess the joke's on both of us. Because, when he goes home, we're all right there, and most days, we're laughing our faces off.

Bildungsroman

❈ 1990–1994 ❧

Sometime in 1990, when I was ten, I wore an Outfit to school. I thought it was a good Outfit, but maybe someone else, someone who understood clothes, should have weighed in. A formal slim black skirt, a pink jersey crop top with green enamel buttons and an asymmetrical, ruffled hem. It was a massive departure from my usual oversized jeans and T-shirt, the uniform I wore so that I didn't have to think about my clothes, but on this day I thought I'd try something different. For emotional safety, though, I kept on my tube socks and sneakers.

Brad F.—tall, blond Californian idiot Brad F., crush of many (but not me) at the American International School in Riyadh—clocked me as I walked down the stairs. He looked— honestly?—perplexed. This wasn't the response I was going for. "Why didn't you shave your legs?" he asked me. *Oh, dear God,* I thought. *Good question.* Why hadn't I? Maybe I didn't know it was an expectation. Maybe I thought we were too young. I knew my mother waxed her legs, but she barely had any body hair. I had my dad's coarse, wiry hair, all over, and I hadn't much thought about it, because it was usually covered up. Or maybe because I was wrestling with bigger issues: back home, Srinagar was a mess, and here in Saudi, troops were gathering all around us after Saddam Hussein's invasion of Kuwait. Yes, I had a lot on my mind, but middle school stakes were high, and Brad made a fair point—not that I'd award it to him. My overdeveloped sense of gender injustice took the wheel. "Why didn't you shave yours?" I said as I stormed past. In retrospect, it was a powerfully feminist statement; maybe it made him think for a while, if he was ever capable of thinking. But I tucked it away in my mind and thought: *Okay. Must learn about hair removal.*

My relationship with the opposite sex thus far had been mostly combative, in the manner of small children. I was sitting in my third-grade social studies class one day when Mrs. Woseley informed us that we were starting a new project and had to pick partners. The class heartthrob was Mateo S., a bright-eyed, olive-skinned Peruvian boy, whose parents were petroleum engineers, like so many of my peers' parents. He leaped out of his seat that day to ask me if I would be his partner. The force with which he launched himself across the room probably had more to do with a sugar-heavy lunch than with any sort of affection for me, but he did plant a wet kiss on my face when I agreed. As his mouth left my damp cheek, I slapped him; he raised his palm to the stinging red spot, and I slapped him across the other cheek. I blame being a little younger than my classmates and still registering boys as gross and dumb. But I was also (and remain) rattled by sudden movements.

Luckily, Mrs. Woseley, busy behind her desk, didn't notice my behavior, but our classmates certainly did, and by the time I made it out to recess that day, the older girls were huddled in groups, dispersing when they saw me. Asha M. walked up to me with an accusatory gleam in her eyes. "I hear you kissed Mateo today." I rolled my eyes and cleared up the situation, but nobody wanted to hear the truth. (In an event unrelated, I hope, Mateo's family moved back to Lima later that year.)

In fourth grade, in Mrs. Vance's class, the only boy who paid me any mind was Hani K., the local irritant. He was a loud, hyperactive, wiry little guy who never knew when to shut up, and when the teacher told him he'd have to be quiet in class or see the principal, Hani started passing me notes. It began with a few notes a day, maybe three or four, and escalated to sixteen, all of which said a version of the same thing: "What are you doing?" Not having had the presence of mind to throw them away and deflate his mischief, or the chutzpah to ball them up in my mouth and spit them back at him—which is what I wanted to do—I raised my hand in class one day and asked if I could sue him.

Much to my pleasure, Mrs. Vance said I could file a formal complaint. I'm not sure if she sensed a teachable moment about the American legal system, or if she was just so used to a range of eccentricities at this school, where each kid arrived with their own cultural handbook. I walked in the next day with a tasseled scroll, upon which I had listed a terrifically boring rundown of every note that Hani had ever passed me. The relief I sought, outlined at the bottom of the scroll, was simple: move Hani to the other side of the class. A trial ensued, during which Hani sat there glum, mumbling to himself as he was examined and cross-examined by our peers. The jury voted in my favor, and Hani never wrote a note again. I felt beyond victorious, although later would have to shush a twinge of regret that I had stifled him so.

At this age, I reserved my worst frostiness for boys, whom I still found pointless. But to the girls in fifth grade, I sent out hopeful tendrils. I had a falling-out with my best (and only) friend at the beginning of the year, and, on top of the Kashmir situation and growing tensions in the Middle East, I was generally nervous. But I was also ready to have some friends who weren't books, and started to recognize some kindred spirits. Connie, a Hawaiian Chinese girl I couldn't believe picked me back; Mel from Georgia, who had a heart as big as the bow her mother put in her hair every morning; and Mwana, who claimed that she was so agile on the playground because she climbed coconut trees to reap the fruit for the entire village back home in Kenya. I squinted, knowing she had a cheeky sense of humor. "Aren't your parents engineers?" I asked, and she laughed at me. "Yes, but someone's still got to get the coconuts!" She was definitely messing with me, and I liked her a lot.

Things started to shift one day, after library, when I walked back to class behind Connie and grew alarmed at a red stain spreading across the seat of her white jeans. She was trying to cover it up with her stack of books. I pulled her aside. "Connie, you're BLEEDING." "I know!" she hissed, panicked. She didn't know what it was. And then she ducked out to the nurse and disappeared for the rest of the day. I shared this with my mother, who sighed and filled me in. I was rattled. It was too soon for us to be women. Wasn't it?

I started to see the effects of puberty seeping into most of the girls, their heads now turned by this boy or that. But my own logic hadn't softened. When the girls were starting to giggle and preen more, I genuinely could not understand why anyone would rather talk about boys than read or splash around in the pool. I stopped being able to hang out with most of the girls altogether the day Mel "confessed," quietly, "I know that everyone says they love Joey McIntyre, you guys, but I want you to know that I'm different. I actually do love him." Maybe I would have had an idea of what she was talking about, or a greater affinity for our first mega boy band, if the "Step by Step" VHS that Dad tried to bring back from London for me hadn't been seized at the airport by immigration officers. And then, one Halloween, when Dad picked me up from trick-or-treating, I had forgotten my violin at Mel's house. Mum was irritated. I went to my room, sorted through the candy, and when I went to the bathroom, I saw it: a spot of blood in my underwear. I ran to my mother. "I think my period made me forgetful," I told her, and she just stared at me: what a way to deliver that information.

By sixth grade, I was finally starting to think about boys. Or, at least, one in particular, and it was for him I had worn the Outfit. Jaime Ramirez met all my emerging criteria for good people: He was polite to the teacher, got good grades, seemed well-liked by his soccer team—things I found commendable. He had a deep tan, and shiny black hair he was always brushing out of his eyes. But the je ne sais quoi? He had a little sister, with whom he was very close, and he treated her kindly. Thus, he created the prototype for my lifelong affinity for "keepers." In any case, he didn't notice my Outfit. When I came back from recess, my teacher, Ms. Ellis, who must have been used to the hormones afflicting the sixth grade, threw a pity compliment my way. "What a fantastic shirt!" she said. "I'm not used to you dressing up." I grunted a response. I had wanted to wake up Jaime, not Ms. Ellis, who liked me already.

Sirens went off just then, and the class lined up to walk glumly to an air-raid drill. I strapped on my consulate-issue gas mask as we sat in line in between the shelves of the library, waiting for an all clear. Saddam hadn't sent any Patriot missiles over to us during the day yet—he was only stirring things up after nightfall—but I guess you never know what a murderous despot might get up to. I saw Jaime down the way and folded my furry legs in, self-conscious. The kids were grumbling—it wasn't a real war, they all said. Ms. Ellis, who had been a Marine, said it never hurt to be prepared.

We were in silent competition for who could be the most nonchalant about the drills, but I was terrified at first. I remember running into my parents' room the first night the sirens went off, shrieking, "But I was going to be a doctor!" My mother burst into laughter and said, "You're not going to die." "Are you sure?" I asked, wiping away my tears. "Everything is going to be fine," she said. She was, unfortunately, an old hand at air raids from her childhood, and her confidence in my safety was contagious. "Well, the war didn't feel like a *real* war," Mum recently told me via FaceTime, from Michigan. "You went to school, you could play outside, the disruption was only at night." I didn't share her nonchalance, but I was small and didn't have the words for what I was feeling—it simply seemed easier to avoid death talk in favor of, say, my first crush. And besides, I wasn't allowed to be scared. If I got scared, Punit might be as well, and I couldn't bear that.

My spirits were low when I got home that day, after the drill. All I cared about was peeling out of that dumb skirt. I asked Mum if I could wax my legs, and she hesitated. Or could I shave them? I asked. She worried I was too young to be thinking about that kind of thing—was it really important? I didn't want to have to talk her into it, so I sneaked Dad's razor blade that night and shredded my knees to bits. *Probably better just to wear pants,* I thought.

We went shopping that weekend to replenish our emergency war supplies. We hadn't exactly had enough of an emergency yet to deplete them, but curiosity had gotten the best of me, and my brother and I had been snacking on the contents. So we wandered to the Sarawat supermarket. My mother's matter-of-fact attitude toward the goings-on was evident in what she put into the box. Along with a few tins of staple goods, we had some pâté, assorted exotic dried fruits, and a number of international foods we had never tasted but wanted to. Plus whatever we kids threw in there. It was like we were stocking up for Christmas.

The next week, back in my jeans, I showed Jaime that I loved him the only way I knew how: by bickering. About what, I don't know, but we each ended up muttering about how weird the other one was. "No, you're weird"—really witty stuff. Even Ms. Ellis's patience had limits. She kept us all in for recess. As she walked to the front of the class, she looked unusually stern, her clenched jaw offsetting her choice to wear a stud earring in one ear and a dangly Christmas ornament in the other. "Now, look, kids," she started. It was time for a serious talk. She had heard us tossing around the word "weird" at each other, she said. "'You're weird, that's weird, isn't Ms. Ellis so *weird*?' I think the word you're looking for is 'interesting,'" she continued. She asked if we liked her earrings, shaking her head so the Christmas ornament caught the light. We loved them. We loved her. We loved everything about her. She was the kind of teacher who inspired an ardent devotion. "Well, they're not weird to me. I think they're interesting. You want to use the word 'interesting' as well, because 'weird' can feel hurtful." We filed out to recess, enlightened.

Meanwhile, at home, my brother, now five to my ten, was emerging as a stone-cold genius. Our nightly routine in Riyadh included waking up to blaring air-raid sirens. The family would stumble down to our makeshift bunker, a large storage closet under the stairs. There we strapped on our gas masks, tried to get some rest on the floor, and then crawled back up to bed at dawn. After a week of this, Punit had had enough. He asked me to help drag our twin mattresses to the bunker, then fell asleep on his while wearing his gas mask, and that's how we did the rest of the war: well rested, on our backs. Comfort, and common sense, can come from the most unexpected of places.

As Mum predicted, there was a certain rhythm to the raids, a reliability that was soothing, in a way. We fielded calls from home about what was being shown on CNN and Star News. "It's not as bad as it looks," promised my parents. The war seemed like it was happening behind a glass door, and it was. Saudi oil was valuable, but our version of the war felt like hearing neighbors fight, while bracing for an object to be thrown through the window. Our relative adjacency to danger allowed me the distraction of standard middle school agita. Come every morning, I could turn my mind back to matters that seemed more urgent: If Jaime and I bugged each other so much, why did I want to be around him? Why did boys make girls so crazy?

I started to understand this when I radio-controlled my befuddled dad into buying my first CD (Pearl Jam, *Ten*) at a music store, which only men could enter, in 1991. As I listened to Eddie Vedder crooning in the dark, the lower half of my body warmed right up. Eddie was a universe away from Joey McIntyre, but I understood now what Mel at school had been talking about. Whereas Joey's appeal lay in his childlike face and sweet young voice, I was drawn to Eddie's low, urgent rumble. Now, here was a guy who could take care of things, I felt. The uncertainty I was steeped in—conflict in my far-away home, the war, the torture of becoming a woman—called for a guy who could take care of things. And in the lyrics—about homelessness, about the horrors of state psychiatric hospitals—his sense of justice eclipsed even mine. I squinted at the album cover, which gave me only the barest sense of what he looked like. In my pre-internet, pre-TV days, there weren't many other photos readily available, so his voice was all I had to go on. But what a voice. By the end of the album, as for so many anguished adolescent girls discovering Eddie, all of my neurons were on fire. I suddenly understood—like, *really* understood—what I wanted from Jaime.

And in a move familiar to anguished adolescents all over the world, my parents disrupted our love story. Albeit unknowingly. The escalation in troops was worrying, and just because Riyadh felt safe now, they said, didn't mean it always would. So they flew us to India to see out the end of the war. We were away for the few weeks it took to end, and I came back to a tragedy: my friend Resham told me that Tiffani M. told her that Heather T. had her eye on Jaime. "Heather T. looks like she smokes cigarettes on field trips!" I screeched. But even as the words left my mouth, I knew she was going to get her way, and I was devastated.

In seventh and eighth grades, with Jaime lost to me forever, the other boys at school felt like annoyances by comparison. I recently reconnected with one, my friend Pheroze—I think he'd be comfortable with my calling him the class clown, albeit a very smart one—who described me thus:

> *I remember you took classes really seriously and seemed annoyed if other people in that same class did not—if they interrupted the teacher or flow of the class. Not a "teacher's pet" but an emissary for the school; focused on using the time in class only for the lesson. And you were not cool with anyone—student or teacher— who didn't take it seriously. [But] I distinctly remember a shift around the middle/end of 8th grade.*
>
> *We had French in Mrs. Dupont's class. . . . [She] had a fun class environment, and I was really comfortable in that class. Mustafa and I really liked making Mme Dupont laugh. Not everyone thought we were funny though—But I remember that in the first few months of that class you sometimes looked back at us and I could tell that you were holding back a laugh but holding onto being serious. But then I remember like halfway through the year you started laughing. And that was the goal post for me and I think Mustafa too, because it was special to make you laugh.*

"Surely, they had crushes on you," interrupts my husband. "That's how you talk about someone you had a huge crush on." I brush this off. You don't understand how unpleasant I made it, I tell him. Pheroze heartily confirms this—"*so* unpleasant." My husband hadn't seen my oversized eighties glasses, the nest of my hair, the scowl. I wasn't stirring up romantic feelings in anyone back then, during the reign of the supermodel. I suspect the pleasure in making me laugh was more akin to winning approval from the teacher. My husband—obviously blinded by his huge crush on me—is not convinced.

The year I turned thirteen, I started to notice that I had a body, unfortunately. Riyadh wasn't an easy place to be a girl or a woman back then—I can't speak to now. So I, a girl becoming a woman, was frustrated. Inside the compound walls we were allowed to wear whatever we wanted, in a simulacrum of American life. And some things about expat life in Riyadh were glorious: We traveled constantly—Cairo, Geneva, Berlin, all a short hop away. We went bowling in marble-lined alleys, manned by white-gloved servers, or spent the day at the Diplomatic Quarter's serene wave pool. We were kept in a bubble, and as such, life there always felt temporary, detached from reality. But in reality, outside the compound walls, I draped myself in loose-fitting clothes, covering every inch of skin. I didn't go out often, other than to school or the market, but even the market was tricky. The area where we bought our electronics during the week was often referred to as Chop-Chop Square, because of the public beheadings that sometimes happened there on the weekends. The names of casualties, if there were any, were delivered in a monotone on the evening news. These grisly bulletins were infrequent: the threat of losing a head or a limb prevented most visible crime in the Kingdom. But the most significant dampening presence, as I got older, was the *mutaween,* religious police wielding large sticks, shouting that I should cover my head.

Though I tried at first to hide in my oversized clothing, eventually no baggy sweatpants could disguise what I considered the ravages of puberty. Some men in public areas, used to seeing women completely covered, were greedy for any glimpse of flesh, even if it was just a face and hands, or the slight outline of a maturing body. Men started to bump up against me in public, sometimes circling around me in a store and into my path. After an episode at the supermarket where an old man walked by and quickly grabbed my bottom while my parents were picking out croissants, I decided that I'd be more comfortable wearing an abaya, the long black cloak that all grown women wore in public, which felt like a layer of protection against wandering hands and eyes. I rarely left the compound after that, but if I had to, I felt safer enveloped within an abaya.

I also took solace in the nurses' compound—a subsection of the larger compound where all the nurses lived and no men were allowed in. Women sunbathed and swam topless; others planned parties or gave haircuts as a side business. Here lived a particular woman, a spry Filipina nurse who baked a moist chocolate cake with a ganache so delicious that everyone on the compound knew to order weeks ahead for a birthday—a large Bundt, so they could eat half and keep the other half in the freezer. The nurses' apartments smelled strongly of delicious home cooking. Each apartment contained two women, usually from the same country, and usually having left entire families back home. Missing their own kids, they welcomed me into their lives and homes.

One fall, I saw flyers around the women's pool announcing a costume parade. The nurses had one every year, but instead of dressing up as sexy detectives or the like, they showed up pretending to have a variety of ailments that they saw all day at work, and the others were supposed to guess what the ailments were. It played out like a terrifying game of charades, by way of Tim Burton. One had progeria (an early-aging disorder), and another gave birth to a bloody mass of bandages between her legs. The most alarming was a woman who ran out in a black tutu and pigtails, skipped into the spotlight, quietly set up a mini–tea party with dolls and bears, and then collapsed, eyes rolling back in her head and foam streaming out of her mouth, heaving and jerking in a seizure. A second woman rushed out from the wings with a spoon, jammed it between her tongue and teeth, and escorted her away. Somewhere between riveted and terrified, I leaned over to ask another nurse what this one was supposed to be. "Epilepsy," she responded. Nobody was surprised when the woman in the tutu won. Even with the horror and confusion I felt that night, their compound seemed an idyll to me. A female utopia. A place where these women could be their most *interesting* selves. And they didn't seem to feel their bodies were unfair burdens. At the ladies' pool, I saw bikinis, I saw sunbathing, I saw generous padding and knobby bones and armpit hair. I felt their un-self-conscious acceptance of the body's intrinsic power, and hoped that someday I could be there, and not in my awkward, embarrassing shell.

Away from the compound, school chugged on. Jaime had somehow grown even more handsome, but his relationship with Heather was still holding tight. I ran around the track after school and saw his shiny head bobbing, golden limbs a blur as he zipped across the soccer field—he was now captain. Although my friend Sheri would later describe me as having an "Oh, I didn't see you there," third-glance kind of charisma, it became clear that in the middle school hierarchy he was way out of my league. I knew I'd never have him, whatever "having" was, but, thanks to some fresh hormones and my dreamy pal Eddie Vedder, I had started to enjoy the wanting. After my final laps, I liked to press my face against the gym wall, letting the sandstone cool me off. I was flushed from the running, yes, but also from the steady warmth of a now three-year crush.

Eventually, it was time to move again. Even though I never told them of the men who made me uncomfortable, my parents knew high school would be a good time to go somewhere else, and Dad gave us a choice: with Kashmir out of the picture now, should we aim for England or America? My fondness for London still held, and Mum and I both said England. Dad thought about it, then made a good case for the expanse, the endless opportunities available to us in the United States. Convinced, or at least curious, we packed up for another big move, and left for New York on my fourteenth birthday. At the end of my last day at school, I gathered my things after science class, walked into the hallway, and stopped short. Jaime was waiting there, and helped me carry my books back to my locker. "It's going to be strange with you gone," he said. "Why, no one to fight with?" "No, I'll miss you," he said, as he watched me empty out my locker. I looked up, frowning, to realize he wasn't teasing. My heart fell to my feet. I really had picked well, even if I hadn't yet figured out my timing or technique. "I'll miss you, too," I said.

Mother Sauces

This is how my mother made me a plate when I was a baby: she mashed rice, yogurt, meat, vegetables, and sauces together in a tiny little *thali,* a rimmed steel platter, and fed me by hand. As I got older, my plate started to look like a grown-up's: still on a thali, but not mashed up. In the center, always, a mound of rice. *"Batha khyov?"* Kashmiris ask, after one another's welfare: "Did you eat rice?" Piled around the rice, chunks of meat and at least two kinds of vegetable, all in colorful sauces. The sauces soaked into the rice, and I would mix together small handfuls, or *mindoos*—a little rice, a little sauce, a dab of yogurt in every handful—and eat it all down. After the thali was clean came my second, favorite helping: only the sauces. I ladled them in, as full as I could get the thali, sloshed up to the rim. Sometimes I mixed the sauces together, sometimes I left them distinct. My hand was my spoon, or I tipped the edge of the thali into my mouth to drink it all down. Sometimes I added a swirl of yogurt and called it "soup," sometimes not. It wasn't until the sauces were done that I considered the meal over. Others might be too stuffed from second mounds of rice, or even have moved on to dessert, but not I. I wanted the good stuff.

Sauces still hold me in thrall. Something about the concentrated essence of a food, the tincture of essential ingredients. Something about how they warm a vessel, and how that same warmth then travels down my throat and into my belly. I can cradle a bowl in one hand, heating up my fingers, while I spoon with the other. If it's actually cold out, I hug my food to my chest before eating, the direct heat over my heart a substitute for my mother's smile as she fed me.

A few years ago, in a miscalculated attempt at re-creating that warmth, I bought six pounds of chocolate chips, which I hid in strange places around the house. It was early in the pandemic, and I had read too many magazines that hinted I could lift my family's spirits by surprising them with baked goods. Twelve months later, five expired pounds remained. When it comes to comfort food, what I crave isn't usually sweets, or melted cheese, or creamy pasta—it's still those warmly spiced sauces my mother made me. The thalis may have disappeared, and cutlery is now a bigger part of my life than I imagined it would ever be, but when I assemble dinner for myself, at my own house or someone else's, my dish is mostly sauce, and it sends me looking for a bowl.

What I put in the bowl is the variable. "What are we thinking for dinner?" my husband asks every night, whoever's cooking, and I sigh—soup, it's always soup I want. A brothy one, a creamy one, a spicy one, it almost doesn't matter. Soup can be fast, and most days, with work, and the kids, and the seemingly endless number of forms to fill out and broken things to fix, it's always dinnertime before we've had time to think about dinner. And I just want soup. But I also don't want my family to be sad, so we make other versions of warming foods. Simple Indian stews, a bouillabaisse, avgolemono. High-liquid, low-effort meals, I guess you could say. Simple things they can spoon over rice, things I can drink straight from the bowl. But if I really have the time, and the forethought, and no rusty pieces have broken off the dishwasher that day, I make Kashmiri food.

Our cuisine, passed down by word of mouth within our insular community, is somewhat misunderstood even among Indians. Kashmiri restaurants scarcely exist in the United States, and the Kashmiri dishes you find on Indian menus are wildly imaginative. (Tomatoes? Cream? In rogan josh?!) But it's pretty simple. Kashmiri sauces are, for the most part, of three varieties. The yellow, kalia, colored with turmeric and cumin; the white, yakhni, flavored with fennel, ginger, and yogurt. And the red, with Kashmiri chili powder and cinnamon. The last is the foundation of rogan josh, our traditional lamb dish, spicy and rich, whose recipe my mum holds hostage in Michigan.

Mum's rogan josh, deep red and thickened with a dab of yogurt, was inherited from Mahi Kak, the man hired to cook three multicourse meals a day, with twenty-five cups of rice, for her large family when she was a girl. Eleven cousins and their six respective adults dined together every night at Matamaal, and the work of feeding everyone must have kept Mahi Kak young, because, after losing all his teeth over the years, he supposedly grew a new set, in his nineties. ("Teeny-tiny! Like baby pearls!" says Mum.) My Nanaji famously considered domestic duties a distraction from his three daughters' and six nieces' schoolwork. So Mahi Kak fed them until they left the house as brides, one by one.

My grandparents hosted a weeklong *wazwan* feast to accompany each wedding; for a stretch in the 1980s, after I was born, there was one nearly every summer, and no matter where we lived at the time, we went home for wedding season. A giant tent would be erected in the yard, the ground draped with long white tablecloths for eating and lounging. Sitting on my Nani's lap while she sorted rice from stones, I'd beg the bride to paint henna on my fat little hands, then smudge the ink until my palms were solid orange. (I was so substantial as a toddler that Babbu Mamu called me *lokut hend-wend,* "little watermelon," because, as he put it, "if she falls over, she'll roll away down the street.") Eventually, I learned to sit still with a book, turning pages with my elbow, until the henna set. But the highlight of every wedding, for me, was lunch. Each day of the celebration, we'd sit down with giant steel thalis in front of us and await a procession of cooks, or *waza,* ladling dish after dish from steaming tureens.

Days with religious ceremonies were vegetarian: huge yellow slabs of paneer, fried and simmered in our yellow sauce; bright-green kohlrabi, our veggie staple, simply prepared with mustard oil and hing; chunks of sliced lotus-root yakhni. But on the nonreligious days, I'd wake up dreaming of rogan josh, with lamb chunks as big as a man's fist. At lunchtime, I'd eat so quickly that the gravy would drip down my arm; relatives would tease that I'd gone "Angrez" (English), in forgetting how to eat neatly with my hand. "Bring her a fork!" they'd shout, laughing. To top up, I'd mash the marrow from the bones into my rice and yogurt and shovel down the glorious mess. I'd learned, young, the charade of covering my thali with a waving hand as a waza approached to serve seconds and thirds, insisting that I'd had enough. (It was a game of chicken: Would he dump a ladle of hot stew on my hand before I could move it?) Once we were fully stuffed, a server would come around with water so that we could wash our hands, and I'd fall asleep right there on the ground, with the grown-ups chattering over tea around me. Years later, when I planned my own wedding, these were the scraps of sense memory I wanted to replicate for my guests: giant hunks of rogan josh; sauces running down our hands; after lunch, a nap in the same spot where we ate.

It's been over thirty years since those weddings, and Kashmir remains a sweet, complicated memory for me. But a confession: I've rarely cooked my own rogan josh. Mum perfected her recipe as an immigrant mother in her London kitchen, re-creating her memories of Mahi Kak's cooking, half a world away. For as long as I've been raising my own family, though, my mother has brought rogan josh to me, in frozen bricks, whenever she visits. Periodically, I've asked her for the recipe; I even recruited my husband to extricate it from her. Each time, she would hem and haw, saying that she cooks with her eyes. "This much," she'd say, gesturing to a pile of fennel powder. "Stir until it's red enough." Without setting quantities of spices, I'd ask, how could she know she'd gotten it right? Not by tasting it: she's a vegetarian. Fundamentally, I think she wouldn't share the recipe because she liked to be needed. And I'd play along, because I liked needing her.

I still needed my mother, badly. But she lives across the country, and I hadn't seen her for a year, the longest I've ever gone without her cooking. My six-year-old says that most pasta "doesn't taste like anything." Our toddler picks at melted cheese like we're asking her to eat candle wax. I feed them their combo of Indian, Mexican, and vaguely Mediterranean flavors, with pizza and Happy Meals thrown in. I look at my toddler and wonder if she'll ever see Kashmir. She'll certainly never experience anything like those summer weddings. But she had enough teeth now to try her first rogan josh. So I called my mother to ask her again for the recipe. I reminded her that we had gone without the dish for a year. She murmured something about shipping me a batch. I pushed back, invoking Kashmir's disappearing culture. I emphasized the importance of preserving our cuisine, especially since I'd married outside of the community. I used all the same guilting tricks that Mum has been known to wield against me, and eventually she broke: she would walk me through the recipe over the weekend, on Zoom.

At our appointed time, my mother ghosted me. Over the following two days, a constellation of improbable technical difficulties and impressive avoidance skills conspired to make her unavailable. When we finally connected, she told me, breathlessly, that my dad's phone number had mistakenly been ported to her phone, so that hers no longer existed. Finally, standing in her kitchen in Michigan, she walked me through the recipe, approximating measurements, approving them by sight, and peering into the screen as I held it precariously above a pot of sputtering oil, so that she could sign off on the exact shade of red. We chatted while the food simmered, and when I lifted the lid after half an hour, she quietly admitted that the rogan josh looked perfect.

I ladled some into a bowl, and held it in my hands, the warmth traveling up my forearms. I slurped a bite, and there it was. It tasted exactly like hers. But it didn't feel quite right. It wasn't the same as my mother cooking me dinner, and that feeling would have to wait. For now, I steamed some rice for the kids' lunch. I was looking forward to seeing the sauce run down my girl's chubby little fingers, and, afterward, watching her nap.

My Mother's Rogan Josh

Serves 4–6

INGREDIENTS

- 6 tablespoons neutral cooking oil
- 1 tablespoon whole cumin seeds
- 6 whole cloves
- 4 cinnamon sticks
- 4 black cardamom pods
- 3 bay leaves
- 2–2½ pounds lamb leg, ideally bone-in, cut into 2-inch cubes
- Salt, to taste
- 3 tablespoons Kashmiri red chili powder (for a milder dish, substitute a blend of paprika and standard chili powder)
- 1 pinch asafetida (hing)
- 2 tablespoons plain yogurt
- 4 tablespoons ground fennel seeds
- 1 tablespoon ground ginger
- 1 teaspoon garam masala
- 4 green cardamom pods, crushed with a mortar and pestle
- 1 teaspoon desi ghee

DIRECTIONS

1. Warm oil in a large pot over medium-high heat. Add cumin seeds, cloves, cinnamon, black cardamom, and bay leaves. Fry for about 30 seconds.

2. Add lamb cubes to the pot and fry until they're brown on all sides, about 10 minutes. Season liberally with salt.
3. Stir in chili powder and asafetida, then yogurt. Cook for 2 more minutes.
4. Stir in fennel, ginger, and garam masala. Cook for 3–4 minutes.
5. Add water to almost cover the lamb, about 3½ cups.
6. Place lid on pot, and cook over medium heat until the liquid is reduced by half, approximately 25 minutes.
7. Reduce heat to a simmer, and cook, uncovered, until the meat is tender and the gravy is thickened, approximately 10 more minutes.
8. Remove from heat, add crushed green cardamom, and stir in ghee. Cover until you're ready to serve, preferably with mounds of basmati rice.

A Toothache

I had a terrible toothache the summer my great-aunt Indra was murdered, but that wasn't the worst part. The worst part was the water at her house in Delhi. It was saline, the texture slippery on my tongue. It felt thicker to me than normal water, and I had difficulty swallowing it. In early July, the monsoon yet to hit, the air in Delhi was a wall of steam. Woozy from the heat, I needed to drink, but I couldn't choke down any liquids.

That summer of 1990, when I was ten, we still thought the situation in Kashmir was temporary, and Delhi, where most of my family had landed for the moment, felt like exile. Not just because everyone ended up in short-term housing—the unluckiest in refugee camps, the luckiest with actual roofs over our heads—but even after the members of my close family settled in and took in that we'd be away awhile, Delhi felt off.

The water in Kashmir had been clear and refreshing, the good Himalayan stuff. We didn't just drink it; we rolled around in it. Our annual picnic in Pahalgam meant cuffing our pants to the knee, stripping our socks, wading into the bracing water of a mountain stream, sitting in the summer sun on a wide, flat rock with ice-cold, crystal clear water running over my feet. I defy you to find a tourist photo taken in Kashmir before 1990 that didn't take place in, or near, a babbling brook. What I'm saying is, we knew water.

But Delhi water was not the water we knew. It tasted thick and salty, like the tears that ran down the back of my throat when I stifled a cry. Maybe that's dramatic, but I was a dramatic youth, even at ten. It was early days of accessible bottled water in India, and I dared not ask for it, because I thought everyone would tease me—the girl who had stayed away for too long, the fancy girl who needed nonordinary things. When we first left Kashmir, when I was tiny, we had made the unspoken agreement that, in exchange for going far away, we'd take India with us. Abroad seemed like a scary, lawless place, with its short skirts and arts degrees, but we'd never change.

Because assimilation, wherever we were, was anathema, I felt that part of my job when in India was to pretend I was local. I probably stuck out as a comical foreigner on sight, but I tried hard not to. So, faced with an undrinkable glass of water, I pretended everything was fine. I sneaked away to the kitchen to add a dash of orange squash, but it wasn't enough to mask the taste. Neither was Rooh Afza, the Persian rosewater cordial we otherwise diluted and drank by the gallon. I didn't like fresh cream-on-top milk, so accustomed to Western homogenization was I, so I suffered in thirsty silence.

Not that this helped me fit in. Life abroad had inevitably chipped away at the pieces I carried of my homeland. We had been living in England, then Saudi Arabia, where I spoke mostly English, so my Hindi sometimes slipped. When I sensed it was going, I marathoned Bollywood movies until I felt I could hold up my end of a conversation again. I had rehearsed lines in my head before I saw my cousins each summer, working out how to explain the rules of freeze tag, or the plot of a book I liked and wanted to share. They spoke perfect English, but it didn't matter to me. Kashmir was my *real* home, the one we'd come back to, someday. But feeling at home hadn't been that difficult in Kashmir. Delhi, now, with its unfamiliar congestion, its chaotic energy, was less comfortable.

This trip to Delhi hadn't been planned. We were living in Riyadh when Mum got a call in the middle of the night, and I heard her quiet crying. I don't think she told me what had happened, exactly. No one gave me all the details. I was told a robbery had gone awry, and Indra Auntie was "no more." We flew to India two weeks later and stayed at Auntie's home, where I pieced together the details from snippets of overheard conversations and newspapers that were quickly whisked away. Indra Auntie—my Nani's sister—had just moved into a new house with her husband and hadn't had time to put her jewelry and cash in the bank. The house painters had killed her, along with a worker inside the house, while her husband was at the office. They had slit her throat and stolen everything, before being apprehended on a train a few days later.

So I knew, even before I had all the details, that the adults around me were dealing with weightier problems than my newfound aversion to tap water. Not just sorting out the aftermath of Auntie's sudden death, the paperwork, and the half-unpacked house, but also my Asha Masi, my mother's darling youngest sister, who was pregnant with her first baby. Indra Auntie, unable to have babies of her own, had partly raised Asha Masi in her house, almost as her own daughter. This happened a lot back then; I don't really know what to tell you. And because of their special bond, she had been looking forward to having a new baby in the family, her "own" grandbaby, before she died. But instead here was my mother, the eldest sister, stepping in to help Asha Masi get through the last month, now a horrifically stressful one, before the birth.

I could tell that the most helpful thing I could do was dissolve into the background. So I read. Mum had let me pack a suitcase full of library books for every trip, but they were never enough. We went to a corner shop to pick up a pile of *Chandamama,* a classic Indian children's magazine that featured a heady mix of mythology-heavy comics, morality tales, trivia, and patriotism. Its Technicolor episodic segments ran for decades, and my favorite was "Vikram-Betaal," the ongoing tale of clever King Vikramaditya and his nemesis Betaal, a ghostly vampire who hangs upside down from a tree, inhabiting and animating dead bodies. "Vikram-Betaal" was based on the *Pachisi,* a desi *Decameron* of sorts, twenty-five tales written in the eleventh century by the Kashmiri poet Somdev Bhatt, and the mechanism of the story frame works thus: whenever the good and honest king tries to capture the *betaal,* he is told a long story, ending in a riddle. If the king can answer it, the betaal gets to go back to hanging from the tree.

It doesn't seem to make sense at first glance—why would Vikramaditya answer correctly?—but almost jells when the betaal further explains that if the wise king lies about not knowing the answer, his head is hexed to roll off his neck. Though the explanation barely holds up, I didn't care. I couldn't get enough. Maybe I identified with the sense of being trapped, the futility of expecting to be able to control my own narrative, the never-ending story to which King Vikramaditya devoted so much of his life. I, too, would definitely let a ghost vampire tell me a bunch of weird stories. I, too, would be clever enough to figure out the riddle. And I, incorrigible teacher's pet, wouldn't be able to pretend I didn't know the answer. The long-suffering king and his tricky nemesis would keep me good company during that summer, which was not going to be a fun time. It was a long season of just me and some broken grown-ups in the house where the aunt we loved had been murdered.

Indra Auntie had spent much of her adult life in Ranchi, then an industrial hub in the Eastern state of Bihar (now Jharkhand), where her husband worked as an engineer in steel manufacturing. Like much Indian industrialization after the Raj, the plant was set up and supported by teams of Russian engineers. Nehru and Khrushchev had developed a special relationship after Partition, in the late 1940s, and the two countries forged a strong cultural bond. I still meet Eastern Europeans who can break into the popular Bollywood songs of the time. My best friend's mother, Irina, remembers tearing up in Kiev when she saw the melodramatic love triangle in *Silsila,* the story of a man duty-bound to wed his dead brother's pregnant fiancée. *"Hathi mere sathi!"* a Romanian cabdriver yells, finding out I'm Indian. "Elephant, my friend!"

Camaraderie with their local expats had led Indra Auntie to learn then teach Russian in Ranchi. To me, she was a glamorous lady, with never a hair or a stitch out of place, and I loved being near her, breathing in her cosmopolitan air. Mum and I had made a few trips there when I was a baby and a toddler, spending an inordinate amount of time at the library next door. Enchanted by the smell and feel of the books, I started to crawl around, then pull myself up on the shelves, and, eventually, walk. I begged to go back to the "libelly" every day after that, seeding my lifelong obsession with books and the pleasure I take in the musty smells of a well-loved collection. As I grew into an avid reader, Mother Russia got its claws further into me via an innocuous-looking magazine called *Misha.* It was colorful and chock-full of folklore, jokes, comics, and visions of the USSR as a perfectly run wonderland. A communist *Chandamama,* as it were.

Russian culture loomed so heavy in India that it popped up in mid-1980s names: kids called Tanya, or Nikita, or, my favorite, Sasha. Also from Russia was my favorite doll, which Uncle brought back from Moscow at Indra Auntie's behest: blue-eyed, flaxen-haired, with eyelids that opened and closed. She was strikingly mod, dressed in a sleeveless gingham A-line dress only just covering her rear, which was clad in a tiny pair of white hot pants. I must have thought something of this, for I drew her a nail-polish bindi, and she was the doll for whom I would crochet a full-length flamenco gown before long. After Uncle's retirement, and the Hindu migration from Kashmir, Indra Auntie wanted to be in Delhi, closer to displaced family, and that's why they had come. We had all hoped that Delhi would be a safer place, even if it felt strange to us. But her death was a startling reminder that no one was truly safe anywhere.

. . .

Indra Auntie's house, after she passed, seemed normal. Most of the rooms were arranged within a second-floor apartment, with an unfinished first floor they had been working on but had halted when it happened. I was asked not to go downstairs, but you tell a quiet, curious child that and it's almost a directive. One day, when the grown-ups were busy, I went down to the first floor and pushed open the bathroom door. It had been sanitized and then abandoned—no sign that anyone had been left there to die. At the time I felt numb, with a buzzing in my ears. I was hardly prepared to absorb the situation in Kashmir, let alone the loss of a woman I had idolized, the heavy sadness around me, the evil and desperation of the men who had done this. Overwhelmed, I closed the door and went back up the stairs, carrying the numbness, the buzzing with me. I went back to my reading, the only coping mechanism I had, and never went downstairs again.

And I remained thirsty and hot. Fortunately, into that stifling, swampy summer came the monsoon. Fresh water fell out of the sky in sheets. We hadn't had monsoons in Kashmir, and it was the first thing I found to love about Delhi. Looking out the window, I knew, rationally, that the rain came from above, but it was as though the entire sky—above the roofs, in front of my face—had turned into an unbroken, endless column of water. I loved the drama of it—the noise, the tropical smell, the temperature. My memories of rain were mostly from England, where it had been an ever-present, chilling drizzle, not this warm, shocking deluge that now carried errant bicycles down the street.

As I watched the chaos from the front window, I had an idea. Swelling with hope, I asked Mum if I could collect the rain to drink, and she pointed to the brownish fug above us, a miasma of chemicals and dirt. The air here was filthy, she said, and my body had already warned me I wasn't ready for it. I had barely made it outside Indira Gandhi Airport before a tickle in my throat unfurled into a full-blown cough. I felt discouraged, but she went on: "Just not the first batch," she warned me. "Wait for clean air."

"The air in Kashmir was different," said an older friend recently, her eyes lighting up. "I wished I could bottle it." It's comforting to hear that my memory isn't far from the truth. For one thing, Srinagar hadn't been automated enough for large-scale pollution. Although it seemed like 80 percent of the people I knew were engineers, we were slow to warm to technology, because we're fundamentally opposed to fixing anything that isn't broken. Symbolic of this was our *kangri,* or "Kashmiri central heating"—the wicker basket full of live coals that Kashmiris carry under our wool cloaks to keep warm during subzero winters. Kids have teeny-tiny ones, painted in bright colors, with little scoops for stoking the cooling embers. When I was born, we were still taking tongas, horse-drawn carts, across downtown Srinagar's bridges. Well, "across" is generous. On one end of the bridge, the passengers would alight, cross the bridge—next to the horse, which was being led across—and then clamber back on, to save the horse some energy over the swell. So coming home for the summer, in the past, had been about filling up my lungs with that crisp mountain air.

Calling Delhi "home" all of a sudden felt wrong, as though I had been picked up at my house, dropped down the street, and told to pretend I lived there now. I grimaced at the thick chemical cloud I was hoping would be washed out of the sky, and got to work. I set up a plastic tent outside to collect the next day's rain, and eagerly waited. The air, though more humid than at my real home, was starting to smell fresh and clear to me, finally. I settled in, again, with my *Chandamama*.

I recently tracked down the July 1990 issue, which I must have read so many times that summer, in an attempt to revisit that headspace—an immersive reader, I tended to internalize anything that I enjoyed. I cried myself to sleep at sad stories, had nightmares after scary ones—still do. I flipped to "Vikram-Betaal," wondering what funny little ideas might have been implanted in my mind during that strange visit. "Dark was the night and weird the atmosphere," it began. "It rained from time to time. Gusts of wind shook the trees. At the intervals of thunderclaps and the moaning of jackals could be heard the eerie laughter of spirits. Flashes of lightning showed fearful faces. But King Vikram swerved not." I laughed out loud, thinking of how vigorously I must have nodded. Weird rain, check. Eerie atmosphere, check. Ghosts? Well, remained to be seen.

While I originally read that story, and waited for a clean rainfall, my focus turned to problem number three: the ache in my mouth. A filling had fallen out of my baby molar, and the tooth had cracked, infecting my gum. My mother gave me a clove to put in there to ease the pain until I could get back to our dentist. As I poked my swollen gum with the tip of my tongue, tasting a metallic tang, I knew it shouldn't hurt that much. Mum doesn't remember any of this today, and I realize I might not have told her how bad the pain was or how consistently blood trickled into my mouth. The ache felt active and alive, unlike the rest of me, numbed by the coldness I'd carried upstairs from the bathroom. But I kept going back to the kitchen, using up clove after clove, until I could ignore my toothache as well.

I wish this could be a story about the spirit of our treasured aunt guiding me through my ups and downs, something sweet and heartwarming. But it wasn't anything like that. Her life ended abruptly, and the only haunting I felt was in who I became after that summer. I carried that numbness with me, becoming someone who likes things the way I like them, as though to inoculate myself against further uncertainty and fear. I love my systems. I know everything from how many grams of carbohydrate I can consume to avoid an afternoon crash (twenty-six per meal), to the exact amount of caffeine I can tolerate every morning before I start to freak out (eighty milligrams, before noon). But in my thirties and after, my little quirks coalesced into an underlying mania, and sometimes they run me ragged; my ears buzz as I double- and triple-check that the doors are locked after my husband has already locked up, or obsess over my children's oral hygiene.

After a long internal debate about whether to get a new piece of jewelry, I immediately put it in my safe-deposit box at the bank, never to see it again. On some days, I don't even wear my engagement ring outside the house, fearful it'll draw the wrong kind of attention. This is funny, because, as an often harried mom in my forties, I also don't think anyone is looking at me. But, deep down, I can't shake the "lesson" I learned that summer, that any sign of prosperity is a beacon for evil. "Why won't you wear a necklace?" asks my mother, who finds a bare neck both unbecoming and an insult to our culture. I demur. I don't say it out loud, and I know it's not rational, but I don't need my throat slit for a bauble.

"You're so . . . cheerful," said an old boss last month, not exactly as a compliment, and maybe that's true. There's nothing like a danger-adjacent childhood to make one feel almost oppressively grateful to be alive. There may be something I don't like about my house, but at least I have a home, when others don't. Every single day that I wake up and go to bed safely, I am astounded to be drawing breath. When my kids come back from the playground or school in one piece, I want to kiss the ground. When they leave for school, I hug them tight and stomp out the tendril of fear that doesn't want to let them go, as a parade of grisly scenarios stampede through my head.

It's not an easy way to live. Though I manage to mask most of it, I brim with fear for the children, and any time I am away from them, or they are away from me, I fill each second with work, to distract myself from my white knuckles. As a counterbalance to my pervasive fear of losing everything, I feel so lucky not to have lost it *yet* that it's almost difficult for me to complain about anything. My daily concerns don't seem important when people are losing their homes and lives. I am fortunate. If something bothers me, I convince myself that it shouldn't, that it doesn't.

Except that the things that do bother me have tricky ways of peeking out. While I was thrown right into the mechanics of it, I never got to process the loss of Indra Auntie. It happened so quickly, I always think. And then there was so much to do. And everyone was so sad, and the baby was coming, and the apartment was unfinished, and my toothache, and . . . and . . . and . . . So I tucked away my grief and moved on. But the water won't let me.

The tap water in my current, grown-up family home is also hard, reminiscent of that summer. I use a built-in water filter most of the time, but if I ever make the lazy mistake of not wanting to walk downstairs, one sip from the wrong faucet takes me right back to the half-finished bathroom in Delhi, its tiny window, a spindly ray of sunlight worming its way through chemical clouds to illuminate one corner of that cursed space. I gag, every time. And though tap water is bad enough, it can't compare to French mineral water: the closest simulacrum to Indra Auntie's and my betaal.

I moderated a panel once, a women-in-business thing, in which an event producer asked what we wanted to drink, and I said water was fine. She ran back carrying a bottle of Evian just before we were whisked onstage, and I paused, whispered, "Is there anything else? I know it sounds crazy, but Evian makes me ill." I saw the looks the panelists exchanged—I could tell they were weighing what level of jerk I might be. "I'll take tap," I clarified, but then the lights turned on, and I was fine, because I had to be. Just thirsty, and a little embarrassed.

The aversion has gotten worse. At a bed-and-breakfast for our tenth wedding anniversary, I mistakenly left my water bottle at home, so I poured myself a glass of Santa Barbara tap and hoped for the best. It barely got to my lips before the smell made me gag. I swallowed enough to take my pills, shuddered, and retched, like a cat with a hairball. Even to my husband, who barely notices any of my quirks anymore, this looked troubling.

I'm not quite sure what to do about the water. Ignoring it hasn't worked, and neither did ignoring my toothache. A month after our trip to Delhi, my dentist back in Riyadh yanked out that rotten baby molar. As soon as my adult teeth grew in, I insisted on having them sealed up, swearing I'd never have tooth trouble again. I brush twice a day, I floss, I never skip. No cavities. On my last visit, my dentist's feedback was that I only chew on one side of my mouth, and I need to switch, so I don't grind down my teeth unevenly. I didn't know how to tell him I can't, because I'm haunted by the ghost of a toothache I had thirty years ago.

My past may be catching up with me, but tiptoeing around discomfort did work, at least temporarily. The monsoon I harvested that summer kept me busy, out of everyone's hair, out of my own head. Unfortunately, the water I distilled with my makeshift tarp ended up tasting a different kind of awful: flat and strange. I realized I had just spent two days collecting the stuff our laundromat used to iron Dad's shirts. Defeated, I walked into the kitchen to figure out what I could make, and it came to me in a thunderclap: *nimbu pani,* Indian limeade, made with limes, sugar, and a pinch of salt, had always trumped all others for me. I squeezed the tiny, potent limes, stirred in the sugar, and omitted the salt this time. It tasted perfect, balanced. The lime cut through the slipperiness and tempered the salinity, so the water felt less like tears. I mixed a pitcher and drank it all down, refreshed, for a time.

Fed Is Best

"I wish I could be more like you," said my friend Liz, the last time she was over for dinner. "But I just . . . tidy too much." I did not take offense. It's true that presentation has never been my forte when it comes to entertaining. In law school, I proposed a meal for my two shy housemates that morphed into a rowdy Indian feast for twenty-four friends, with mountains of chicken tikka marinating in a (clean) black trash liner. A pasta dinner I made later that year ended with us climbing a billboard in downtown Detroit, balancing a jug of Carlo Rossi six stories above the shell of old Tiger Stadium. In my empty Ann Arbor apartment after graduation, guests sat on the floor and ate a massaman curry with their hands that dissolved their plates into papier-mâché and stained the crappy carpet orange. We covered up the stains with an even crappier rug. My food was just this side of passable, even as I collected and dog-eared piles of used cookbooks. But I welcomed challenges and I loved to feed people. I trusted that, if the company was good enough, the food just had to be edible, and chaotic dinner parties cemented my friendships through my mid-thirties.

But after having my first baby, I lost myself. Thirty-two weeks of prenatal nausea, choking down crackers and bananas, spiraled into postpartum chaos, low milk supply, an under-weight baby, and a severe, lengthy depression. A lifelong non-crier and non-panicker, I was a stressball of tears and distress, trudging an endless treadmill of pumping six times a day, wak-ing to his hungry screams every twenty minutes around the clock. I wanted someone to chart out exactly when I would be able to recognize myself—a countdown to reading, cook-ing, traveling again. Food, my great joy, became just a vehicle for calories. Slabs of supermarket turkey meatloaf sustained us while my forlorn cookbooks gawped at me from the kitchen shelves, like so many volumes of a dusty to-do list. *Play with us,* they moaned as I scurried past and avoided looking directly at them. *Remember how much fun we used to have?*

By the time our son was eighteen months old, he had become my universe. It's a universe I slowly replenished with reading and travel, but the era when I cooked anything other than his quick meals—turkey quesadillas, steamed broccoli—was a foggy memory. A part of me rejected cooking, because I'm a working mom and I won't be tied to a stove as well as chil-dren, damnit, but I had always loved the aura around the cama-raderie of cooking—it was how I caught up with old friends, how I expressed my affection, how I turned acquaintances into my near and dear. Nobody had ever made me cook. I still bought piles of cookbooks, out of some hope to re-create the photo essays within, only to shelve and avoid them until a day when I had "more energy." Every once in a while, I'd roast meat or blend a soup and feel a twitch of my old culinary longing.

And then, as with my previous bouts of depression, a chink appeared in the clouds. Things started to feel more manage-able, and instead of just looking at cookbooks, I wanted to dive back in. After ignoring them for a year, lazily flipping through one or two before wiping away my drool and ordering in, I wanted to see and taste what was inside them again. Like reclaiming a dormant passion for distance running or tap dancing, cooking the way I did pre-baby took diligent training.

I turned first to the neglected books bursting from my shelves. Thirteen were uncracked, which meant planning thirteen dinner parties. In pursuit of growth, I picked three-course meals outside my comfort zone. No two-step soups. No one-step chicken. No Bittman. I posted a Google spreadsheet asking my friends to sign up for open Friday nights, strong-arming them into being my lab rats, but really seeking to reconnect with friends I hadn't spoken to in almost two years.

The results were mixed. Some highs entered the canon, for sure: *The Silver Spoon* is flawless, and *The Adobo Road Cookbook* took me back to my high school boyfriend's Filipino kitchen. I became intimate with the collected works of David Tanis and Einat Admony. But the lows were almost more fun. A "definitive" Spanish cookbook was disappointing, the flawed translations resulting in a gazpacho that made my Spanish friend Amaya screech, incensed. Searching for answers, I found comrades in online reviews:

> . . . *as we say in Spain* Si esto es la Biblia de la cocina española que baje Dios y lo vea, *(Literal translation) If this is the Bible of Spanish cuisine may God come down and strike me.*

And every week, without fail, I ruined dessert. Hervé This's "foolproof" chocolate mousse became a chalky pudding. I squashed a soufflé, which I should never have attempted. I flattened a flan. The only dessert out of all thirteen that I mastered was the "Homemade Kit Kat" from *Balaboosta,* which was essentially melted chocolate poured over cornflakes. The issue was that dessert, to me, demands a terrifying level of precision, and I've never been a precise cook—more of a "Let's marinate meat in a garbage bag" cook. Women who bake well intimidate me. They're so polished; organizing their books by color, blending signature scents, "creaming" butter, whatever that is. I decided to stop beating myself up about it. Halfway through the dinners, I started asking my guests to bring dessert, just in case. And by the end, I accepted it. Dessert, like breastfeeding, like staying calm in the face of a mewling newborn, is not my superpower.

That sweet little baby is going to turn ten soon, and I'm still just awful at desserts. Every once in a while, I'll get excited by a muffin recipe, and we'll go for it, but my son makes me promise not to substitute any ingredients. He's been disappointed by too many low-sugar hacks, or my using whatever flour I have on hand. But he's been joined by a sister, and, once again, the line-cook nature of the job—slinging grub at a yowling mass—is leaving the cookbooks dusty. The two children, when home, eat a shocking thirty-six eggs a week. We scramble five almost every morning, to pile on buttered toast, and the rest get folded into endless muffins and pancake-type things. And that's just the eggs! The kids' bodies are like clown cars, an unfathomable amount of groceries—two gallons of milk? three loaves of bread!—tumbling into their wide-open mouths before they careen around the three-ring circus of our unkempt house.

Not that I haven't tried cooking some new things—thanks

to pandemic lockdown boredom, we've done the challah, the Thai, the Indian, pizza from scratch. But as they get bigger, and hungrier, and work deadlines interfere, I become so tired of cooking. After hundreds of meals and snacks every week, the inspiration well runs dry. They don't like takeout, and I don't even want to look at groceries. Which is why I decided recently that it might be time to teach my son to prepare his own meals so that I don't have to. He's pretty good at making me coffee on our one-touch machine, and last month I watched him handle hot toast with oven mitts. Who am I to stifle his natural talents?

I figured that we'd start with breakfast, and that we need to leave some eggs for the rest of California. Though he prefers a warm meal in the morning, we'd also keep fire in my domain, for now. But how about a parfait? We layered yogurt, fruit, and granola in a glass, and it reminded him of the rainbow sand sculptures they made back in kindergarten. He tasted it, suspicious, and beamed: "Like digging up blueberry fossils!" he said. He rolled his eyes when I asked if he knew how to "make cereal," so we moved on to a lunch classic: PB&J. He slathered two pieces of bread and slapped them together, marveling, "Everything tastes better together than it does apart." His baby sister, in her high chair, was impressed, staring at her own plain roll like it was cardboard. Wanting to be part of the conversation, she interjected whatever relevant words she could summon: "Peena buttah! Toost! Silly!"

As they chattered on, a siren sounded in the distance, and both kids' ears perked up. "Fi' truck!" she shouted. "Oooh! Or a police car!" he told her, thrilled. The noises of a problem far, far away. "What do you think the police are doing, Mama?" "Oh, you know, chasing a speeder, that kind of thing." I waved it off, impatient to move on.

Satisfied with my answer, he asked about his favorite hot sandwich, the grilled cheese. To sideswipe the burn aspect, I heated up the waffle iron, because I'm a Fun Mom. The cheese oozed out, crisped up into a golden halo around the toasted bread—an instant success story.

Then it was on to the next day's menu: "How old do I have to be to make a hot dog?" he asked. "That depends on your standards," I told him, and taught him that old after-school trick: microwaving a rubbery sausage for forty-five seconds, toasting a pillowy white bun. He swallowed it seemingly whole, and quickly "cooked" another; the scales fell from his eyes as he realized my culinary magic is entirely attainable. "Can we make chicken soup next?" Absolutely! And out comes our pressure cooker. We chopped up a mirepoix, which I now realize I can buy pre-chopped, if I really want to put my feet up. I briefly drifted into a vision of reading magazines while my child makes dinner.

What else should we put in the soup? "Ginger? Garlic!" he suggested, with newfound culinary confidence. I grabbed both. See, look how easy this could be! He begrudgingly allowed me the contribution of a bay leaf, but before I added the broth, he had a thought: "This chicken looks too good for soup," he said, peering in. "Could we just make it . . . chicken?" We could indeed. We sealed the pot, cooked for fifteen minutes, and sat down to a complete meal that tasted not unlike Zuni Café's chicken bouillabaisse. He insisted that we call it

"Not Quite Chicken Soup," and that I share the recipe with other kids—my child readers who cook, you see.

When I put him to bed that night, I asked him what made him feel grateful. It's something we've gone over every night since the world shut down and he couldn't easily access the friends, playgrounds, and outdoor spaces that usually make him happy. He sighed, reached deep. "I'm grateful the universe is still alive and the sun hasn't exploded." I try not to tear up. We worked hard to make things as normal and loving as possible inside the home while riding out the pandemic, but even this small child knew we were in the middle of a major crisis. I told him that I agree, that I'm so proud of his special mind, and proud he's becoming so independent. I closed his door and collapsed on top of my bed, unnerved by the growing frequency of the sirens I dismissed outside. We were now in the wake of George Floyd's murder, which shook up Los Angeles like a soda bottle, and I wondered what would happen next.

The following day, my son asked for another grilled cheese, and I said, "Why don't you try it on your own?"

His face fell. "Can't you just make it for me?"

"Because it tastes better? Because it's made with love?" Yes, I was fishing for compliments, but he just looked at me like I was not very smart.

"No. Because I can't reach the bread."

Oh. I am not very smart.

I cleared out the bottom shelf of the fridge and filled small jars with yogurt and berries. I put single servings of milk in the fridge door, the fruit on a lower shelf. Cut-up veggies and bread where he could reach them. I stocked the freezer with waffles to toast, for a change of pace. We were getting this figured out, and I knew I wouldn't be his line cook for much longer. I day-dreamed happily of him feeding his little sister someday, the way I had fed Punit. They were on their way, I thought, if we could just cement these life skills.

But all our progress came to a halt as the nation exploded in a tidal wave of civil unrest. That night, while I was tossing and turning, the soda bottle finally exploded: a tank rolled down the street to the soundtrack of helicopters and gunshots in our neighborhood. Los Angeles buckled under so many years of unresolved pain and fury, and my desire for the kids to grow up faster felt selfish and shortsighted. In my impatience to cross a few tasks off my list, I had forgotten what a blessing it is to be able to spend mealtimes with a family. I felt for the protesters, so many of them kids who had grown up experiencing their lives as a wearying incline, and I felt for the mothers who, hear-ing sirens, couldn't dismiss them as a fun sound, far, far away. The mothers who wish they could be making sandwiches for their grown sons but no longer can.

Now I wake up grateful for the incessant daily needs of my small children.

"What would you like for breakfast?" I ask my son. He rubs his sleepy eyes. "I think I'll make some toast."

"I'll make a scramble," I say, and get to work alongside him, our time together fleeting, urgent, a gift. He has the rest of his life to cook. For now, my baby needs eggs.

How to Be Alone

Given everything that happened, I should have been a tough little kid, but my heart took a while to harden. When I was nine, we also moved twenty-two miles across Riyadh for my dad's new job, and it meant a glossier compound, with a movie theater! But I missed our little neighborhood, and I missed Miryam, who had lived just downstairs. The girls on my new street had an energy I didn't understand. They were all of South Asian extraction, but had moved from the United States. They rolled their eyes at my naïveté in regard to their shared childhood allusions. "What do you mean, you don't know the Bobos jingle?" they sneered, as we hung out on the corner, balancing on a low stone wall. I felt foolish and left out. I had only been to America once. They surrounded me to scream it in my ears: "Bobos! They make your feet feel fine! Bobos! They cost a dollar ninety-nine!" I allowed it, eager to make new friends, even if they seemed a little mean, but I seized up inside. I didn't like loud noises, and I didn't like that these girls made me feel scared and lonely.

The old compound had been so tight-knit, and I was invested in our relationships there. Since the age of six, I had come to see Miryam's home as an extension of ours and knew how lucky I was to have a second family downstairs, especially so far from our actual one. I loved her mother, Huma Auntie—she had a soothing, sonorous voice, and such good taste. She dressed beautifully, smelled so good, and was partial to a color called dusty rose. She set an elegant backdrop for Miryam's silliness. Her daughter was always the first to throw the Barbies into shocking outfits, then out on the town in the back of a makeshift "limo." Miryam lived to make up a song. "Chicken Cluck-Cluck" was the one we called to each other from up and down the stairs, if we could make it through without giggling. A little sister, she had a buoyant spirit I admired and tried to emulate. I was more familiar with the energy of her much older brother, who hung out somberly nearby, the weight of the world seemingly on his shoulders.

I missed that lightness and connection at the new compound, where even my new ride to school was overwhelming. Miryam and I had carpooled with two other families, in a compact white van. This compound had its own fleet of school buses, bright white with blue stripes, with all the sociological discomfort a bus full of kids could whip up. "Do you know what sex is?" asked a girl named Sara that first week, fourteen years old to my nine. She and the older kids, the ones in the back of the bus, had been giggling at a joke, which I asked them to share. I had my eye on the girls in those last seats—they tittered and whispered, they were friendly with boys, they accessorized. Every day, I casually moved one seat back, first incorporating myself into their field of vision, and then into their conversations.

"Obviously I know what SEX is." It was when two people were naked together, which Miryam had overheard from her big brother.

"Hmm. Have your parents ever had it?"

"DON'T BE DISGUSTING."

She didn't tell me the joke.

When we got to school, I hurried to the library to grab the "S" encyclopedia volume. Stomach turned, but mystery solved, I couldn't look my parents in the eyes for weeks. I did notice that the back-of-the-bus girls modulated their conversations to a solid PG-13 so I wouldn't be left out, which was thoughtful. But I missed being with Miryam: the laughing until we were breathless, the faith that I could tell her anything in the world and she'd receive it without judgment. I thought a lot about what I wanted from the people in my life, what I wanted to give and receive. I wanted people to be kind, and like me for me, and never let me down.

But every normal thing in those years turned muddy with sociopolitical drama. When a mosque was looted in India, some of the compound kids weren't allowed to play with me, because it was "our" fault. When homes in Kashmir were being set on fire, kids in the neighborhood told me we deserved it. I had to ride the bus with those kids the very next day, with the expectation that I'd keep cool. I felt abandoned and attacked on a monthly basis, buffeted by headlines, but I knew, on some level, that no middle schoolers were coming up with these ideas themselves. What was I going to do, argue with their parents? I just wanted friends.

One of the girls on the new bus, the aforementioned Sara, intrigued me most of all. Every morning, she tore sheets out of a lined notebook and wrote erotic fiction notable for its precise timing ("After fifteen minutes of nude kissing, they made love for ten more"). She passed it around the back of the bus and at school until the paper fell apart, then started anew. Sara was usually buried in her writing, so I knew I'd need a singular act to grab her attention.

My chance arrived in the form of a chain letter another girl handed to me at school. I had never seen one before but immediately recognized it as an early networking opportunity. "Copy this letter and give it to ten people, or you'll have ten years of bad luck," it warned. "If you share it with ten friends, all of your dreams will come true." I copied it out longhand over lunch and marched a copy straight to Sara on the bus back home. She read it and stuffed it into her backpack, sizing me up.

That night, the phone rang in the middle of dinner, and Dad picked up. "Your daughter is spreading superstition, and she needs to stop," Sara's father told him. We should be reported to the religious authorities, he said. We were guests in the Kingdom and should be ashamed of ourselves. I got a reluctant talking-to from my parents, who reminded me to know my audience. The injustice! I wanted to snitch about Sara's pervy stories, but that would risk exposing that I had read them, so I didn't push back. I filed it under things I'd never understand about grown-ups, and moved back to the front of the bus, where life was less tricky.

After all the confusion of in-person aggression, the simplicity of the ensuing crank calls was almost refreshing. One time, the phone rang and a boy jabbered a stream of nonsense into my ear. "Get out of the country," he said. "You don't belong here, go back to where you came from, you people shouldn't be here"—that kind of thing. Startled, I showed the phone to my parents. I didn't have to explain what was going on—they could tell from my face—and in that moment I grasped that it wasn't the first time this had happened, just the first time I'd picked up. It made me wonder what the kids around me were hearing from their parents at home. It made me want to fold smaller, into my own company, which, right now, felt like the only company I could trust.

But I missed Miryam so much. We were attending the same school but not in the same grade, and it wasn't easy to get together—our mothers couldn't drive, and our dads worked late hours. But I needed her like a baby needs a comforting blanket. These new, loud American girls didn't understand me. Miryam would, and sharing my new life with her could make it all better. So I found her at recess, to discuss a visit—and that's when she let me know she wasn't allowed to play with me anymore.

I stood still, outside the library at my elementary school, staring down at the textured vinyl flooring that prevented high-energy kids from skidding all around. It smelled acrid, metallic, that post-recess mix of tween armpits and sport socks. Focusing on the orange bumps, the whiff of kids bounding in from the playground, helped take me out of my feelings. I didn't want to cry at school. "I'm not Indian, I'm Kashmiri," she said to me, mysteriously, before walking away, and I realized the break had something to do with my being Hindu, and her family being Muslim and invested in the idea of Kashmiri independence. I couldn't even be mad at her, because she

looked sad about it. Still, I didn't understand. I knew we had
had some trouble back home, but what did I have to do with
it? What did she? She slipped out the door at the end of the
hall, and after years of spending every free moment together, I
never saw her again. I remained confused: People supposedly
turned to religion for a sense of community, some social order,
an explanation of the unknown. But if religion was what told
adults to tell their kids not to play with me because of news
happening thousands of miles away, I didn't want any of it. Not
theirs, and not mine.

I broke the news to my mother, who sighed, sat with it. She
must have been expecting it, considering the things that had
been happening in Kashmir. And she must have been lament-
ing her own fracturing friendships, like with Huma Auntie,
while trying to comfort me, in the best way she knew. "I don't
know if you should trust people the way you do," she murmured, stroking my hair as I wiggled away. "You can trust your
family, but . . ." Here she trailed off, wanting to save me the
heartbreak that she had grown up with.

I was hurt but mostly puzzled. Given the trouble back
home, and the pervasive low-grade cruelty of the girls at the
new compound, how had I not seen any of this coming? More
important, how could I ensure it never happened again? I
hadn't spent one second thinking about religion. My parents
were scientists, often rational to a fault, and, other than major
holidays, Hinduism was just a piece of our background that
barely related to our daily life. But as home burned, it started
to make people a little crazy, and I wanted none of it. "Well,
you can't trust Muslims," I heard family friends say under their

breath, and I rolled my eyes. "That's what they say about us, you know," I argued. How could anyone be right, if everyone is the enemy? "You'll see," they said, their voices low.

After Miryam left me, I wasn't alone, exactly—I could still go outside and meet up with the neighborhood girls if I really wanted to—but I didn't like how it felt to compromise. I wanted a deeper, more trustworthy human connection, and I couldn't rely on them for it. I never knew if they'd greet me warmly or scatter, like they had when their parents forbade them to talk to me. These were not the kinds of friends I wanted. So, without Miryam, without friends I could trust, I had to learn to rely on my own company, and I learned to like it.

In lonely times, in new places, Mum had been great at making our family the nucleus. Who needed to go out looking for fun? she said. Who needed to be invited to a party? We were our own party. And I liked my family; my little brother was fun, and I found purpose and solace in helping raise him.

And I also had books. I got a lot of praise for all the reading I did as a child, and I read in big, fast gulps, like an addict. And, also like an addict, I did it to escape. To be briefly in a world not my own, to tut at someone else's problems and soar in their triumphs. I tried to read things as far away from my own experience as possible, whether Enid Blyton's Famous Five books, in which the biggest problem was that the bottled milk didn't stay cold enough in a brook, or Malory Towers, about a British boarding school that made me yearn for my own tuck box. And when I had finished all my books, I sneaked into my mother's stash—finally devouring her copy of *The Thorn Birds,* with its randy priest, which supported my emerging hypothesis that religion was a sham. "You were so well behaved," my aunts and

uncles say now. "Your nose always in a book." "Look at Didi,"
my cousins were told. "She's always reading—why can't you
read that much?" *I wasn't behaving*, I want to tell them all now.
I was dissociating.

"You're not friendly," said my mother, as I got older. Not an
insult, just a statement of fact. She simply meant I wasn't in
the habit of making friends, and she was right. I had experienced a mind-meld with Miryam in first grade, and that was
my standard for friendship. Until I felt a connection again, on
par with the one I had shared back then—a true friendship—I
had my family and my books. I recoiled at most friendly gestures, turned my nose up at company. I didn't want to tolerate
company; I wanted lasting love. But friends could break my
heart, and books never would.

I enjoyed sitting, alone, with my thoughts. "What are you
doing?" asked my college roommate Tory, watching me lying
down on my bed once, immobile, for an hour. "Oh, just thinking," I said. Like I did as an "unfriendly" child in Saudi Arabia:
wandering around the neighborhood, finding a tree to read
under, flowers to gather, leaves to dry in the sun and grind into
a fine powder between two rocks. Heading over to the pool,
which had ladies' hours, when the mean girls would be there;
and family hours, when I could go to be surrounded by people
in my loneliness. And I loved watching people. I loved watching them so closely that I could figure out which brother and
sister might be in a snit at each other, depending on how they
shared a pizza at the snack bar. Which parents seemed to like
each other, which parents seemed to be just tolerating their
partners. Maybe it was easier to frame my disconnection from
other people if I thought of myself as an observer, a tiny social

scientist. Part of me thought that, if I could just figure out what made people tick and why, I would be spared any future heartache.

Once, I watched a nurse eat a burger with an entire bottle of ketchup. *So that's a kind of person,* I remember noting. I watched older boys towel off and go play basketball at the courts just next door. I could tell which ones were kind—one interrupted a game to bring his little sister a Popsicle—and which were not, like the boy who only grunted at his parents while grabbing ice cream money from them. I learned almost everything I needed to know about people just from watching them at the pool, and though they might have wondered what a ten-year-old with a furrowed brow was doing, taking mental notes, my age shielded me from any questions.

In those lonely days, I spent all my time reading about people, observing people, trying to understand people. I still couldn't figure out why the Miryam thing had happened, but I kept turning human nature over like a worry stone. What did that amount of ketchup mean? Did the woman love ketchup, or hate the burger? Was that how her family had served burgers, or had her mother only allowed her a small dollop, so that, when she went out into the world, she told herself she'd have as much as she wanted—a whole bottle, even? I learned to watch every person with this level of detail, creating mental files in my head, so that I could make sense of them.

. . .

I did eventually make a neighborhood friend, a quiet Irish girl whom I met at the rec center and let, tentatively, into my world. She was also partial to lying around on the playground

equipment and talking about our secrets: which boys were
stirring up what feelings, that kind of thing. Her parents didn't
seem particularly religious, which was a relief. *This is the kind of
friend I want*, I thought, lying on the playground sand with her,
while we watched clouds pass by. I felt safe and connected, I
felt enriched. This was friendship. Recognizing this, I slowly
sought out a few more friends at school. First Connie, Mel,
Mwana, then Lisa, a blonde musical prodigy. The through line
was their trustworthiness, and the fact that none of their family backgrounds would prickle against mine. But in expat life,
friends came and went; everyone moved away, so it still didn't
pay to get too attached.

I lost touch with most of those girls over time, but Lisa and
I exchanged letters for years. I loved hearing about her mas-
tery of mathematics, her side hustle as a music teacher, life in
small-town Utah. Her family was religious, but it was a religion
that hadn't interfered with my life. And then, one day, a pack-
age showed up from her, a Book of Mormon. All that old stuff
came rushing back—feeling othered, not being good enough
just as I was. She was wondering if I'd be interested in talking
about the book sometime. I dropped it off at a donation box
and didn't write back. I didn't want friends who thought my
soul needed saving. I wanted friends who liked me now.

So I waited for the right ones. And, in the meantime, I
watched, noticing patterns and filing them away. It helped that
my parents are charming people—the kind whom everyone
seemed to speak tenderly about and wanted to be close to. I
saw why, if they weren't my own parents, I'd want to be friends
with them, too. So, in the next series of moves, I put together
a little mental scrapbook of how to connect with new people,

and I went after them like a girl possessed. I developed a series of overly familiar icebreakers. I overshared, just the tiniest bit, to make people feel comfortable sharing with me. I sent in my brother, and his smiling face, to warm up rooms of strangers. I asked questions more than I talked about myself. In asking these questions, I usually found out what was missing from people's lives—a book recommendation, a plumber—and I had information handy, to fill the hole. I followed up when I liked someone, and said, "We're going to be friends!" It worked every time. I learned that people liked to be courted. I could make anyone my friend, and I would make anyone my friend. I slipped right into being my mother, and I still am. "Oh, gosh, sounds like her divorce is going well!" I'll say, after we get out of a grocery line, or "I have a great tree guy" to complete strangers, when I grab the mail.

"Unfriendly," my butt. I'll show you unfriendly.

. . .

Somewhere along the way, though, connecting with people became a compulsion. It became a feedback loop in which I needed people to be drawn to me, and I felt the small "ding" of reward after each connection. On the one hand, I think I was trying to build a community I'd never had—a "chosen" family—but I also treated it almost like a video game: Can I make this person like me? That person? What about that guy down the street who never smiles? How many interactions will it take? I set goals with difficult people. *We'll see about that,* I thought, when a writing teacher said she doesn't hang out with students outside class. We hung out after class. Collecting friends made me feel special, and worthy, and indispensable.

When I entered the workforce, I was often sent in to deal with high-maintenance colleagues or clients—I was known to have a magic touch with the difficult. The magic touch was just asking them what they were actually upset about, because it was hardly ever work.

A therapist friend recently asked me if I play an instrument, and I joked, "People," but it wasn't really a joke. I identify people, or at least the people I want to connect with, and I connect with them. "It feels manipulative; am I manipulative?" I asked her, and she laughed at me. She assures me that, as long as I don't have a dastardly plan in mind (do I?), it's okay to navigate people the way I feel compelled to.

But as I have collected so many sparkly people in my life, it has drained me, especially now that I have two small kids and one tiny sliver of bandwidth for anyone outside my house. It took a lot out of me, maintaining these friendships, but I purposefully set them up to be ones in which people needed me more than I needed them. And I never asked them for anything back. By my mid-thirties, I had made hundreds of friends who could never break my heart. Who relied on me for favors. Who could never abandon or hurt me, because only I understood them, or could fix this specific mess. And then, after the kids, I started asking myself questions about the quality and depth of these friendships. Would we be friends if I didn't check in every few weeks? And who checks in on me when I'm having a hard time? Do I care about the people in my life more than they care about me?

I ask my husband these questions, and he asks if I'm being rational. Maybe not, but it's my fear, sometimes. How many of my friendships would be alive, I say, if I hadn't identified and pursued them? How long would those friendships have lasted if I didn't make most of the effort? I can count on one hand the friends who call me to see how I'm doing. I've worked myself into a simmer about this, and he tries, delicately, to dissuade me. He says sometimes I put an energy out into the world that says I don't need anything, that I don't need anyone. So maybe people think I'm always okay. I tear up thinking about how not-okay I am sometimes, and I see the smile on his face, because he is extremely fluent in the language of feelings, and relishes the opportunity to dissect a Big One.

"Oh no you don't," I say. "Don't you go enjoying this."

He claims not to.

"You love being sad!" I point out, correctly.

"I don't love being sad," he says. "I love intense emotions washing over me."

I shudder. I honestly can't think of anything worse.

Crawling into bed, I force back the tears in my eyes, still grumbling at him. Well, most people are limited, I mumble. And I'm kind of a lot. I don't know if *anyone* could put the energy into a friendship that I do.

"Is that really what you think?" he asks.

Maybe.

"So what's the answer? Caring less?"

No, that I cannot do.

Still, it might be time to reevaluate the data I've collected as a lifetime amateur sociologist. I can read people well, but instead of some crazed effort to win them all over, I can turn my critical gaze inward, and start to think more about what my own needs might be, and my own requirements for friend-ship. No flakes, I decide at first. No one who's bad at making a plan. I want to surround myself with people who care how I'm doing, who reciprocate, whose kids (if they have them) get along with my kids. I want loyal-to-the-death girlfriends—as loyal as me—and easy family hangs.

I try something new: not checking in on every one of my contacts, waiting to see who initiates contact without my constantly making the rounds. It means a lot of friendships fall by the wayside, and though I'm sad to lose contact with people at first, within a few months I feel lighter. More of my friendships now feel like two-way streets. They feel healthier, more supportive, and less of an obligation, as friendship should be.

In a heartwarming parallel, Mum and Huma Auntie have found their way back to each other as well, after more than thirty years apart, and have been nudging me to speak more with Miryam. We've exchanged a few messages, but it's bittersweet—she seems like a lovely woman, with some nice memories of me, but all we have in common is a relationship that tore a hole in my belly that I'm still trying to fix. I wonder if anything would be different had we been able to grow up together, or at least be in touch, that whole time. But I never saw her after that day. "You did see her," says my mother, shocking me. "She came to sleep over at our house, a year after that fight." I'm confused, and she tells me our dads eventually backchanneled to get us together, agreeing that politics should never have gotten in the way of our friendship. But I don't remember that, I tell Mum. I've blocked it all out, because by then it was too late. I already felt like I couldn't trust anyone. My mother thinks about this quietly, her face falling. "Those were some sad years," she says.

American Sigh

꒰ 1994 ꒱

"You haven't been the same since you started watching that awful show," said my mother. The show was *My So-Called Life,* and she was convinced, after overhearing a few episodes, that it was giving me ideas. I tried to explain to her that I had the ideas already—I was a high school sophomore when it began— but she told herself it was the only explanation for my new-found surliness. And, wow, was I surly.

I moved to the United States in the middle of my freshman year of high school, on my fourteenth birthday. "The middle of your freshman year!" so many Americans have screamed to me, horrified. "That must have been a nightmare!" Agreed, it was absolutely a nightmare, but not for the reasons anyone thinks. My first morning attending high school in suburban New York, Mum walked me to the bus stop, just to be safe. Her overwhelming impression of America was that kidnappers and murderers lurked behind every bush, poised to shoot unsupervised minors, with their widely available guns. While waiting, we stared at the snow on the ground, she with tender-ness and recognition, I more in wonderment, because I hadn't lived near any since I was a toddler. Mum and I leaned over the little bridge at the end of our road to watch a creek below. This was the detail, she said, that had made her choose our rental. It reminded her of Kashmir. The bus arrived, and I kissed Mum on the mouth, as I always had, and boarded. Avoiding eye contact, I sat down toward the front, armed with a book, and quietly rode to school.

I showed up and walked through my schedule, which was fine. The students were friendly; the teachers had gotten my transcripts in advance, and knew I wasn't going to give them any trouble. At lunch, a nice girl named Hillary asked if I wanted to eat with her friends, who were also very sweet. "It couldn't have been that easy," says my husband, who grew up twenty miles away from there, but it was. I only remember one small speed bump: the daily fire-station siren that announced it was noon. On my first day, I jumped in my seat, my heart in my throat, assuming there was an air raid. Some other kids calmed me down, and I was surprised and touched by their kindness. After the constantly changing winds of a childhood abroad, establishing a social foothold in a normal American high school felt relatively simple.

But the cultural shift was jarring. Saudi had never felt like a permanent home; it had been a detour on our way back to Kashmir, and now we were even farther away from whatever faint sense of home I had left. In those pre-internet days, I hadn't been immersed in American culture. We had only just gotten satellite TV in Riyadh, but I don't remember seeing much other than a ten-year-old run of the soap opera *Santa Barbara,* with its shades of teal and peach and its low-stakes drama. Maybe life in the United States would feel less thorny than life had been so far, I thought, and welcomed the idea. But when I left a rigorous International School in Riyadh and landed in the middle of a regular public school in a regular town in New York State, my system couldn't handle it—the gum under the scratched-up desks, the disdain many kids had for being at school, their kindness to me aside. *Where else would they rather be?* I wondered.

America felt so far away from everything I had known, and no one here seemed to have any sense of the larger world. "What was Saudi Arabia like?" they asked, without guile. "Did you have to ride camels to school?" I tried to describe my life before, but the marble bowling alleys, the casual international travel—it was too alien. I might as well have been describing another galaxy. Home, to these kids, had different rhythms. The town was very Italian and Jewish, firmly middle-class, at the time. It had one red-sauce place, a local bagel shop, a diner, and a Friendly's. There was one other Indian girl in my grade, and we became friends. I was glad to meet someone who had a sense that human existence didn't begin and end in New York. But even so, and with everyone being so sweet, I came home that first week, threw myself on the bed, and moaned, "Nobody here even cares about learning!"

My parents seemed different in America. They had always been so self-assured, captaining a watertight boat over rough seas. We were sealed inside, my brother and I, safe and warm. Then we got to the United States, and, for the first time in our collective lives, the sea outside was relatively calm. I wanted to take a dip in the water, which to my eyes was warm and placid, if a little murky. But my parents sensed only sharks, and their fear for my safety for the next few years of high school was somehow more difficult than all the storms we had weathered together. Now they huddled close, faces tense, lines of worry and confusion deepening with every unfamiliar challenge.

My father, by then, was an internationally recognized pediatric nephrologist, who had defined a new syndrome that was named after him and everything. He was recruited by a medical center in New York that had negotiated his US training-for-certification process. What normally would have taken six years—redoing his residency and a fellowship—turned into two, albeit at trainee pay. There wasn't much room for financial extras, and I usually knew better than to ask. I do remember one serious conversation about whether we could spare forty dollars so I could go on a field trip to the opera with the orchestra. We could, just barely, but when the group had dinner beforehand, everyone else had multiple courses while I savored every bite of my French onion soup. I watched *La Bohème* at Lincoln Center, rapt, maybe reminded a little of my once-bigger life.

By the beginning of my sophomore year, I had a solid foothold on what it meant to be an American teen, which dovetailed with the on-screen presence of Claire Danes: her crimped bob and opaque tights, the knitted brow and wobbly chin telegraphing her angst. *My So-Called Life* spoke to me, as it did to so many young women my age, because she was so profoundly dissatisfied, without a clear understanding of what might soothe her. While I related to her indeterminate longing, I questioned every one of her choices. Why that dum-dum Jordan when sweet, reliable Brian was right there? Rayanne was gonna drag her right down and ruin her chances at college. What a luxury, I thought, as these kids whipped up season-long plotlines based on a crush, a note, a strange teacher. What a luxury to be so preoccupied with little things. What a gift to go home to understanding parents who sigh, reasonably concerned, in contrast to my parents' lockdown mentality. How nice to fall asleep worrying about whether someone likes you back, instead of whether every life decision might lead to the crushing disappointment of generations of forebears. How cute.

But when my mother caught glimpses of the show, all she saw were red flags, her worst fears come to life, and her face was a mask of alarm. If only she had been able to see past them to who I actually was. "Maybe a drink would loosen you up," joked a jock-y kid at school while I was tutoring him in biology. "I don't drink," I said, prim. "Because I like to feel like myself." There were squares and there was me: a pile of wet sawdust thrown on the shimmering flames of normal teen conversation.

My parents, now fearful of what might befall me, had battened down the hatches, allowing me to leave the house only for school. I wasn't allowed social events, and I wasn't allowed to ride in anyone's car. After our years in Saudi, where I could wander around the compound with my friends from homework until dinner, I felt confined at home. I don't blame my parents for those difficult years. They grew up in a world where unfair circumstances seemed to fall out of the sky: wars, deaths, fires, floods. Hypervigilance was in their blood. When my mother wanted to apply to medical school, she was told her birthdate didn't meet an arbitrary cutoff, so she had to apply to PhD programs instead. My father studied for a year for an entrance exam he scraped the cash together to take in Malaysia, only to have the rules change that next year and his results thrown out. After forty-odd years of having the goalposts constantly shift, all they knew was to buckle down and control what variables they could. And after the extreme safety of life in Riyadh, everything was a variable—especially, they thought, for a young girl.

So that's when I started my double life. I knew, rationally, that my life outside the home was wholesome Americana. My friends were good, dorky kids: most of them members of the tennis and cross-country teams. Hangouts, more often than not, revolved around baking brownies and chitchatting about school. My classmates were confused about why I couldn't join general hangs. "You don't really . . . do anything," they said. "Why are your parents so hard on you?" they asked, and I defended them: "It's not their fault; they've come from a very different place and were raised in another era." But at home, I raged. "WHY?" I screamed at them, more than once. "Because hanky-panky" was often the response. Because drugs, because alcohol, because derailed futures, because teen pregnancy. "How do you know I'm not a lesbian?!" I yelled once. My mother was shocked and then laughed knowingly. "Oh no, no, you definitely aren't," she said. Their caution enraged me. Did they not see me? Did they not understand how I had been raised? Didn't they know that I wasn't going to walk out the door and fall into a pile of heroin needles or a pint of whiskey? I was so driven, and my peer group was so hopelessly dedicated to clean living, that I don't remember making one irresponsible choice in all of high school.

But my parents' fear was real, to them. So I spent as much time as I could away from them, at school—at track, in orchestra, in pit orchestra, in chamber orchestra. I didn't even like playing the violin that much, but it gave me an out. The only other thing I was allowed to do was go for runs in the neighborhood, during which I would sometimes pop into my boyfriend's house—because I suddenly had a boyfriend. He walked in on me reading *Anna Karenina* before a class once, and then we were dating. That's how nerdy a couple we were. If that sounds easy, too, that's because it was. What were the minor blips of high school romance compared with the random ostracism and heckling I was used to? My boyfriend was the sweet, smart captain of the swim team. His mother, a Filipina nurse, reminded me of the women I had worshipped in Saudi—so competent and warm. I'm sure she understood that I wasn't actually supposed to be there, and she had raised two girls of her own, but her friendliness and silent support gave me a model for how I wished my parents could be with me. But as I snacked at his house—a warm cheese bread, or leftover penne alla vodka, a family favorite—I knew that the only thing that could change my parents' minds was time.

The adults at school, unlike my parents, appreciated me, because I loved being there so much. AP European history was taught by a tiny old Italian man, who took an uncommon shine to me. He called me "Princess," bowed when I walked into class, often read my papers out loud to the class as examples. During exams, he would wait for me to hand in my test paper and then start chitchatting, about his day or about an article he was currently reading, which he would snip out of conservative magazines and newspapers and hand to me. During one final, he was particularly incensed about something *The New Yorker* had published. He was canceling his subscription because he believed the liberals had taken over and were pushing their agenda on him, specifically. As soon as I had finished the exam, he handed me the offending article, explaining his anger in a loud voice that caused me to shush him. "Everyone is still taking their tests," I said. Looking at me with wonder, he said, "You're so considerate." Then he grimaced at a student in the back of the class and stood up to walk to my friend Ruth, who was absentmindedly picking at a hole near the crotch of her jeans. He silently, disapprovingly handed her an article about the dangers of teaching teens about masturbation.

After the warm embrace of school, I dragged myself home, tensing as I got ready to scurry up to my room, with my parents moving heavily around the house, watching me. I was allowed to have people over, but generally barred from going to anyone else's place. "We don't know their parents," my mother said whenever I asked to go anywhere. Who knows what their standards were, how they lived, if they owned guns? "But they can come over here." Ruth sometimes rode her bike over to do homework, and stayed late. My mother liked her a lot, so she'd turn on the burglar alarm on her way up to bed, so that Ruth couldn't leave: Mum didn't think a kid biking home at night was safe, and trapping Ruth was her solution. When I asked them to let up because the constant monitoring was too much, they pushed back. "We're not American parents," they'd say, as though that would be an insult. "We'd never let you ride your bike around at night, not caring where you were or when you came home."

If a boy called, they hung up after the first syllable. If I wanted to go to something special like a school dance, I had to procure permission months in advance. And the more angry I got about it all, the more my parents tried to tighten their grip.

Once, I wanted to see what would happen if my friends just showed up to take me to homecoming, without my having had the whole series of conversations. When the headlights shone in the front window, my father said I could leave, but when I came back I'd be grounded for six months. *Grounded from what, exactly?* I wondered, so I went. And then I didn't go anywhere else for six months.

I hated feeling I was making them unhappy by just existing, but I also didn't believe that anything I was doing was intrinsically bad. My boyfriend (whom, obviously, they didn't know about) wrapped himself up in a giant box at my locker for Valentine's Day, for Christ's sake. This was the wholesome teen content of most parents' dreams. I was a C-story, too tame and reliable to make it anywhere near the universe of Claire Danes's character, Angela Chase. Living like this cleaved my heart and my mind. Frequent fights ended with me curled up on the bathroom floor—the only room I could lock myself into—sobbing for hours, wondering if they would ever understand me again, or if our relationship was over.

After I was all wrung out, I'd wonder if it would be easier for everyone if I had never been born, or if I could evaporate, somehow. I heard my brother once trying to help my parents through one of my spells, when he was around ten. "You know she's a little crazy," he said. "She'll be okay." I couldn't even be mad about this. I was definitely the crazy one, I agreed. I teemed with uncontrollable hostility and sadness. He was always smiling, a pleasure.

And I loved my mother so much. One day, after school, Mum told me she had been having a snack with her tea, and a raisin went down the wrong pipe; she'd thought she was going to choke, she said, but finally coughed it out. This kept me awake that night. I wished I could be easier, but I couldn't. And through it all, my parents, on their sealed-up little boat, wrung their hands, feeling helpless, believing they were doing the right thing. "Better safe than sorry," they said. "Sorry isn't the only other option," I screamed.

The only escape, I knew, was college, and I was in a rush to get out. At least in this area, my parents and I agreed. I was intensely focused on my schoolwork and test scores, because, frankly, I was wired to be. I missed a few questions on the math SAT, and we conferred about whether I should take it again to get a perfect score. In these moments, fretting about the decimal points that we all thought would make or break my future, I felt like we were a team again. But I hit all the benchmarks, got all the A's, raked in my merit scholarships; of that part, they could still be proud. "Why were you so hard on me then?" I ask them now. "You were out of control," they say. "We had to be." I tell them I was furious because they wouldn't let go. We sit, silently, every time this exchange comes up.

They fretted, and I fumed, counting down the seconds until I left, and at college I finally had room to breathe. I didn't feel at home, exactly, but neither did anyone else, and I was comforted by the sea of students around me, all equally puzzled about who we were and who we were going to be. The distance from home was good for our entire family, especially my parents. I still felt alone in the warm, less murky water, but I felt more comfortable exploring the unknown as I paddled toward a distant shore. And I didn't have to look back as much. My parents weren't flailing their arms anymore. They'd sometimes peek at me, call out, curious. They'd ask how the temperature was. They never dived in, and they still worried, but we eventually achieved a détente.

They felt they could now turn their attention to my brother, who was in junior high. But it is said that no siblings are raised by the same parents, and Punit and I definitely did not have the same parents. Four years after our move, they had settled in, formed a community. They knew the parents of the kids he was friends with, and had relaxed into the culture. I often weighed in, the third parent, who had "grown up" in America. And I reassured them in ways I wish they had been reassured when I was in high school: "He's a good kid, Ma," I said, when she worried. "You've raised him with judgment and values. He's not going to careen into your worst vision for his future. And certainly not with all of us around him on high alert." They listened. They relaxed their rules, and my brother had a much more conventionally American upbringing, although he claims it was less *My So-Called Life* than *Freaks and Geeks*: hangouts, school dances, spring break in Florida, even. But still, I was a phone call away, not just their reckless little swimmer now but one who helped drag them, inch by inch, the last few miles to shore.

Lo Sandwich

I think about this sandwich a lot: a soft white roll, football-shaped, palm-sized, sliced at an angle. One folded piece of ham, half a boiled egg, and a generous dollop of mayonnaise. It cost two thousand lire—then about a dollar—at the bakery in Sesto Fiorentino, not far from Florence, and was only available from 2:00 to 5:00 a.m. The bakery had other midnight offerings, too—pizza al taglio and the like—but nothing beat the sandwich. When I bit into one, I tried to notice and hold on to the feeling: *This is happy,* I thought, each time. I hadn't always been happy.

I was a great college student until I couldn't get out of bed. I hadn't expected to love the University of Michigan. My ranking-obsessed, tunnel-vision brain had allowed me to apply to only three schools: one Ivy, one for literal rocket scientists, and one Michigan, because my parents were moving there. I assumed I would go to the Ivy, because I thought I had done everything right. But then I got waitlisted, and after I collapsed in a dramatic heap, I scraped together enough self-righteousness to send them a letter pulling myself out of consideration.

I visited the school for rocket scientists, assuming I would study rockets and then attend medical school, like I had always planned. But I was struck by how unhappy many of the students seemed. "Sleep, party, or study: pick two" was the joke, one in which they took pride, and that made me nervous. I liked to sleep. I didn't know much about Michigan other than that they were offering me a scholarship. "The people here seem . . . happy," I said to the wholesome freshman with whom I stayed when the university flew me out to Ann Arbor. She, like me, had been academically driven, and turned down other schools to go here for free. She popped a birth-control tab as she made her way out the door, tossing me an extra key. "Yeah," she said, smiling. "It's a good life."

I didn't want to take on a mountain of debt to go be a sad rocket scientist. This was one practical reason why I accepted the scholarship to Michigan. But the other reason was that lightness I felt on the campus, a potential well-roundedness, the idea that worlds existed beyond the beeline to medical school. I consulted, once again, with the girl I had stayed with. "It's not like the other schools I've seen," I said gingerly, and she smiled: "There are a lot of cute guys here." I nodded. That wasn't what made my decision—of course not. But it did hint at something mostly unexplored. So I accepted the scholarship, and I loved it. Until I got sleepy.

My first semester had been fine. Organic chemistry was a bust—I'd have rather taken more literature classes—but reading was fun and felt like cheating. Work was meant to be, well, *work.* In my second semester of college, though—the "weeder semester," everyone kept calling it—I slept, and I couldn't stop. I thought I was just tired. I was enrolled in core premed classes, and in a lecture hall of hundreds, I couldn't connect with the professors. My peers, other type A valedictorians from around the country, formed study groups to obsess over problem sets. I just wanted to stay in bed with my books, and when I wasn't reading, I slept. At first I thought it was the weather: "Too cold to walk across campus," I said. Then I wondered if I was sick, because I was sleeping through my morning classes, through meals, into the afternoon, sometimes through the night again.

I was amazed. I had been a terrible sleeper forever; the smallest noise would wake me and keep me up for hours. I've never really shaken my body's vigilance for sirens. So sleeping through the night was, at first, a marvel. But no matter how much I slept, I never felt rested or refreshed. I barely ate, other than a bag of Cape Cod potato chips, or a small container of grapefruit juice cocktail I picked up at the convenience store nearby, where I elbowed my way through hordes of friendly students stocking up on beer for the weekend. Everyone was drunk and happy at Michigan, it seemed. I drank, I went out, but none of it worked for me.

The missed classes piled up, until I was clearly going to fail out of all of them. "Sleep, party, or study" applied here too: I had made my choice, but I didn't even enjoy sleeping anymore. I don't remember much from that time; it was a semester-long fugue state. But I know that, when I dragged my stuff home at the end of the year, my parents were holding my report card, apoplectic. I had gotten straight D's, with a B+ in Hindi, which I'd already spoken. I didn't have an explanation but swore I'd do better. I wasn't sure how I could stomach a return to form, though. I had been feeling lost and unsure in class, which confused me. I had always excelled at being a student, and if I wasn't good at that, I didn't know what else I had to offer. I was starting to feel the first stirrings of a break from my chosen academic path. And the long, dark winter days and heavy-drinking culture had decimated what was left of my happiness.

I was put on academic probation, and had to get my GPA up to keep the scholarship. But the summer semester offerings were, fortunately, low-lift. I signed up for yoga and Italian 101. A literary seminar, I think. I looked for small, cozy rooms, not lecture halls, in an attempt to ease my broken mind and body back into school. I didn't have the vocabulary for depression then, but I knew I needed to wrestle myself away from those sad, lost feelings, and away from another long sleep. Yoga was a good start. It woke my body back up, reminded me that I had arms and legs, that I could move those arms and legs to take me out of my short-circuiting brain. As the semester went on, the professor bookended our sessions with calming meditations, and I felt my nervous system start to reset. It felt good—and foreign—to lean into something that wasn't painful. Taking classes I liked, just because I liked them, restored me. I hadn't really enjoyed using my body since those long hours at the pool as a small child.

And Italian was a revelation: an excitable, warm language, taught by an excitable, warm department. One of my teachers was a chain-smoking terror from Bologna named Beatrice, although we called her "Bea." An even five feet tall, curvy, with a severe brown bob and mischievous little squinty green eyes, Bea looked like a disoriented street urchin but was actually a PhD candidate in Chinese literature. Her previous job, in Italy, had involved translating Chinese pulp fiction—"splatter" novels—into Italian. Bea had the kind of past that she hated explaining, because she thought it took too long. I knew that she had lost half of her body weight, seemingly by replacing food with cigarettes. She never once touched the dessert we shared at coffee, puffing out her cheeks and shuddering ever so slightly. I'm not sure how she avoided all those desserts, considering that she often moved class to cafés, because she wasn't allowed to smoke in class. Then there had been the matter of her rent-free apartment in Venice.

"How did you avoid paying rent?" I asked suspiciously, certain she had been a squatter.

"The landlord . . . He liked coffins," she responded, slowly pulling at her Camel Light.

I sighed, exasperated, and she hurried through the next part.

"So I slept in a coffin with my hands folded over my chest."

"Did he watch you sleep?"

"Sometimes," she conceded. "But he stayed by the door."

"You must have had some other job skills, Bea!" I exclaimed.

"I did, but it really wasn't the same after my plane crashed," she said, lowering her gaze to her knees and mistakenly ashing on her lap. We never got a further explanation, but I knew I wanted to seek out more people like her.

My scholarship covered tuition for the summer but not my living expenses. So I worked at a hippie clothing store, selling long Indian cotton dresses. It was straightforward work, but physically taxing, eight hours of standing a day, outside, dealing with constant foot traffic. The owners brought in trays of hearty vegetarian food for the employees. I soaked my feet in an ice bath each night while shoveling a pound of moussaka into my mouth, because I was hungry again. The job wasn't rocket science, but when I look at a photo I have from then—

in a strappy purple dress, shoulders glowing from the sun—I remember the warmth, my full belly, and my new Italian friends. It felt like the last semester had been a bad dream, and I was starting to wake up.

As I entered the next school year, I stared with new eyes at the kids around me who looked forward to orgo lab. I thought about my own father, who loved his job with a singular passion, and recognized that I didn't share it. Pursuing medicine, for me, would have meant turning my back on the thousands of other things I wanted to explore. And mustering up the passion for medicine was an uphill struggle. Maybe it was all the yoga, but for the first time I started to wonder what would happen if, instead of beating against the competitive current for once, I gave myself over to the universe. What if it had a plan for me, and I gave it the space to unfold? So I made the first impractical decision of my life.

My parents were understandably confused when I told them I'd be majoring in Italian and not going to medical school after all. They pointed out that an Italian degree didn't normally lead to a bunch of job offers, but I had planned a workaround: I'd go to law school afterward, I told them. Still, they weren't convinced. "Isn't that just reading and talking about it?" said Mum. "Who goes to law school?" Back in India, when they were young, it had been a last-resort profession for people who didn't have the grades for science careers. "Presidents?" I said, honestly not having done a ton of research. I was just stalling, really—creating some space so I could follow this feeling, but giving it an end date. Who knew where law school would take me, but at least I'd be—well, yes—reading, and talking about it.

My parents accepted my plan, and I bought myself a few years to figure out who I was.

There was the small question, though, of my never having been to Italy, and I wasn't sure how I would ever get there: my scholarship required me to stay in campus housing for all four years. But then a celestial loophole opened wide: the lady at the study-abroad office told me that the Michigan program in Tuscany was housed in a villa that they considered a campus dorm. Confirmation came through from above: I could go to Italy for my entire junior year, and it would be paid for. I just had to pay the airfare with my summer earnings and work in the villa while there to cover spending money.

It's cliché that Italy was the balm I needed, but the cliché exists for a reason. I landed at the airport in Florence, and, like generations of students before me, felt immediately comfortable, for no tangible reason. "But it feels like India," I said to my mother when I called her from a pay phone to tell her I'd landed. A little chaotic and dilapidated, but bustling, warm. And the endless talk of food felt familiar. Between classes at the Villa Corsi Salviati, a seventeenth-century estate just outside of Florence, fifty-nine other students and I peeked into the kitchen at the end of the dining hall, where Chef Nino muttered and whirled, preparing our daily impeccable sit-down lunch. We whiled away afternoon hours with homework, waiting for the clang of the dinner bell, before descending like a pack of puppies on a sausage.

Nino took dinner seriously, coursing out a soup, then a pasta, followed by an entrée and at least three sides. After the past years of hastily slapped-together dorm food and microwave ramen, it was restorative to be fed and taken care of by him. Dinners in the villa dining hall came with a jug of unfiltered olive oil from the groves on the grounds, thick and cloudy. We sopped it up with bread, stirred it into soup, and drizzled it on everything else. I alone must have gone through a liter a month. After dinner, we wandered into the night, which often ended at an after-hours hip-hop club with a Senegalese DJ. At closing time, we tumbled out of the club, sweaty and euphoric, before dragging ourselves back to the villa. One night, as we stepped out of a taxi, a fellow student smelled bread, and we followed the smell to the back door of a local bakery, where a bemused baker introduced us to Lo Sandwich, and the new peak of my happiness.

I was so content in Italy, and not just because of that sandwich. I had thought, for too long, that things had to be painful and difficult to be worth pursuing. I believed that there would be some kind of reward at the end of moving through a cloud of discomfort. This narrative, shored up by the Immigrant Dream my parents had achieved, was so baked in that I felt suspicious and guilty when I was happy, or when my classes felt interesting and easy. It seemed to me that my happiness was at direct odds with my parents' happiness, that either they could be happy or I could, but never all three of us at the same time. I was learning that seeking out my own interests—letting them inspire and motivate me—felt so much better than being tired and sad. I wanted to see what would happen if I followed the good feelings instead of eternally rolling a boulder up a mountain I didn't even know whether I wanted to climb. As I binged on neorealist cinema and collected endless annotated translations of Dante, I felt guilty about enjoying my new life this much. Actively seeking out joy felt like flying right up to the sun.

Then, shortly before the year abroad ended, my energy flagged. I fell into bed around eight, and dragged myself out twelve hours later. I was tired again, and worried that it meant something dangerous. One morning, I woke to a clanging bell, which I thought was a fire alarm, only to realize I had slept through the entire night and day, and it was dinnertime again. This scared me, but I knew it was because I was dreading a return to normal campus life. What would happen when I stepped out of the fantasy that had been keeping me afloat? I was worried that a return home would mean falling back into that awful, sludgy feeling that kept me under a pile of clothes and blankets, in the dark, away from people, as I slowly erased myself from the world.

I knew I had to let go of my dream life in Italy, but desperately wanted to remember how I had lived here—pursuing simple pleasures, connecting with people and things that fed instead of depleted me. If I could maintain that as a baseline, I thought, I might be able to stay out of the pit. While I stared down my cultural expectations, applied to law school, left the intimacy of a small program to return to the anonymity of a cavernous lecture hall, and though I couldn't take the villa home with me, I hoped against hope that I would be able to summon the feeling it had evoked.

Dance Yourself Clean

I woke up to screaming, one sticky summer night in Rome, and it was even louder than usual. I stumbled into the hallway and saw my roommate, Teo, pulling a naked man out of his bed. Teo's girlfriend, Katie, stood nearby, topless and shrieking. I watched as Teo dragged the man out of the apartment and pushed him down the stairs. I groaned.

"Guys, could you keep it down? I have to work tomorrow."

They apologized, but whisper-shouted the rest of the night. In the morning, Teo was gone.

I hadn't been able to stay away from Italy for long. A few months into my legal training, it was dawning on me that I simply did not understand it, and never would. When I tell people this, they laugh, assuming I'm exaggerating, because I was allowed to graduate. But that was a miracle, because even though I did the homework and took notes in class, the words were a jumble. Legal principles remained opaque, and exam papers were often my best guess, covered up by competent writing. I don't remember one single thing I learned, other than the difference between assault, which creates apprehension in a victim, and battery, actual physical contact. But that comes up less often than you'd imagine, even.

I had thought I would wrap up law school and do the stable corporate thing for a while, but noticed far too late that those jobs involved mountains of paperwork, or representing corporations against wrongdoing, or both. The starting salary was great, if I was willing to be an exquisitely bored bad guy. Those first few months, I already knew I couldn't do it, but I was forty thousand dollars in a hole, and if I left now I'd have to hurry up and decide on yet another career. In the logic I was using at the time, it made a heck of a lot more sense to stick it out, take a few years to formulate a next step, and at least graduate with a degree. But, once again, I didn't connect to what I was studying, and, as I'd done the last time, I ran away. Missing Italy, I emailed every American lawyer in Rome until one kind soul created a summer internship for me.

In the classifieds of a low-fi website for expats in Rome, I found a room on the quiet side of Trastevere with a couple: Italian Teo and American Katie. I sublet from their roommate Jason, a stringer at *The Boston Globe,* who had been quite friendly on email but seemed frazzled and curt when I met him at an ATM near the apartment so I could pay him for the entire summer in cash. Later, my new roommates dismissed him as a "downer," and, to be honest, he did seem much older, more uptight, than someone in their early twenties should be. I wondered if newsrooms did that to people. "Good luck," he had mumbled as he rolled his suitcase down the street. "Good riddance!" Teo and Katie yelled out the window at the empty cobblestone street below.

Teo couldn't abide a downer. He was a pin-thin, dead-sexy drummer in a grimy punk band. Katie was a petite, bespectacled redhead with a pixie cut. We were instant friends—she

was a sweet ladybug of a girl, and I felt a maternal urge to protect her—but Teo made me uncomfortable. He had an unsettling way of staring at me silently, letting unease spill out of his
head and onto my face, before answering a question. Although
his English was technically perfect, he spoke in jagged phrases,
like language reflected in a broken mirror.

By day three, Teo's strangeness had crystallized into obvious
alcoholism. He took off after dinner and was gone all night,
then came home wasted, to a barn burner of a row. Repeated
nightly. When I asked, their friends said that was just their
"thing," but I felt for Katie, who cried herself to sleep every
time. I not-so-gently encouraged them to break up, and after
that fight, the one that ended with Teo throwing a male visi-
tor down the stairwell, they finally ended things, and he
moved out.

After Teo left, the air changed, literally. Fresh flowers and
bubbling pasta sauce replaced the stink of his smoke-filled
Peroni bottles and sweaty T-shirts. I went to work every morning and called Katie over lunch, the Mastroianni to her La
Loren, and asked her what she'd be making for dinner. On my
way back from the bus, I would yell up to our window from the
crooked cobblestone street, and Katie would drop down three
or four euros from our kitchen change jar so I could go to
the corner store and get a couple of tomatoes, an onion, some
plonk. If I found more change in my purple pleather tote, I'd
throw in some peas or a can of "good" tuna. I watched as Katie
sautéed the onion, added the tomatoes, then tuna, then peas,
and tossed it all with some pasta. It tasted better than made
any sense, and was my introduction to the Italian tradition of
cucina povera, or "poor cuisine"—proudly, intentionally scraped

together with spare change, some bread crumbs, a saggy vegetable or two. I loved the care she took in creating something so delicious out of such simple ingredients, the attention she paid to making sure I was well fed.

As Katie cooked, we'd talk, and after dinner we'd go up to the sixth-floor terrace and make evening plans over a twinkling view of St. Peter's. And what plans! On a combined weekly income of about two hundred dollars, we had to be creative—taking long chatty walks through the city and way-off-peak day trips to Florence and Siena, attending catered events with my colleagues, wandering into the piazza, and hitching rides to wherever anyone we knew wanted to go. One night, after a beach bonfire in Ostia, we fell asleep in our designated driver's car and woke up to a sunrise on a cliff above Naples, 150 miles away. It could have been glorious if I hadn't had to be at work in three hours, and if Katie had been able to see the view, but her glasses had gotten buried in the previous evening's Lido sand.

We one-upped each other with grand, if free, gestures. Katie loved the Red Hot Chili Peppers, but we didn't have enough money to buy their new album, so I begged a musician we knew to play it on his guitar in exchange for spaghetti on the roof. I thought I had won the best-friend contest until she met me at work one day and said we were going to see Sonic Youth play the Palladium. We definitely didn't have the money for the tickets—did she get it from Teo? I worried about his influence over her as we approached the venue, and she shushed me as she walked me behind the stadium, up a hillside, and into a clearing populated by happy ragamuffins. We perched on the slope, with a perfect view of the stage from above the retaining wall. My delight was doubled by the mozzarella sandwiches she pulled out of her pockets as we sat down.

Four months later, my internship ended. I left in tears, with promises to write. I returned home to the first twinge of Ann Arbor's endless winter, dreading my second year of law school. Both Katie and I were bereft; circumstance had torn us apart right as we were building the world's greatest friendship. But then a stroke of luck: Katie wanted to move back to the States, she said, and my roommate was graduating. Did she see a future in Ann Arbor?

Katie moved in, and at first I tended to her as if she were a neglected stray. I introduced her to my friends, and she fed and charmed them as she had me for a few weeks. After that, my rosy image of her began to crumble. The spirit that had been so free in Italy seemed reckless at home. She up and drove to New Orleans with a guy friend after a conversation at a dinner party, and moved right back after it fizzled. That take-her-anywhere amiability became a lack of identity as she picked up the style, interests, and sometimes even accents of her new friends.

So, because it's what I did whenever I was sad, I ran away. A friend in college had started an electronic-music label, with a roster of DJs who played in underground venues across Detroit. I knew that dancing made me feel good, and law school and the Katie situation made me feel bad, so I threw myself firmly, recklessly into the good feelings, flailing around warehouses and basements until four in the morning, the music loud enough to drown out any other thoughts in my head or worry in my chest. In retrospect, the dancing probably kept me from careening back into depression—the chemicals of movement flushed out my anxiety about the future. When my friends now hear about the years when I went out dancing every night, they assume I was some kind of club kid. Oh, there were no drugs, I'm quick to mention. A little vodka here and there, maybe. But the dancing was the drug. It kept me out of bed.

But after 4:00 a.m., there was still class, and there was still Katie, and she became the screen upon which I projected all my unhappiness. I started to see her cheerful flightiness, which had been so charming in Rome, as desperation for attention. I never stopped to think that she had shed an entire old life, and was only just figuring out her new one. I just thought it was annoying. Her flexible schedule, so convenient when it meant I could come home to a cozy Italian apartment, devolved into drinking beer in front of the TV all day. Sophia and Marcello became Edith and Archie, and our relationship disintegrated. She moved out. I felt pain and anger, yes, but also relief, at a problem having snuffed itself out.

I know now that Katie wasn't the problem. I know that it was easier to be irritated at her, and wish she'd change, than to examine myself. I can see that I was immature and selfish, and I regret having dragged her into my whirlpool of sadness. She's one of the only close friends I've had in my adult life with whom I've not maintained a relationship, and I know now that I was deeply unhappy, while she wasn't, and I envied and resented her free spirit. I still think about her, and our friendship: Was I a bad person for cutting it off? Why did her behavior bother me so much? Was it even as disturbing as I remembered? I feel that it almost certainly was not, and I hope I've learned a lot more about friendship, and myself, in the twenty years since.

But, recently, I opened the Travel section of *The New York Times* and read this:

> *The dog was not house trained, but after a day of pounding Peronis, neither, really, was my roommate. His fights with his girlfriend wrought havoc on our dishware, and the vagabonds screaming Roman threats outside, demanding the money he owed them, invaded my dreams.*

I looked up the author's name and laughed. He's now the *Times'* Rome bureau chief, but years ago was the stringer at the *Globe* who sublet his apartment to me and then ran far away, cash in hand. We reconnected online and marveled about our shared experience, which, it seems, was real. I understand now why he had the tired eyes of a much older man. Neither one of us slept much in that apartment. And, like him, I'll always love Italy, and I wouldn't have loved it nearly the way I did without Katie. But, like so many souvenirs that make sense in their country of origin—ponchos, braids, summer flings—Katie's presence in my life might have been easiest left in Rome: a fond, uncomplicated memory.

Phantom Threads

"So I'm in Daniel Day-Lewis's office for lunch. . . . He's eating an airport salad at his desk, and I'm sitting on the couch, across from him," I tell my friend Annie, a therapist. "We're trying to have a conversation, but he gets distracted by the wallpaper peeling above my head. He hates the wallpaper, and he *really* hates the peeling. Then lunch is over, and I've gotten nothing done. That's the whole dream." It's been six months since I woke up from it, and I can't stop thinking about it. I'm hoping Annie can help me figure out why. As I rush through the plot points, I feel sheepish. I don't know if there is anything more boring than hearing about other people's dreams, no matter how enchanting the dreamer finds them. Dream lives are such a collection of nonsense—a trippy word salad—that I tune out immediately whenever anyone brings me one. As when my toddler starts telling a nonsense story that also has no basis in reality, I nod and smile, thinking about other things, then dutifully chime in at the end. "That's amazing!" I say. Or "Wow, your brain is working overtime!" But I don't mean it. I don't really care what anyone's dreaming about.

Until I got to know Annie. I first met her at a playground in our neighborhood, because our firstborns are the same age.

She was warm and low-key in a way that was instantly familiar, and we were soon a fixture at her funny little Venice bungalow, with the kids bopping around for entire afternoons while we caught up and made them dinner. She was such an empathetic presence, even as a relative stranger, that my feelings easily slipped forth: about losing myself after parenthood, about all the murky dissatisfaction that surrounded the shift. As I shared more with her—the times I couldn't get out of bed, the heaviness of everything being just too difficult—I realized that sharing the hard parts made me feel better. This was an epiphany, although it perhaps shouldn't have been.

I didn't know anyone in my community who had ever seen a therapist. I had always thought it was for people with actual problems, like people who had been kidnapped, maybe, or who hated their families, or both. When yucky feelings come up, Indians traditionally get irritated, then talk ourselves out of it. We count our blessings and move on with our lives. But as I talked more to Annie about the Mom stuff—the scary, angry, worrying parts, the lying awake at night freaked out by everyone's mortality, my own shortcomings, my other dreams on pause—I felt lighter, and suddenly I saw the point.

She texted me the number for my first therapist: a mother of two, and a perfect fit. "When was the last time you felt like a child?" Pam asked me in one of our early sessions, and I stared back, blankly. I've never felt like a child. Over the next two years, she pulled me out of what she saw immediately was a clinical depression. She helped me find myself again, but even better: after thirty-some years of not having the vocabulary to talk about my feelings, I started to line them up and experience the sweet relief that came after examining them. I grew less restless, more at peace, and I resolved to teach my kids how to do the same.

Now I'm a therapy convert, thanks to Annie, and this is how she tricks me into sharing my dreams, because she tells me I might learn *even more* about myself. It sounds like some LA nonsense, and I'm not convinced. But when I tell her the Daniel Day-Lewis one, Annie laughs. "Well, first off, that does sound like him." She is uniquely qualified to make this joke, because she once worked as the nanny to Mr. Day-Lewis's children. As a young theater producer in New York, she made ends meet by nannying and assisting prominent celebrities. But by the age of thirty, tired of the pace and uncertainty of show business, Annie sought out something more stable. Her love of storytelling drew her to the Joseph Campbell Archives at Pacifica Graduate Institute, where she earned a master's in marriage and family therapy.

The intersection of Carl Jung and Joseph Campbell is where she fell in love with what she now calls "Dream Minding," a method she uses in her client work. Jung believed that dreams were from our unconscious and that their symbols and imagery could help us work out problems in our conscious life once they were unpacked and discussed, she tells me, and Campbell also viewed dreams as a source for learning about yourself. Even the most personal dreams contain archetypes and mythological themes—fear of death, being tested—that under examination can teach us about our inner selves and how we connect to the rest of the world. With her Jungian foundation in place, Annie has now been doing dreamwork with clients for eleven years, first one to one with clients, and now Dream Minding workshops with small groups.

By the time she asks me to share a dream of my own, our families have been intertwined for years. But I haven't had any peeks into her professional life until she, nine months pregnant, invites me over to discuss Mr. Day-Lewis. We get comfortable in the living room of her home, a warm, cozy Craftsman in the West Adams neighborhood of LA, while her toddler is napping and before she needs to pick up her six-year-old from school. Annie's instructions are deceptively simple. I'm to share a dream, and then we'll go through the objects and symbols one by one, playing close attention to how each one makes me feel.

Annie points out that the dream has stayed with me for a reason, whereas so many dreams evaporate upon waking. "What does Daniel Day-Lewis mean to you?" she asks, and that feels ridiculous enough, but I give it a good think. Well, what he means to us all, obviously, the pinnacle of creative achievement. The desk? "Oh! It's my old desk from when I was an agent." The sad salad? Food for sustenance, not food that tastes good. An afterthought. "But why an afterthought? Why is that important?" she asks.

Aha. When I had an office job I didn't love, deciding what to eat for lunch was a highlight of my day. It was a break from suspecting that what I was doing wasn't the right fit, my little midday reward for tolerating the job, as so many of us take. But now that I'm happier, I get so absorbed in my work that I sometimes forget to eat—for the first time in my life. She nods, nudges me along. "What does the wallpaper mean to you?" she asks. I giggle, but then get sober, recognizing it as the exact paper from my friend Beth's bedroom. A eureka moment. "What does Beth represent to you?" says Annie. Beth, a costume designer, is . . . "creatively engaged and fulfilled." Would Beth be agitated if Daniel Day-Lewis didn't like her wallpaper? A teal fleur-de-lis design? She absolutely would not. She'd cover another room in it.

I start to think about what I'm wrestling with at work. I've been eager to establish a safe foundation, so I've been taking on projects that land on my desk, instead of following what drives me, and me alone. I'm so grateful to be doing what I want, finally, that maybe I've focused too much on grasping for a foothold. I haven't been listening to my inner voice or truly following my own curiosity. This gives me a lot to think about, and shifts my priorities. Isn't that what Daniel Day-Lewis would do? While I'm reflecting on this, Annie's ancient dog, Bear, wanders in and falls asleep in the middle of the floor, twitching, probably, with a dream of his own.

Annie calls Dream Minding a "shortcut to therapy" for people who might hate the idea of therapy. Generally, the therapy-averse are much more comfortable talking about facts than feelings, and retelling a dream is a recitation of facts, "which we can then unpack together to connect in a slow and gentle way to your real, waking conscious life. It's not shining a bright light on an issue that might be making you uncomfortable. It's much gentler, like unpacking a poem." She smiles cheekily at me—she knows how resistant I can be, which is clearly why she's been trying to get me on board this dream train.

The marvel of Annie's approach is how quickly it becomes habit, and how easy it is to slip into a meaningful conversation. When people bring up dreams in conversation now, it's a fun game to play. "Let's list the objects," I say. "How do they all make you feel?" It's a magic trick, watching the awareness wash over their faces. A glorious new path for me, an inveterate meddler, to play armchair psychologist—with a real therapist's approval! I've even tried it with the kids. I notice that sometimes, when our eight-year-old son might not want to talk about his worries directly, he'll at least be able to process them through exploring a scary dream. And not just dreams. Last week, our three-year-old came up with this story, to which I would normally not have paid close attention, but now Annie has me intrigued by the brain's symbolic workings:

"A witch put the bird inside a stew and she eat it," she begins, and instead of tuning out, I'm taking mental notes. "She spit out the bird and her tummy hurted. Then she can walk. She walked on a bridge and saw a goose. She putted the goose inside the stew. Oop she slipped, she almost fell in the stew but only her feet got wet. Then lava came from the volcano outside. It went under the bridge to the witch bird's house floor and the witch bird fell in the lava. That's the end."

I'm excited about the opportunity to work through some of the things she might be worried about—this is a text rich with symbolism. Maybe I can dive inside her funny little brain, find out what it all means to her. What an incredible way to get to talking about her internal life at an early age. Frankly, I'm proud of myself for even thinking of it. I start my quest. "How do you feel about witches?" I nudge. "They're strong and friendly," she says, shoveling penne into her mouth. And the . . . gooses? "Gooses are pink and purple—they're my favorite color." Stew? "Is delicious. She gave the stew to her neighbors, and they all loved it." The tummy ache is "because she liked it so much she ate too much." I ask about the lava, but she's moved on. "I don't want to answer any more questions," she says, grumpy.

"I want to play with someone who wants to play with me." So I get down on the ground, and pretend I'm a customer at her store for "things that spray."

As I bite the inside of my cheek to stop from pushing my daughter on the witch-bird front, I realize I may have been overzealous. But I'd do anything to protect my kids from the buzzing numbness, the bouts of endless, enervating sleep I went through before I knew how to manage them.

After my first therapist moved away, I met with nine more before finding The One. Arti is a queer South Asian woman who is close to her family. She mentions in our first meeting that she's convinced her own father to go to therapy. "I want that," I say. Not for my parents to embrace therapy, necessarily, but to be able to talk to them about sad memories and uncomfortable feelings that we've mangled for forty years. "It all feels so indulgent, though," I tell her, a little embarrassed. "So American." She smiles. "Pain is passed down until someone has the bandwidth and resources to feel it," she says, and I immediately have to lie down. I'm reeling under the weight of generations of forebears who didn't have the time or tools to deal with the emotional impact of their incomprehensible challenges. The part of me that's embarrassed by my emotions, and embarrassed to tell anyone in the family about them, is the part that needs it the most. "You're doing this for your kids," she tells me. "This"—the sleepless nights, the inexplicable panic, the ever-present, debilitating fear of loss—"begins to end with you."

She teaches me to sit with my horrible feelings, and I hate it. But, eventually, I acknowledge the deep well of sadness that follows me around—it's right next to me; it probably always will be—and I learn how not to fall in. I still sometimes feel the breath of my old friend Despair, and I greet him, a cloudy scribble, aloud: "Well, if it isn't my old friend, Despair." I remind myself that waves of sadness pass, and he eventually goes silent. The latest character to emerge is a pit of anxiety. It looks like a literal peach pit, and we're still learning to coexist. We'll get there. But I wish it hadn't taken an entire lifetime to begin.

If the children can just learn to express and process their feelings in real time, I think, they'll be safe, better than me. Less scared. Rational me knows I can't protect them from disappointment or catastrophic life events. But I jump at any chance to discuss what's going on in their hearts and minds. And perhaps I can be too eager, too vigilant, in my constant overcorrection. Playing with my daughter—and following her lead—is a reminder that I'm already doing the work, and sometimes I need to let a witch bird just be a witch bird.

The Last Frontier of the
American Dream

∂{ 2004 }ⴲ

A low-energy alligator hung, entirely still, in the small pond of his enclosure. Through its Plexiglas sides, we could see his stubby little legs dangling, useless. His face above the water was menacing—those beady killer eyes—but underneath, the rest of his body floated around like a sleepy baby in a pool. The effect was that of an inverted iceberg: scary on top, ridiculous down below. "Emmett doesn't move much," said our tour guide, Ariel. "Doesn't eat much, either." He subsisted on one rat a week, which didn't seem possible. Ariel shrugged. "He's not into swimming around, really. His owner raised him in a bathtub, and when he outgrew it, we got the phone call." I was mesmerized. Would he move if I got closer? Nope. Farther away? Also no. If my children screamed? No. He just floated there, on his transcendent plane, content: a leathery, Lebowski-esque Dude.

I had only ever known Sylmar as a convenient fast-food stop off the 210 and the 101, on the way to Palm Springs. It is a dusty pocket at the base of the San Gabriel Mountains, just north of Los Angeles proper. But we had heard through the parent grapevine that children loved this institution, the Wildlife Learning Center. The website said my kids could touch a sloth, meet a porcupine, feed a giraffe. It sounded like a good way to kill some time, and make some memories, all of that. But they really undersold the alligator.

As I watched Emmett glide by, I marveled at what had brought him to LA. But what had brought any of us? I'd often contemplated. My own path to California sometimes seemed equally random. In the spring of 2004, eighteen years before I met the alligator, I had two problems: I was in love with someone who didn't love me back, and I had just earned a law degree I didn't want to use. Everyone seemed to expect that, if I left Michigan, it would be to move to New York and shackle myself to a petroleum company or some finance monsters, to earn my keep. I vaguely, dreamily thought I might work in publishing. It would make me so happy to be near books, but I couldn't afford rent and loan payments on an entry-level publishing salary in New York. So, when a friend from college moved to Los Angeles—which was much cheaper than New York at the time—I tagged along.

The West Coast gave me an opportunity to reset. California freaked people out, and I loved that. I had visited a friend there once and enjoyed the foreignness of it. The plants, the sun after all my time in Michigan—if they weren't perfect for me, at least they meant a change. I had felt the weight of family expectations for so long, and LA felt so far away, that I could figure out what to do with my life without anyone's interference. With the promise of a job in an agency mail room, already a huge leap of faith for my parents, I hopped into my Civic and drove across the country with a broken windshield and somewhere in the neighborhood of $350. I was trying to outrun my fate.

I started that agency job, and shared a one-bedroom apartment with a willowy redhead I met on Craigslist. She was never around, but she was kind, and paid half the rent. I once walked into the apartment to see her painted blue, with half of a teapot strapped to her head. It was my introduction to the idea of Burning Man. Her sweetness aside, I had made grave errors in choosing this apartment, which was on a busy intersection. The crosswalk chirped around the clock, a waking nightmare for a person who can't sleep through a sneeze. My only social interaction outside of work was with a friendly neighbor, who invited me over out of pity, but also because he was assembling a photo album to take to an immigration interview, to prove his marriage wasn't a sham. "Come for Thanksgiving," he insisted, in the middle of spring. And, a month later, "Can you make it to a cocktail hour on Thursday? Wear a Christmas sweater."

I got home so late from work that I'd have to park many shadowy blocks away, and run back home with my keys in weapon position (this was a decade before a fancy jam place gentrified the neighborhood). Then, as I approached home, I'd be greeted by the elderly men who liked to sit on the stoop next door. They'd shout their greetings in Spanish, after which I got yelled at for not replying in Spanish. "Your parents spoil you!" one of them said, in English. I didn't have the words to respond, so I slunk back home, honestly a little embarrassed, and crawled under my covers. My exhaustion began to overpower even the chirps of the crosswalk. Usually, I stayed in bed just until morning, but on Fridays I crawled into bed until Monday.

One night, after staring down a negative nine-hundred-dollar balance at the ATM, I fell into a deep sleep and woke up, around midnight, to the squeaking of busy mice. I blearily wandered into the kitchen, rescued a bag of brown bread, and passed out clutching it, only to find in the morning that a mouse had burrowed a little tunnel through the loaf. In tears, I reached for my jeans, where I knew I had one piece of gum that might tide me over until I got to work and could gorge on free peanut butter from the office kitchen. But the gum was gone, the mouse having gnawed a hole in my pocket to get it. Everything was terrible. I went back to bed, my life a waste.

Looking back, I wonder why I didn't ask for help. Pride, maybe. A strong desire not to let my parents be proved right in their misgivings about my unconventional career path. This is exactly what they wanted to avoid with their emphasis on a reliable professional degree. They never wanted me to be broke or lonely. But I couldn't reach out. I had gotten myself into this mess, against my parent's wishes, so I'd get myself out.

When I was nine, and prone to sensory overload, I had slipped out of my brother's fourth-birthday party in search of some quiet and fallen into that neighborhood fountain. There's a self-deprecating version I tell of the story that paints me as an antisocial klutz. But if I dig a little deeper, it was really because I was wondering whether anyone would notice if I left. As I leaned into the fountain, I thought about how long it might take them to look for me, if they ever did. After I dried off and sneaked back in, I was probably disappointed they weren't missing me, but it was easier to turn that into pride at getting myself out of a scrape. I was driven by a stubborn desire to shake a fist at the universe, to scream a silent *I'LL SHOW YOU* when challenged. So, even at rock bottom, miserable about the mouse that had eaten my last piece of gum, I was too proud to ask for help, or admit that my California dream wasn't unfolding as I had envisioned. And another, quieter part of me knew that things had to get better, that hope lurked around a faraway corner.

. . .

I thought about my mouse-nibbled jeans as I read everything I could at the Wildlife Learning Center in Sylmar—taking notes on every plaque, like a real weirdo, while my children wandered around, only half as interested. I was suddenly in love with Sylmar, and looking up its history did not disappoint. After being considered a vast wasteland at the turn of the twentieth century, the town had sprouted the world's largest olive grove by the 1950s. Obviously, a bunch of delusional Californians had taken a barren ghost town and made it into a backdrop for dreamy Mediterranean-style picnics. The settlers of that dusty place had seen promise in a field of nothing, just like I had known in my twenties I could make something of my own pitiful mess.

Putting my notes away, I turned a corner past the plaques to see a bald eagle sitting on a branch. The majesty of it made me gasp and clutch my chest. Had it just . . . alighted there? Was I having some kind of heat-induced vision? It hopped from branch to branch, seeming content. I was worried it could fly away, and looked up for a net, but there wasn't one—it had been found next to a highway, with a broken wing that never healed. A second bald eagle—a second bald eagle!—hiding in the back, hopped up. Surely both couldn't have broken wings? That seemed like too much of a coincidence. "No, that one has vertigo," said our guide. She continued: "But they have each other!" Their backstories were much less sad in a pair.

I wondered if the first eagle had even known whether it was lonely before its buddy came around. I certainly wouldn't have admitted as much when I first moved to LA. I showed up with a head full of knowledge and a decent amount of self-regard, but was nowhere near fully formed. I had been a student for so long, I hadn't picked up the real-life skills of a young working-woman. My bed was a mattress on the floor, next to a pile of my clothing. I've already mentioned that I wasn't one for upkeep, or fashion. I was still fine eating mostly peanut-butter sand-wiches and soup out of cans. I didn't know any different. But then I met Jenny, another assistant at the talent agency. She never made a mistake at work, while I took naps under my desk and misplaced million-dollar checks. Jenny and I barely knew each other when she helped me with some professional mess I brought on myself. I asked if I could buy her dinner as a thank you, and she almost said no, because she thought I had a grumpy face.

After a late night at work, she met me outside the office, in a Kelly-green coat and a string of pearls. I wore threadbare men's corduroys and hand-me-down sneakers. Like a real jerk, I assumed she was too pulled together to be fun, and I was dead wrong. I loved Jenny immediately. The child of Russian Jewish immigrants who grew up in a "not-cool part of Brooklyn," she had wiring that overlapped mine in all the right places, and we seemed to have the same idea of what a friendship should be: dependable and not showy. In both of our communities, even niceties like "please" and "thanks" aren't exchanged among relatives—they're just words, met with a snort, or a dismissive "You don't need to thank me—we're family, not strangers." Or "Anyone can say I love you," as my parents pointed out when I was growing up, "but isn't it more important to show it?" She was raised the same way.

After a year in the entertainment industry, encountering all stripes of extreme, confusing behavior, I hadn't made any real, close friends. Jenny exuded such competence and good judgment that I felt relieved, even safe in her presence. Neither one of us felt we could call our parents with any real problems—they'd worry too much—but we could turn to each other. Our shared immigrant foundation made me feel like I had known her my whole life. By the end of dinner, I had decided that, if I couldn't be her, at least I could keep her nearby, forever. I plied her with a bottle of cheap white zinfandel that tasted like a Jolly Rancher, and proposed moving in together. I needed out of the mouse-riddled one-bedroom before they ate what remained of my belongings.

Jenny was living with a Fabio-looking software programmer whose only piece of furniture was a Bowflex workout machine, in the middle of the living room. Jenny thought I was deranged, because we had just met, but I knew our lives were meant to merge. I changed her mind by inviting myself along to her weekend plans, and waiting for her to agree. This took until Sunday. I couldn't believe my luck. "I hope we never run out of things to talk about," I told her, as we browsed online listings together. "Eh, there's always gonna be someone to trash," she joked, and we've been family ever since.

The two of us alone couldn't afford the three-bedroom house we wanted to rent, but we didn't have any other friends, so we advertised online for a third roommate. A nice-seeming girl committed herself. She was a professional "background worker," or "extra." Unfortunately, she had to back out almost immediately, but we begged her to come to the lease signing so we could lock it down, and promised to find a replacement before move-in. She did attend, and did a bang-up job in the role of responsible tenant. "This would be a good place for our emergency kit," she murmured to the landlord, opening the hall closet. We got the house.

We moved in to no power the first night, because we were too clueless to know we had to have it switched on. We didn't care—we were barely in our twenties, and so much happier as a pair. We just watched the BBC's original *Pride and Prejudice* on Jenny's laptop, with stolen Wi-Fi. Overjoyed at our luck, I looked around Jenny's tasteful room, which had been inspired by a recent cover of *Elle Decor*. We were operating on the same budget, but she had somehow conjured up an upholstered headboard, matching table lamps of blown glass, a vintage rug— things not even on my radar back then. My bare mattress and one rickety nightstand couldn't compare on the design front, but I did slowly add a bed frame and some hangers to my room. Eventually, I even had curtains. At first I was confounded and amused by all the grown-up-type things Jenny did, like running errands before noon and returning with barely distinguishable paint swatches, or trying out different bulbs to cast the perfect light. But I became an eager participant in time. "Thank God for Jenny," my mother says, often. "She made you a person."

I half argue with that, because, surely, I was a person before, but I adored Jenny for her loyalty and discretion. She wouldn't have just buried a body with me; she would have tucked me in with a cup of tea and done it herself, to assure me plausible deniability. But the depth of our affection for each other might not have been visible to the untrained eye. "You never say 'I love you' to each other," said Jenny's beau (now her husband), back when. I rolled my eyes.

"To call it 'love' would be an insult," said Jenny, going back to our shared salad.

. . .

I was still gazing fondly at the eagles in Sylmar when my son announced he needed the restroom, so we went looking for the bathroom. We followed the faint tang of urine in the air, but ended up at a cage full of little fluffy chattering monkeys with a yellow tinge to their fur. "That's because they rub their pee on each other," said our guide. My son asked about a monkey who remained off to the side, peeking through a barrier. "And that little one's in a time-out, because he talks too much." The little outcast gazed longingly, sweetly at the others, waiting to be allowed to rejoin.

As my heart went out to the little guy, I also chuckled, because he brought to mind my own voluble friend, Adam: the only person in the universe who would genially shrug off being compared to a pee-covered monkey. When Adam came into our lives, Jenny and I had just started living together and weren't letting a lot of people join our tight unit. We didn't need any other friends, we reassured ourselves, as we spent every night in with a cheap bottle of white and some DVDs. And when we met Adam, it still seemed improbable we'd branch out. Adam was a fast-talking former finance guy from New Jersey, who had quit his money job to follow his showbiz dreams. He had helped me out with a work favor, and though it took a lot to get me out of my house for a night of socializing, he harangued me into meeting him for a drink. I'm still not sure why I agreed. From what I could tell, he didn't have many friends, or at least didn't like the ones he had. I took Jenny with me, as insurance, and I'm realizing now that the light in his eyes when we walked up was because he'd been searching for one pal and found two. Once we got past the Jersey accent, the double ear-piercing, the level-eleven, brain-splitting enthusiasm for almost anything, we found a sweet, devoted friend, one whose mother was a librarian, who wanted to discuss Eugenides with the same fervor that some boys devoted to—I don't know—sneakers (he may have discussed sneakers as well, but never around us). As a trial, we invited him to a dinner at our house, and he showed up early, and helped clean up. The next time, we trusted him to bring ice, and he's been showing up early, with ice, for almost twenty years.

Together we formed an unlikely three-legged stool, and its stability was my foundation in Los Angeles. I, a lawyer who didn't want to be a lawyer. Jenny, a New Yorker who didn't want to be in New York. And now we had folded in a finance bro who didn't want to be a finance bro. Which is probably why the Wildlife Learning Center sang to me, with its alligator who didn't want to be an alligator.

The kids and I proceeded through the maze of spacious animal enclosures, charmed by the backstory of each one: The twenty-foot python who had gotten too big for a studio apartment. The prairie dogs that weren't allowed to have grass because they kept tearing it up, but they kissed each other nonstop on the cheek, shouting, like so many tiny Sicilians. The giraffes who had to be kept apart because they liked to kick each other. The foxes, tons of them, everywhere, had been abandoned by their owners, one by one, because they didn't behave like dogs, and smelled so much worse. But in a place that should have felt as hopeless as a late-night bus station, or my first sad apartment, I was enchanted by the camaraderie of the staff, the way they talked, loving and exasperated, about their eccentric wards. All these strange little animals had started out uprooted and broken, in a way: unwanted, unsure of their place in the world. And, like us, they'd ended up with friends and a future.

· · ·

The first time my mother visited me in Los Angeles, shortly after I started feeling less miserable about living here, we sat at a sunny beach café, eating breakfast. I was trying to show her what she might enjoy about the city—who can complain about brunch outdoors?—but her eyes followed the gorgeous waitress around. "The poor girl," she whispered, eventually. "Doesn't she know her dreams won't come true?" Exasperated, I called my friend Emily, the one who had lured me out here, and unloaded. "My parents think everyone here is nuts," I told her. "Are we nuts?" Emily reminded me that everything out here felt scary to our parents, because nothing we were striving for made any sense to them. Like the gold prospectors before us, like the man who dreamed of starting a bakery for dogs in an outdoor mall, I had grown up a mismatched puzzle piece who dreamed of a bigger life. But here, people had found their gold, and that dog bakery was thriving, despite everyone's skepticism. Their incomprehensible leaps had been worth it. "California is the last frontier of the American Dream," she said, which helped something click for me: I wasn't disappointing my parents. I had done exactly what they had done—moved westward in search of something different. I was a direct product of their wanderlust and curiosity. And when they first moved, I bet their parents thought everyone around them was crazy, too.

The final animal we met at the Wildlife Center that day was Pauley, their sloth, hanging in a mist-controlled room by himself. Born into a zoo, he had been sent over because none of the other sloths at the zoo liked him. "Their loss," said our guide. This—more than the other tales, for some reason—touched me. That an odd little creature, like so many of us, hadn't been wanted at home, but found one amongst a passel of other weirdos in a faraway part of Los Angeles. He had found love in a hopeless place! Or he had at least found the space and support to be whomever he wanted, and to be taken care of by people who embraced him, just as he was. Pauley was a big hit with the entire family, and once we got home, I looked up the center on my computer. They had a vibrant online presence, dominated by close-ups of Pauley's large, soft eyes. My daughter asked me to click on a link, which led to his own social media page, where he's living his own Angelino dream: ten thousand Instagram followers and a dazzling array of professional headshots.

The Culture

◁ 2004–present ▷

I should have run when I saw how they cut the fruit during staff meetings. A man in a slim suit, like all the other men in slim suits, had grabbed a green apple and was now slicing off each cheek, then the remaining slivers off the sides, as he filled us in on the weekend's box-office numbers. Another took a banana, and instead of just eating it like a banana ("looks like I'm eating a . . . well, you know"), sliced it into chunks, which he ate with a fork. Nobody seemed to think this was strange. A third man, an older one, fortunately not eating any fruit at all, said something like "What we've learned from this weekend is that women want to watch movies, too." I was used to that kind of statement—it barely registered. But the fruit? That was disorienting.

"You are miserable," said my former boss Sharon as I murmured in faint protest. "Every day you come in here with that grumpy face, and you make me look at it." Her words were laced with love and concern, and she was absolutely right: the job was not a fit, and it wasn't really about the fruit. I was a talent agent at a massive Hollywood agency, representing emerging comedy actors and writers. My job was to make my clients' dreams come true. I loved that part—talent spotting, and getting people started on their paths to fame and fortune—and I'm certain they'd tell you now that I was good at it. But that was the only part that worked for me.

I had first wanted to run when, still in the mail room, I had to drive home a partner whose car wasn't working. I wound my way up the hill, nervously, in my old Honda. She wasn't bad, I thought. She had been quite friendly. We made our way through the gate and into a circular driveway that had, until recently, belonged to America's sweetheart—whoever America's sweetheart was at the time. "Is there anything you wish you could change about the job?" asked this not-so-scary-now partner. I thought of my negative bank balance, and told her I wished we got paid more. She sighed, rolled her eyes, and told me that we all work paycheck to paycheck. Her house loomed like a white confection over my dusty Civic.

I should have run when I was an assistant and we all got told off about the water. The Fiji water was only for client meetings, warned a very stern email. And the assistants had clearly been stealing it. We couldn't be trusted, so the water was going to be kept under lock and key. *Look at yourselves,* implied the email. *You should be ashamed.* We assistants looked around the bullpen. Who on earth would steal tiny bottles of water? We shrugged, and got used to asking approval for a specific number of bottles before clients came in. Shortly thereafter, one of the board members was caught loading entire flats into their car.

I should have run when a partner asked everyone over to his house after the Christmas party one year, and loudly announced that any assistant who jumped into the pool with their clothes on could come in late to work the next day. How he got this approved by the board, I'm not sure. I went home.

But a lot of women were late for work the next day, as though it were an actual prize. Many years later, I would be asked by a mutual acquaintance if I wanted to meet with this man and work with him, whose movies had, by then, made billions of dollars, and I couldn't totally remember why I didn't want to. I called a friend and asked, "Was it the swimming pool thing?" She said it wasn't: "He tried to kiss you at that Christmas party, don't you remember?" I had blocked it out, like I blocked a lot of things out. I declined the meeting.

On top of this kind of general derangement—*Entourage* existed for a reason—I didn't enjoy the stuff that was supposed to be "fun." After a long workday, all I wanted to do was go home, get into my pajamas, and curl up with a book. After I got promoted to agent, I was once reprimanded for spending too little on my expenses, a sign to the partnership that I wasn't schmoozing enough. After a movie premiere, I got a talking-to for going straight to my seat instead of walking the red carpet with the actors, a ritual that made me want to shrivel up every time. "There are parts of the job you clearly find icky," continued Sharon, as she watched me curl into a ball on the love-seat in her office, a place where I often went to hide. "But you have to think about whether you can tolerate them, in order to enjoy the parts you like."

Once I was an agent, I should have run, or at least said something, when one of the male partners grabbed my shoulders as I walked by his office and told me to stand up straight. I was comforted by a woman nearby who said he also yanked on men's ties, so I shouldn't think of it as sexist. I didn't think it was sexist; I just thought it was bullying. What I found sexist was the way one of my colleagues loudly called me a whore after I declined to stay up and "party" after dinner at a corporate retreat. I almost argued, but I was tired and wanted to get away from him.

I didn't even run when one partner had a barbecue at his house and his octogenarian contractor asked us all to come to lunch the next week so he could talk to "some young people." I was the only person who went to lunch, and he took out his checkbook and asked if I had any debt. About seventy thousand dollars left from law school, I said, and he told me he could pay it off. I asked why he'd do that, and he sat, silent, like I should have known. I thought I was just being nice to a friendly old man. I guess I was, but lunch was the limit of my kindness, so I walked out, shaken.

But I didn't run. Because tolerating things I didn't enjoy was, for a long time, my superpower, one I had cultivated since an eventful childhood. See, the thing about a hard time is that it's supposed to end. Mental-health professionals like to say that we're all floating around the world like little rubber bands, and then we encounter a challenge, which makes us stretch, grow, and bounce back. That's how resilience is meant to work. But what if there's always something else? What if you move countless times over three continents, lose a homeland to political turmoil, lose a favorite grandparent in a grisly accident, lose a sister-in-law to a brutal murder, and then spend a war falling asleep with a gas mask on, under the stairs, while sirens blare? What if most of this is clustered in a five-year span, all before high school?

What happens is that you get used to it. My little rubber band eventually stretched out, taut and brittle, but seemingly forever. By many metrics, I'd had a blissful upbringing: boundless love, laughter, globe-trotting adventures, the best family anyone could ask for. But a lot happened. And in powering through the discomfort of constant change, I became inured to it. Resilience without any waning period turned into endurance, and I became adept at snuffing out my own vulnerability and discomfort before I even felt it. I grew into someone who could live anywhere, befriend anyone, be anyone, do anything; the harder, the better.

If no one understood me, I'd learn a new language. If my accent was a barrier, then—poof—I would sound American. If my bank balance cratered one month, I'd figure out how to reverse it. And for this, my unflappability, for executing my plans in the face of resistance, I was praised. "You don't have to worry about her," people told my parents, and everyone swelled with pride. So that's how being fine, no matter what, became my only setting, my identity. I chased the high of conquering things that seemed impossible, which led me to the entertainment industry, and agenting. Cracking the codes to its impenetrable world made me think I was winning, then thriving, until those conversations with my boss, about my miserable face. I could see that I had someone's dream job, but not mine.

And I stayed in it for far too long. I wanted to run when a woman's phone timer went off during a staff meeting and the young men all screamed, "Time to take your pill!" Everyone in the room was laughing, except the woman whose timer went off. She sighed heavily and left the room—and, eventually, agenting. There was a lot of talk of "the Culture" at the agency. Preserving the Culture, making sure new hires (like me) did not disrupt or dilute the Culture. What the Culture was, exactly, I couldn't tell you. It came up so often, and I could only think of my mother's homemade yogurt. Milk heated to a perfect temperature—warm but not boiling. A half cup of old yogurt stirred into the clay pot, which was then wrapped in the warm cuddle of a towel overnight. That culture, the one my mother brought from home, and taught me to nurture, I understood. A small amount of a different substance, which blossomed and grew in a substrate, changing and improving its nature. This Culture at work was confusing, although they did try to educate me. One colleague pulled me aside and told me I could be friendlier. "But we're not friends," I said. "We work together." He conceded, but claimed that was beside the point.

There was so much talk of this Culture that I couldn't quite define it. The men—and it was mostly men—spent all their money on clothes: the suits, yes, but also shiny watches, and jazzy sneakers, an act of individuation that came full circle to conformity. They also seemed to go on vacation together a lot. Was that the Culture? The halls were abuzz, once, with the idea of a rec room upstairs where leadership might be able to put a Ping-Pong table. "Do we need a Ping-Pong table?" I asked. Weren't we all working all day? "Wouldn't a day care come in more handy?" With this I killed the vibe, per usual. I was a ticking Cultural threat.

Also not part of the Culture? Reading. An hour could go by in a staff meeting with people talking about available scripts to direct, movies that were casting, books that were available for our clients to produce or adapt, and I'd pipe up. "What's it about?" I'd ask, and they'd startle, this smooth, bespoke-suited herd. "What's it *about*?" muttered one agent, as if that was irrelevant, and looked around the room for support. And maybe it was irrelevant, to them. Every movie was a series of open jobs to fill with our clients. The material didn't matter as much as the transactional nature of agenting. The "winning," the "crushing it," the "dominating," or whatever shared lexicon they pulled from as they high-fived, fist-bumped, bear-hugged one another after closing a deal.

And I hated it all—thus the grumpy face. When Sharon suggested I could be happier, that I should envision the right life for myself and go get it, my mind was blank. I had been ignoring my feelings to cross off the next goal, through college, law school, a prestigious job. After an upbringing filled with constant change, I was wired to pursue stability above all, but what were my dreams? "Don't you want to write some books, maybe have a couple kids?" she said—gentle, loving—and I froze. It sounded perfect. But how did she know that? It was as if she could see through my clothes. Experimenting with happiness had felt safer in a college setting, where I could change classes each semester. Here, while I struggled to get out from under a mountain of debt, while ruled by an immigrant need for stability, the stakes felt too high. And underneath it all simmered the actual fear of trying. I couldn't write, because what if I failed? Books had been my favorite companion since pre-school. If I tried to write and couldn't, I didn't think I could withstand the heartbreak.

I finally ran when, the year I signed two unknown actors who quickly became massively famous, my bonus was a pittance. I was already getting paid less than my male colleagues, and went to the head of the department to complain. My bonus the year before had been significantly more, which was critical, because my base salary was close to an assistant's, and

I was trying to pay down my loans in addition to my rent. The partner looked at me, puzzled. He was the kind of man who wasn't used to taking younger women seriously. I got the sense he called me a girl when I wasn't around, if he even remembered I existed. To calm me down, he doubled the amount, which was still not enough. It wasn't caring so much about the money as taking a clear-eyed look at what this place valued— what the Culture meant—there was just one way to be, and if I didn't want to be that way, I was going to be uncomfortable, forever. The Culture was made to be replicated endlessly by the same kind of man, nudging out anything that was unlike them, until it became a sea of clones jostling for space. Even if they paid me fairly, I couldn't see a future there. So I finally quit.

I had spent so long buffeted by the waves of external events that once they went quiet I didn't know what to do. Agency life had been brutal. Technically, a lifetime of resilience had made me so tough that I could handle anything. But I didn't want to. So, for the first time, I had allowed myself to say that I didn't want to be there. That it didn't feel right for me, that I didn't know if there was a professional pursuit that might make me happier, but there must be one worth seeking. I knew only that my true love was reading, and being with writers. I knew words on a page made me happy, and I went looking for more of that feeling. The joy I felt discussing ideas, helping mold those ideas into a script, then putting them on-screen, became my new pursuit. It felt so silly, so luxurious all of a sudden, not to be in pure survival mode. To have made the space to think about what was good for me.

I moved on to a production company, and a gentler pace. I

loved working closely with writers, developing scripts for TV and film. But after a few years of producing, and then having a baby, I felt that old dissatisfaction creep in again, the one that I was making other people's dreams come true, but not my own. And this time I trusted my feelings enough not to ignore them. This wasn't the kind of challenge I was meant to power through. It called for looking clearly within myself. The pleasure I derived from work had successfully chipped away at the hard shell of my endurance and let happiness into the chinks, shining a light on the malaise as it nudged its way out. Yet I still couldn't admit what I wanted.

So I spent some time flailing about, groaning, wishing out loud that someone, anyone, would tell me what to do next. After months of this charade, my husband steered me into listing five people whose careers I admired. That was easy. "They're all writers," he said. "Do you think that means anything?" But I could never, I said. Could I attempt magic? Reading brought me such transcendent joy, who was I to think I might bring that same joy to other people? It seemed insane, at the time, like deciding to be God. I just couldn't. "Of course you could," said he, a professional writer (aha!). And the new me, the one who was learning that life could be celebrated rather than just tolerated, decided to try.

So I wrote and wrote, thinking, *If it's bad, no one will ever see it. If it's good, it might change my life.* I wrote a lot of disjointed, maudlin blog entries. I wrote an advice column for people wanting to break into entertainment. I wrote a short film, funded by my last producing paycheck, and shot it in our home. That got me an agent—one I actually liked—and sold my first TV show, and kicked off a screenwriting career. A couple of years ago, I wrote some essays. Those essays allowed me to write a book. It's funny to me now that I had a bunch of jobs in which I was expected to make something out of nothing—an ally from a stranger, a client list from thin air, a slate of programming from a bare desktop—but it never occurred to me, back then, that I was nurturing a transferrable skill set. That writing was creating the ultimate something from the ultimate nothing.

Ever an immigrant, I still find it difficult to say out loud that my dreams are taking shape, without having my old self disassociate. *If you talk about it, it'll all crumble away!* she screams, floating above my head at this very moment. She's maddening, but I ignore her. I have finally figured out what is good for me: To sit in a sunny room, by myself. No pushy colleagues to force small talk. No schmoozing of slippery execs for intel. No stiff upper lip while I wait for a happier time that might never come. I get to create my own work culture now, sometimes wrapping myself up in a blanket to read, some days venturing into the world to take in new ideas, a new culture. Nurturing my own voice, not crowded out by others, and seeing how it blossoms.

I'm still tough; the last few years have reminded me of that. But my rubber band hasn't snapped or frayed; it hasn't fossilized. I know it's not stuck, and this won't last forever. I have some other settings now: content, delighted, disappointed, anxious. One might even call them feelings. Feelings I'm marinating in as I write this book. If these feelings allow me to connect with other readers, I'll have unlocked my dearest dream of all. And if I don't? Well, I'll bounce back.

Astrocartography

My facialist, Talia, is my quarterly indulgence, and not just because she has managed to make my skin look the same for fifteen years. It's because every time I go to her she's buzzing about something new: an energy reader or a crystal interpreter to add to her roster of avant-garde LA healers. I hear what's going on with Bugra, an energy healer who visits annually from Istanbul, and Pati, the astrologer based in Ohio, who helped Talia pick where in the city to move, based on her star chart. Talia knows that, even though I roll my eyes, she might get me with that mention of Ohio, because Midwestern roots are my weakness. At the end of each session, Talia slips their business cards into my hand, encouraging me to call them, to "find my balance." I've never called any of them. I just enjoy her stories. I appreciate the California wackiness of it all, and I love it when anyone loves anything that much, even if it's crystals.

Los Angeles can be a profoundly silly place, but I like a lot of things about living here. The sense that anything is possible, the fact that the children can play outside for most of the year without my having to bundle them up. It's technically a city, but I can live my life at a suburban pace: loading up my electric car with groceries, walking the kids through our wide-open spaces, it feels almost like Michigan, but with better weather. I have developed deep friendships here, I've made a home. But every fall, when Los Angeles bursts into flame, I am taut with dread for weeks. I'm not sure if my fear is well earned—perhaps, after the Kashmir situation, I am especially vigilant about the idea of our house burning down—or if I'm losing my mind, which is what it generally feels like.

The wildfires rage just north of us, in the scrubby hills of Malibu and beyond. We pull out the air purifiers, and keep the children inside, away from the smoke, and guilt and fear chip away at my fondness for the city. "This wouldn't happen in London," I mumble. And people there have socialized medicine. In the depths of my despair—and it is a bottomless, dark hole—I shout things like "We are choking on smoke, within a failed state!" My mind races: Are we supposed to live here? Isn't there somewhere else we could be safer and happy? My husband helpfully reminds me that the East Coast has snowstorms and hurricanes. We can't escape climate change (can we?), but I still question our geographical choices. During one of these episodes, I think of Talia's move, and ask for Pati the astrologer's contact information again.

I stare at Pati's number on my laptop for days, feeling ridiculous. Major life choices are made with common sense and consensus. Not star charts. I am rational! I don't call astrologers, right? I've spent my whole life running away from them, even—and in the Western world, they seem to be the domain of a certain kind of uppity lady. In an online search, I come across Aditi Ohri, a young Canadian astrologer of Indian origin, and ask her why every other astrologer I've found in the United States is a loopy Caucasian woman. "Ahhh. It's the yoga thing!" she says, laughing. Astrology certainly has its roots in our ancestral land, but, because we're immigrants, the relentless push to achieve professional stability often shoves aside any self-reflection or dreaming. Vedic or Indian astrology is practiced by gurus "back home," and if you want to become an astrologer in India, the path is narrow and complex, involving an apprenticeship in a dogmatic and seemingly impenetrable system. Aditi has pursued Western, or "Hellenistic," astrology because she's found it a more welcoming space for the self-taught.

We talk about how edicts from the homeland can also feel stifling. Get married on this day, start a job on this one, put the bed on this side of your room, with zero explanation or context. I realize this is why I've kept astrology at a distance— "auspicious dates" have always seemed like such hokum to me, so limiting, proscriptive, and oppressive, that it's easier not to think about that stuff at all. Aditi says it can seem that Vedic gurus are telling clients who they are and how things have to be, directing people and establishing social norms, as opposed to the Western approach of laying out the elements a person is working with and teaching clients how to use them.

We're all housebound under a smoky purple sky when I next call my mother, and I tell her about my reluctance to call Pati. She gently reminds me that, even though every person in my extended family is some kind of scientist or engineer, all major logical decisions, from wedding dates to move-in dates, have traditionally been cross-referenced against an Indian guru's star chart. I don't usually open up this area of conversation with her. But now I ask her if that's what got her on board with my relationship—did my chart align with my husband's?—and she shakes her head, suddenly dismissive. "I didn't even look," she says. "You guys were a done deal, why mess with it?"

It fills me with love and an inordinate pride that she was able to sacrifice that seemingly small ritual to support my happiness. But she's still curious about what Pati might tell me. Mum is emotionally porous to a heartbreaking degree. If I'm in distress, her face tells me she wishes she could take on my pain. As we FaceTime, from inside our home with the air purifiers going, she wrings her hands. It's difficult for her to see me have a hard time, and she mentions that astrology, though not determinate, might provide me with a distraction, and maybe even some peace of mind. So I finally call Pati, and ask her where I should live.

First of all, Pati Carlson is not loopy. She's also not from Ohio: she lives there to be near her grandson. But Pati has, unsurprisingly, lived an interesting life. When she was six, her father was transferred from Pennsylvania to Belgium, where she attended school in an idyllic one-room schoolhouse in a town called Knokke that sits on the North Sea. The single room of the international school in Knokke at the time held all the kids from first through twelfth grade, and a curriculum that changed based on the students' interests, without regard to their age limitations. She remembers it, fondly, as "a wonderful, wonderful way to grow up, and a wonderful education."

Reentry to Erie, Pennsylvania, was a shock. Pati had arrived there as a self-guided thirteen-year-old with an unfettered love of learning, but was thrust back into a structured public-school environment, like an alien in her own country, and she curled into a self-protective, lonely shell. The only thing that kept her spirits afloat through her difficult period was an emerging interest in yoga, meditation, and Eastern philosophies, for which her mother sweetly bought her books that she devoured. Pati's time in Erie was mercifully brief: her family transferred once again, to Santa Barbara, when she was sixteen. In California, she found her home and her people, including an instant best friend whose mother was an astrologer, and she started to study it in earnest.

I'm pleased and surprised by how my own life mirrors Pati's, even thousands of miles and about twenty years away. The moving, the international school, and then landing in the States as a high school freshman, being thrust into a situation in which I felt foreign for the first time in my life. And then I, too, flopped around, lost in books, until I moved to California, where I finally found my people and home. I don't tell her any of this, just the locations I've lived and the years, but I do silently marvel at our shared emotional arc.

I'm charmed by her self-awareness about how astrology is perceived. It's never been her day job—she laughs heartily—but it's what she has loved. She and her husband built a series of small, successful software and tech-based companies in the Bay Area, where they were happy until they retired and moved to Ohio to be closer to her son's family. Ohio is "comfortable," she says, and she's happy she can be with family, but, realizing there are "places that can make a soul sing," like a small town on the Belgian North Sea, she now devotes her leftover time and energy to location astrology, and its fascinating subspecialty, Astrocartography.

Astrocartography (ACG) is a series of specific mapping techniques laid out by the astrologer Jim Lewis in the late 1970s. To create an ACG map, a map is created of the planets' angles or paths over a global Mercator map. The result is a mesmerizing crisscross of sine curves, each representing a planet (plus the sun and moon), and sprouting from one's birthplace. Each line represents a specific energy—the sun, for example, is fame and reputation, and Venus is beauty and relationships—so you can look at the intersections of various curves on the map and see which locations might be best for certain aspects you want to focus on in your life.

Because I am a dork for any kind of map—in a new city, I'll unfurl a giant one until I can memorize its rough shape—it's no surprise I'm also intrigued by having my chart mapped across the globe. And despite my efforts to remain skeptical, Pati's ACG map makes me gasp. A gorgeous, undulating web of lines, every which way, over Europe, and absolutely none in the United States, except for the West Coast. Pati confirms my amateur read, noting that the sun, Jupiter, and Venus all influence this area. I laugh—I do not know what any of that means—and she clarifies for me: "Fires or not, LA is a good place for you to be." The only other place in the States she'd recommend at all is Seattle, but options in Europe include Stockholm, the Costa Brava, and southern Switzerland. This sounds, to me, like an ideal retirement plan.

But Pati's not done. She also generates relocation charts, which are standard astrology birth charts, recalculated for other places I might have lived or wanted to live. The idea is that a natal chart changes as one moves from place to place, emphasizing different aspects of birth temperament. The aspects of birth planets don't change, but the angles do, depending on how much one has moved, and that shifts the orientation within the wheels of the chart. The shifts in mine guide how each aspect applied to my life. This is where I start to be tickled by the intangible: She can tell, for example, that as a child in London I was friendless, silent, and observant. That I flourished academically, but not creatively, in Riyadh. That I became a miserable, rebellious valedictorian in New York, and found peace and friends in Michigan. But, again, LA comes out on top, with love, career, and creative expression all mapped out here.

I thought that a clear answer would make me feel more settled, give me a measure of peace, but I'm alarmed. Like my mother with her palm reader, I feel I'm being told I'm trapped here forever by forces I can't control. Surely, I can decide to live wherever I want, right? I could be in Sicily next year, or Tokyo, and I'd still have my family and career . . . right? *This is all so silly*, I think. *I can get out whenever I want.* And then the air purifier turns on, its scarlet light a warning about the smoke that's made its way inside, and the morbid part of me wonders if a fire is how I'll end up leaving. Wouldn't that be apt?

But Pati interrupts my dark thoughts with, somehow, even more charts! As she did with Talia's house hunt, she has created a "Local Space Map," which she does for clients who are interested in learning how different parts of their city might affect them in different ways, whether they're looking to move or just curious. For these charts, she overlays an astrology wheel over a local map, and extrapolates the lines of the planets to show which areas might be best for, say, family harmony, creative expression, and productivity. My specific map tells her that my most productive writing days might be in Malibu, which sounds dreamy, and accurate: when I feel stuck on a piece of writing, or just generally life-stuck, I do sometimes make the long drive, to give myself the sense that I am somewhere else entirely.

I thank Pati, and then, looking for a second opinion, reach out to Jessica Lanyadoo, an astrologer I've been following online. Unlike Pati, who feels grounded, Midwestern, matter-of-fact, Jessica is what everyone thinks an astrologer is: unapologetically "woo." One conversation with her, though, and I'm on board with her cool-big-sis energy. ACG isn't Jessica's specialty, but she loves relocation charts, and jumps at the opportunity to read them. The readings and the information she gleans from my charts align with Pati's, and Jessica also worries about my gum health, anxiety, and workload. But does it say I'm supposed to live in Los Angeles? I ask. She comes to the same conclusion: LA it is. For now, forever.

On my regular drive to pick up the kids, I'm grumpy. Now I feel that I can't leave—that there's some cosmic force keeping me here, and that bad luck might befall me if I try. And the cozy elements of my reliable suburban life feel suffocating. The school pickup, the fast-fresh weeknight dinners, the family calendar, the security I've been seeking for my entire life, are a too-tight corset, and I can't breathe. I stare at a sea of red rush-hour taillights, dejected. In these moments, I hate LA. I don't want to be in my car. I crave "real" cities. I want walking for miles, popping into stores, seeing people and things in an unscheduled manner. I want public transportation, and the scraps I get to overhear when I'm a pedestrian. Even though I'm too tired by the end of most days to go out much, I want to feel that exciting things are happening just outside, and I could join, if I ever had the energy to venture forth.

But we make our own excitement, says the little LA cheerleader in my head, the one that always bursts out of me with a pep talk when I meet new transplants who are feeling down. *This place is a mirror,* I tell myself. *If you don't love it, you're not trying hard enough.* But on my least optimistic days, I wouldn't mind living in a place that requires less work for me to love it. Then I feel immediately guilty about being ungrateful. *This is what you always wanted, when you were broke and miserable,* says another voice. *You wanted no weird surprises, and a steady paycheck.* I asked for this. And LA has been kind to me. It's given me a career and a family.

As I watch a plane break free of LAX and wish I were on it, I wonder if my problem isn't actually Los Angeles. I might be deluded in thinking that one peaceful place exists for me. Maybe I've been in one city far longer than I find comfortable. I spent so much time bouncing between pairs of countries: India and England, Saudi and India, the United States and Italy. The continual movement is a cadence I find soothing and familiar. Whenever I felt stuck in one place, we could go to the other. And we always came home with fresh eyes. When I first moved to California, I was glad to be far enough away from my parents that I could determine the course of my own life, but I also worried that I couldn't drive home to see them in an emergency. I felt disconnected from the rest of the world, and definitely from the world in which I'd grown up.

It never occurred to me I'd be here this long. I thought I was just trying some things out, but I never thought those things would keep me here forever. There's none of the relief of bouncing around to some sister city, because LA is too far away from anywhere else I want to be. And the dramatic annual fires aren't helping. An LA native tells me that "the fire stuff" is easy

if I just think of it as a season. Like other places have snow
or hurricanes. "We used to stay home because of the smog,"
he says. "Same thing." His intention is to make me feel better.
And I certainly don't feel worse.

The traffic, and the smoky sky, have finally cleared when I
get to school. The kids are playing with their friends outside,
at last. They tumble into the car, and my gloomy mood starts
to lift. They are so hilariously Californian—mostly clothing-
optional, dust-covered, bighearted, big-idea kids—that I guess
I can think of a couple of small reasons to stay here. My husband and I are trying to build them a safe, steady environment,
like the one my parents built around me. But we benefit from
not having to move them around for work. Though my itiner-
ant childhood made me who I am, I feel no need to replicate
it. I like that the kids might consider this their home, forever.
That they'll be able to revisit their old schools and friends, and
might not inherit my restlessness. I may not have roots here,
or anywhere, but I can help them plant their own. Their lives
in California seem a done deal—why mess with it? "But after
they go to college, we'll move, right?" I say to my husband later,
and he nods. "Absolutely."

Someone Else's Spiders

⌐ 2021 ⌐

I didn't mean to get into a spat with the manager of an anti-quarian bookstore, but this seems to be Oliver's thing. After an unanswered call, email, and direct message to Henry Sotheran's, an institution just off Piccadilly in London, I air my grievance on, regrettably, Twitter, and he responds. "I am sometimes in the store," his tweet says. "But a bit like Bilbo Baggins I frequently vanish to avoid visitors, well-wishers, or distant relations."

That's it.

"I am flying from very far away," I type, in Los Angeles, just barely keeping a lid on it. "DON'T MAKE ME BE TRICKY."

Oliver will like me; he just doesn't know it yet.

Because Oliver is the quintessence of Britishness, and I love England, even though I find this mortifying to admit. Moving around a lot means never letting yourself get too attached to any one place, and definitely not England. The second I say I love England, I know what people are thinking. The Madonna accent, the Goop vibes, the ordering of commemorative tea-cups and setting of alarms to wake up for royal weddings. Lov-ing England, at least in the United States, means drooling all over the Crown while ignoring its tragic expansionist past. So I don't participate in any of that. But it still exerts a pull.

I love the way England worships books. I love the idea that learning might be something to strive for outside of capitalist purposes. I love relatively accessible higher education, and the miracle workers at the National Health Service. I love cheese on toast, and "picky bits" and a full English. I love "tea" as a necessary fourth meal, and endless wordplay. I love the lights down Regent Street at Christmas. In fact, I love every inch of England at Christmas. I love Marmite, and British chocolate, and leathery wine gums. I love a drizzle, and a pint, and how it never gets too cold in winter. I miss the accent I had as a child. And I love Sotheran's as a symbol of all this: the tucked-away, Beatrix Potter–ish lifestyle for which I secretly long. Even if the list of traits that I project upon Oliver is as artificial as a set of commemorative teacups, it fulfills something I badly need.

Though it's mostly on simmer, I live in constant yearning for the feeling of home. Almost nobody I know in Los Angeles is actually from Los Angeles, but they all make yearly holiday migrations to wherever they were born. I've moved so much now that I don't know what a real homecoming feels like, but I've started to piece it together, from watching others. I see my husband settle back into New York, comfortable, rejuvenated by his return, like he's docked into an emotional charging station. I see him stroll around his old neighborhood, take the kids to his old playground. "This is how I grew up," he's telling them. On *this* walk, from his old friend Pete's house after school. In *this* ravine, where he and his friends skipped class. *This* ceiling he stared at when he couldn't fall asleep. All of them the building blocks that put him together.

"Do you want to walk past my old school?" he'll ask, and I do, but I feel a twinge, because I don't often have a happy old place to walk by. Kashmir is gone, at least for me. I spent a lot of time in Saudi Arabia, but that always felt temporary—it's not the kind of place where they used to let expats plant roots. High school in New York went quickly, painfully, and my parents have lived in Michigan for ages, but I only passed through there for college. So, embarrassment aside, if we're talking about the place I've lived that made me the most me, England is the closest after Kashmir. And as I scroll through my Twitter feed every day, it's not that I need to meet this Oliver of Sotheran's, exactly. But there's something about his voice online that jabs a pointy stick into the parts of me that are homesick for London.

First, his enjoyment of the English language itself. On news of a post-Brexit departure from the metric system, he posts: "Look the imperial system is very simple, a Stone is the weight of an English rock, a Pound is as much flesh as you can excise in the time it takes to toast a crumpet, and a Gill is how many fish you can strap to a penny farthing." I chuckle at this on its face, but also because it's funny to remember there was a time when I didn't speak English. *"Hindi bolte nahi, English aati nahi,"* I had told Mum, miserably, after my first day at nursery school: "They don't speak Hindi, I don't speak English." She saw my fresh clothes—I had changed because I'd cried so hard I vomited—and worried that she and my dad had made a terrible mistake.

But within a few weeks, my new best language and I were inseparable. And that love of language led me to, of course, literature. "All I want is a mysterious stranger to bequeath their gigantic, shadowy library to me so I can spend the rest of my life deciphering its mysteries—is that too much to ask?" Oliver puts out there, and my eyes glaze over in rapture, thinking about the first time I fell into a room of books.

When my mother first took me to the John Harvard branch of Southwark Library in London, I gasped. Not just in shock, but in dismay at how I was ever going to finish reading every volume within. "One at a time, sweetie," she said. One at a time. She patiently carried home armfuls of books—first ten, then fifteen, twenty every week—so I could gobble them up, like so many candy bars. Once I could actually read, I remember coming home from school and heading straight to my parents' room, the warmest in the house, to sit in the square of sun on the rug. Mum handed me a favored snack on my way up the tight little staircase—a warm bowl of custard, blanketing apple crumble, if we had it. Sometimes a bag of cheese-and-onion crisps, or half a sandwich in a pinch. I opened my book, always a novel, something transporting, and didn't look up until dinner. As I got older, I heated my own custard, peeled and chopped the apples for the crumble myself, but the ritual never changed. A bowl of food, a patch of sun, a novel.

This was the routine, week in, week out, broken so rarely that I remember the few times that it happened. Once, a friend's mother brought me home. Once, Dad picked me up, because Mum was giving birth to my brother. And once, when I was five, she took me to see a play. "I hear it's funny," she said, bundling me up in my coat; she took my hand to hurry me down the street. Having just gulped down the complete works of Roald Dahl, I was on board for more funny. The play was ridiculous, a farce about a bumbling housekeeper, and I screeched with laughter as she chuckled next to me—whether from the play or my delight, I don't know. I still remember the housekeeper putting a bunch of shirts in the washing machine, fumbling around the stage for the whole play, and coming back just after we thought it was over. She opened the washer and, instead of the crumpled pile I expected, extracted a stack of crisp starched shirts on hangers. I sat there, gasping for air, tears streaming down my cheeks as I processed the brilliance of a setup and unexpected payoff. I had considered the written word only as something to bring to life inside my own mind, so I was blown away that someone had typed out a bunch of words and expressed them as a collective vision that we could all experience. It was almost too much.

Unexpected payoffs keep me checking in on the Sotheran's Twitter feed as well. "I feel like this should go without saying but please do not try and sell us books infested with arachnids, only a very charitable soul would describe the condition of such a book as 'near fine,'" Oliver posts on a late-September morning. And later in the day: "A very nice man earlier made the flattering mistake of thinking I own this place, and politely but erroneously congratulated me on being very wealthy, in the moment I could only think 'Sir if I were rich would I be standing here with my hands full of someone else's spiders.'"

So it's not Oliver, exactly, but what he represents. After a few professional disappointments, and a long period without travel, I feel trapped. I'm rootless and homesick all at once, a mental state that I know only London can resolve. So I go on a weeklong work trip, thinking maybe a visit to Sotheran's can help. I'll find Oliver—who I imagine is rumpled and professorial. What I'll do when I find him, I don't know. Shake his hand?

Ask some questions? I already know I've become too American for this quest—I can see myself bounding in, full Yankee, him mumbling awkwardly before hiding behind a stack, but I still want to try. On my first morning in town, I walk to the store, and my mood soars. It's been sunny all week, which is how London sometimes tricks me into thinking I could live here. I see so many brown faces on my walk, hear so many accents and languages, that I can, for once, relax into a crowd. Back in Los Angeles, I can go a week without running into another Indian person, and when I do, I grin at them, stupidly. Here, I'm grinning at everyone, even if they look confused—as the largest visible ethnic minority in the UK, Asians are everywhere, and I feel like I'm surrounded by my people.

And I am: Although we've been trickling in since the East India Company showed up, Indian immigration to the UK happened in four major waves: The first caused by a post–World War II shortage of laborers to work on the railways. The second, in the late 1950s and early '60s, to work in textile manufacturing. A third during the founding of the National Health Service, thanks to the British medical schools that had been founded in India. And, in the 1960s and '70s, the expulsion of Indians from Kenya, Uganda, and Zanzibar. The delightful result, for me, is that I see Asian faces everywhere— making coffee at Heathrow, reading the news on television, pacing in scrubs at the hospital. We exist in all neighborhoods and every socioeconomic class.

Well, almost. There don't seem to be any Indians at Sotheran's when I get there. It's tucked away in a side street near Piccadilly, with a gleaming glass storefront, not nearly as hobbit-y as I had hoped. But there's still time. I open the door to total silence, and notice there's no dust in the air, or on any surfaces, and plenty of bright light streaming throughout. So maybe it's not the creaky old library I've been imagining. But it's still a place where books are obviously worshipped—polished wood shelves all around me hold immaculate first editions. I'm excited and nervous as I step in, wondering who I'll see first, and if I'll be able to spot Oliver from a distance, but everyone working here seems normal. Two men—one surprisingly young—studiously avoid eye contact until I follow the signs down to Travel and Children's. The four people who work down there are also avoiding me, engaged in long phone conversations, real or imagined. I pay no mind to the avoidance—it's clear evidence that these are my people, book people. This is what we do.

In Travel, I find Klaus, a tidy German fellow who asks if I'm interested in any location in particular. I've prepared an answer for this: guidebooks to Kashmir, I say. From the Raj, ideally. I've been looking for them, in general, because I'm curious to read descriptions of the area that predate my grandparents. He hops to it, the light in his eyes revealing how much he loves his job, and starts to stack them up in front of me. A few are familiar, but he hands me one I haven't heard of before: *Beyond the Pir Panjal,* by an English doctor named Neve. "It might be good to read one not by a military presence," adds Klaus, helpfully. The cover is a shikara on Dal Lake, obviously commissioned by someone who must have loved it well. As I read more about Neve, I find he was a true lover of the area. He built a hospital for the rural poor with his brother, ultimately convincing his niece Nora to join him from England as well. He eventually died there, adored, in 1946. He was a missionary, but we'll set that aside for now—I can't imagine Christians getting very far in a region as skeptical as ours.

Neve is more generous than most Western visitors of his era: a quick library search can give you the impression that every single person stationed in India in the nineteenth century wrote a condescending book about it. But Neve at least understands the context: "The Kashmiris owe much of their character and disposition to their environment and especially to a long history of tyranny and oppression," he acknowledges, adding a bittersweet note of wishful thinking: "In half a century Kashmir has, under Dogra rule, progressed far upon the road to recovery from its sorrows and woes. Time is still required. The habits and customs of generations become a second nature and are slow in passing away. It may be long before we have complete religious toleration in Kashmir. But education and reform of all kinds are steadily advancing, and freedom cannot be far behind."

Klaus looks on as I read Neve's compliments about the locals: "The people are good-tempered, often merry; they have a distinct sense of humour and enjoy a joke." But then it gets real:

> *The Kashmiri is by nature deceitful and given to petty larceny. . . . In spite of his great physical strength and powers of endurance, the Kashmiri is highly strung and neurotic, and he will often weep on slight provocation. In the presence of very little danger he will sob like a child. These people can bear pain much better than Europeans, but owing to want of self-control they make more fuss. Naturally impulsive and huffy, they respond readily to tactful handling. On the whole they are*

grateful for benefits. Their moral sense is fairly well developed.
They readily distinguish between right and wrong. In money
affairs they are close, and the more wealthy are mean. They
spend little, and except at weddings care nothing for show. Even
the rich wear dirty clothes lest they should be thought too well
off. They are affectionate in family life, and very good at nursing
sick relatives. . . .

Kashmiri children are often bright, pleasant and pretty, but
spoilt.

I chortle, reading these passages aloud to Klaus, who is, respectfully, more subdued in his enthusiasm. Neve's anthropological observations are on repeat across other sources.

Mrs. C. G. Bruce, in the Kashmir volume of the delightfully named *Peeps at Many Lands,* agrees:

The natural untrained Kashmiri was not a strong character.
Endurance and patience—the chief virtues one might imagine
all their hardships to have produced in them—are even lacking.
One of the everyday sights is a great big man sobbing like a
noisy child, and a whining and cringing manner is far too
common. Even when they bear pain or trouble it is not bravely
borne. They are very lazy, too, and very dirty. What was good
enough for their fathers, they say, is good enough for them.

Even the 1911 *Encyclopædia Britannica* states that "superstition has made the Kashmiri timid; tyranny has made him a liar; while physical disasters have made him selfish and pessimistic. . . . The Kashmir women have a reputation for beauty which is not altogether deserved, but the children are always pretty." Three makes a clear consensus, I'd think. But I know of a fourth echoing the same sentiments, and many more.

I ask Klaus if he's ever come across *A Lonely Summer in Kashmir,* a 1904 travelogue by a stroppy young woman named Margaret Cotter Morison, who was meant to be traveling through with a friend, only to get a flaky telegram—her friend canceling—when she reached Srinagar. In her recounting, I can see why Kashmir was so attractive to Brits. With its temperate weather and postcard-worthy vistas, Margaret could squint and imagine she was stationed somewhere else.

> *With the polo-ground, tennis-courts, and smartly dressed ladies, one might think oneself in an ordinary Indian station; at the Residency garden-parties, where croquet is played on the softest of lawns, and strawberries and cream dispensed under cool spreading trees, any one would think himself at a country house in England; on the river above the town, where house-boats are crowded close together for over a mile, the sight recalls Henley a few days before the regatta; a row down the town where houses and temples line the banks, where gracefully carved wooden balconies overhang the water, where men and women loiter chattering on the steps, and half the population lives in boats, brings back faint memories of Venice.*

But her views are ruined by the people, "for the most part a grasping, thievish, cowardly set." I especially couldn't get this passage out of my head:

> *Had we been in France or Italy I think I should have feared to trust myself alone on a strange country road towards sundown*

with a crowd of unknown men, for none of my servants were
with me; but in Kashmir one so quickly realises what an arrant
coward the Kashmiri is at heart, in spite of his fine physique,
that I never once during my stay felt any of that bodily fear
which a woman alone is apt to feel in most so-called civilised
countries.

I had to reread this a few times, because surely she wasn't
docking character points for . . . not having been assaulted?
But there isn't another way to read it. These national traits are
reported as fact, truths as objective as the color of a butter-
fly's wing. Though I'll seek out any crumb about what Kashmir
was like before our current state, it's disconcerting to read a
foreigner's narrative of my own people. These books read as
naturalist guides: endless descriptions of the shimmering lake
in summer, breathtaking hikes, rare flora, the overwhelming beauty of the valley. Lovely place, they all agree. It's just a
shame about the locals.

An important part of being a colonialist is believing that one
is doing the colonized a favor. That one's presence somehow
elevates and civilizes the inferior types who were there before.
And for that, colonizers have to see the inhabitants as less than
human. Thus all these descriptions of Kashmiris as slightly
obstinate pets, ones who could use a good bath. Any writer
who could connect to our humanity, a writer with real empathy,
might have recognized that the distrust the locals were evinc-
ing might have to do with a long history of being invaded. That
the coddling of children, the keeping close of family, has been
passed down through centuries of invasions. It's an intergener-
ational wound that echoes even in the present day, infusing my

own childhood training that anyone outside of our immediate community should be kept at a safe, cordial distance.

The British writers—I'll refer to them en masse, as they do us—have a similar disconnect when it comes to the area of Kashmiri art. We've been churning out hand-embroidered shawls for centuries, painstaking woodwork screens, glassy-smooth papier-mâché jewelry boxes with filigreed enamel. Intricate silk rugs. Again, they marvel over what the locals have on offer, but, unlike the treatment of Western art of the time, there is no discussion of the depth behind the humans who make it. The entire country serves as a factory store of high-end goods for the taking. Which the colonies were. A diamond here, an Ife head there—ooh, the Rosetta stone—add to cart. I'm reminded of when I used to take my toddlers for walks around the block and they'd pick up anything that caught their fancy—except, unlike the English, they knew to leave the neighbor's rocks alone.

A little irritable, and not ready to buy, I put the books on hold, thinking one might make a good present for Dad's seventieth, which is around the corner. But I want time to think about it. A decision that should be easy—I should definitely get Dad the gift of historical record—has put me in a strange mood. I've been drawn back to England because of my particular love of it, and been rewarded and comforted by the overwhelming presence of my kind. I do feel a sense of home here. But in this bookstore, which lured me in with its Englishness, I've had a rude reminder that my real home—the one that's more home even than London—has been wildly misunderstood and mischaracterized. That's the push-pull of the former colonies. The familiar overlay of British culture, which feels like our own, mixed in with the sting of the classist, racist history that lies beneath it. It makes me feel guilty for loving England so much, and for having been charmed by the kind of things I'm supposed to reject. In my fit of pique on the way back to the hotel, I pass the British Museum, and glare at it.

Being Indian feels vastly different for me in America, not just because I moved in fully formed, but also because the population felt so uniform when I did. Because of the selective, large-scale importing of "specialty occupations," our community in the United States can feel overwhelmingly made of high-end worker bees—doctors, tech professionals, and the like. For this, we are celebrated, and encouraged not to veer too far from the narrative of the model minority. As a teenager destined for professional school, I had a plot laid out for me: a shiny life, a marriage to a nice Indian boy, two children. It felt safe but not quite right. Surely, there was another story I could write for myself? Something a little less cookie-cutter, less polished?

Existential crises aside, the historical racism in the United States feels different. In America, the people around me might acknowledge that racism exists, that indigenous genocide and slavery were a blight on the nation's history. But "history" puts the country's misdeeds too far in the past. America has a friendly relationship with India, on its face. But Reagan's CIA armed the Afghan mujahideen in their proxy war against Russia in the early 1980s. These guns flooded commercial markets, got into the hands of separatist groups, and ratcheted up conflict in the entire region, eventually leading to the splintering of many homelands, including my own.

As we've seen in the Middle East, America consistently

exports the world's most heavily funded military to protect a hazy democratic ideal, which is often tied to oil interests. Americans may not think of themselves as colonizers, but when political pressure requires that these troops be brought home, the wobbly new "democracies" collapse, leaving a chaotic vacuum in their wake, every single time. It's a disarray familiar to former subjects of the UK and France.

The silver lining to Britain's many historical sins, for me, is that London is bursting with people from former colonies, and damnit, it does make me feel at home. On a meandering walk before dinner that night, I daydream about taking the kids on a long bus ride and pointing out locations from my life here—passing by *this* park I used to visit with my mother, *my* old primary school, *this* corner shop owned by my friend Amit's family. I stop by a Boots pharmacy and pick out chocolates for my kids. I ask the pharmacist (Indian) about a dry patch on my arm, and we're soon friends. I wonder, again, if I should be living here, so I can feel this way every day.

I meet some writers for dinner and hear how they're doing. One, an Asian actress, has just written her first TV pilot, which the channel likes, but with one reservation. "They say my character is unrelatable," she tells me. "So I've tried to make some changes, and—" I stop her there, and gently tell her they're racist. She seems shocked. I press on. They could see a white lady doing all that, I say, weary from two decades in entertainment. The people who decide what goes on TV can see the value in buying our stories, yes, but they still see us as less than, or "other." My words wash over her. I'm almost sad to open her eyes to this unpleasantness; I wish the process could be purer for my friend. "They can handle brown, and they can handle edgy," I say. "But the two together? Seems a bit much." I share that I've just had a pilot die on the vine myself, an Indian family comedy I was excited about, and the projects I've been meeting on since are discouraging. One producer wants a murder mystery at an Indian wedding. Another wants a competitive Bollywood dance movie. A third can't wait to send me her arranged-marriage script that ends in—naturally—a Bollywood dance number. None of these producers are remotely Indian. I am heavy once again with the sense that the people who control programming are interested in stories about Indians—as long as they decide what the stories are. We love the views, these foreigners are telling me again. But let's not ruin them with actual people.

I hear echoes of this at a party later that week. One woman, a comedy producer, bemoans the fact that all their brown and black talent absconds for the United States once they've started to "make it" in London. "There's more of an Asian community here, for sure," I say. "Well, if it's the same there, then why do they keep leaving?" asks this producer, and the answer, as with all things American, is money. Americans can pay to acquire the diversity of viewpoints they haven't fostered. They're still open only to the same six stories, but Hollywood provides more opportunities to tell them. The United States gets a lot of things wrong, I point out, but not capitalism. I say this out loud, pretending it's a joke, and depress an entire table of artists.

· · ·

The next day, I'm supposed to go back to Sotheran's to pick up my books, but I have a terrible stomachache and spend the morning recuperating in bed. It feels like a waste of a sunny, clear day in London, and I'm still cranky about my dead pilot, and the state of storytelling in general. The injustice of it all. But I do have the rare gift of idle time to stare out the window, entranced by the only thing I can actually see: the redbrick building on the diagonal corner. A supine online search reveals it as the longtime home of the editorial offices of a magazine called *Oriental Art.* I keep digging, and the cover article of the issue I find is entitled "Defining Squirrels in Chinese Art: A Case Study from a 14th Century Painting to the Modern Era." It was written by an art historian named Diana Chou. I am immeasurably relieved that the contributor is of Asian descent, and I lie in bed for the rest of the afternoon, getting overly excited about her.

The sheer luxury of knowing that an Asian woman has been allowed to devote thousands of words to medieval squirrels! I imagine her in a set of leather-bound grad stacks, an endless Sotheran's, and I want to be her. To explore what I want without having to defend it, or shape it into what buyers think my story should be. To labor quietly in a gigantic, shadowy library, alone. *I* want to write about squirrels, maybe, I think. Or maybe I want to write a show about an Indian woman who writes about squirrels. As an undergraduate, I almost did a second degree, in medieval and Renaissance studies, completing everything but my required thesis, which concerned "Depictions of the Devil Up to and Including Dante." I never got around to finishing it—law school applications loomed—and when I reach out to the University of Michigan to see if I can still submit one today, at forty-two years of age, I find out the department has folded. It gave me a strange satisfaction in college, to have entertained something so impractical. But I didn't follow through on that impractical, interesting thing, not back then, when I was in training to be a shiny young professional. I lie back in bed, rubbing my sore belly, to wonder why.

When my stomach feels good enough so I can go outside, I walk over to the redbrick building to get a closer look at it, and my tummy rumbles as I approach the Pret A Manger on the lower floor. It sometimes feels like a betrayal to my palate, the magnetic pull of a floppy prawn mayo sandwich and some cheese-and-onion crisps. It's settler food, I know, a pale comparison to the food of the settled, but that Anglo-Indian boundary is a blurry one. Taking it back to my room will scratch a childhood itch: a meal, a patch of sun, a novel, like my after-school ritual. I grab both and scurry back to the hotel, past a crew of people who seem to be taking a beer break from carrying tufted ottomans into yet another high-end Indian restaurant. I smile, they avoid eye contact—my dumb grin or state of dishevelment, who can say—and I remember I still need to email Klaus about those Kashmir books.

I go over the prices in my head. One hundred and forty-eight pounds is not excessive for my father's seventieth-birthday gift, I decide. But am I really going to pay for a beautifully preserved account of how horrible some ruddy colonizers found us? I've even worked myself into a lather at Morison, who got to enjoy a summer traipsing around Kashmir, which I never will.

"Aren't *you* angry?" I sometimes ask my parents, and they make a face that means, *The past is best left behind us.* They feel only fondness for England. My father, an Anglophile, laments the decline of the practice of medicine in London. No one even dresses up for work anymore, he says. What would he be like if he hadn't worn a suit and tie to the hospital for forty years? Who would my mother be without her love of gardens, and china patterns, British comedy, and McVitie's digestive biscuits? Who would they both be without multiple cups of strong tea a day? They wouldn't be my parents, that generation born at the same time as India's independence, many of whom moved to the UK because it felt new, but familiar. I don't know where the Raj ends and my parents begin, but they're more than willing to set history aside, because England gave them so many things they loved: True independence from a joint family unit. Quality time with their perfect daughter, me. A sweet, cheerful son. England holds nothing but happy memories for my parents, and on the family WhatsApp they ask me for photos of the old neighborhood.

I've been too busy to get any, I say, but on day four I finally make it over. The weather is still surprisingly sunny, so I decide to walk all the way from my hotel, near Soho, across town to Southwark, where we lived. I dawdle on my way there; the sun's out, and I'm in no rush. But as I cross the bridge into South East London, I stop many times. To watch the river twinkle below me, to turn around and eye the receding shore. It really is a stunning day, but why am I moving so slowly? I notice as I enter the old neighborhood that I'm stopping an unusual number of times, almost as though I'm trying to avoid getting there. I push through that feeling, which I've never felt before, but, two blocks away from our old building, my legs slow down, then won't move. I sit on a bench a block away and wonder why. And then the tears come, surprising me.

I cry and cry on that bench just outside the hospital campus where Dad used to work, and people shoot me worried looks. I couldn't be more obviously American—only a foreigner would ugly-cry on a park bench—but I'm also trying to figure out what's going on. I loved that flat; I was happy there. Then I understand: that's the problem. "When was the last time you felt like a child?" my therapist had asked that time, and I had answered: never. I thought I was telling the truth. But I now understand that I do remember feeling like a child, once, and it was when we were living in that flat in London. After we left, everything happened—the loss of the house, and political instability, and war, and a murder—and the world felt menacing and exhausting, forever. But when I lived here, I didn't know about any of those things. I cry for the loss of a feeling I've only just remembered having. I almost have to squint to get back in touch with it. But I felt weightless back then, and happy.

My husband calls, a couple of days before I'm due to come back, and asks if I'm ready. Not really, I say, which is unusual for me. I'm usually sniffling for the children by day two away. "Ideally, you'd bring the kids here tomorrow, and I'd get another month," I tell him. And I make my last days count. Stomach healed, tears shed, it feels so good to lean into pleasure. To take restorative long walks alone, where I used to take long walks with my mother. Seeing friends from all kinds of Asian and African countries whose parents do all kinds of things. Combing the aisles at Sainsbury's, caressing Jaffa cakes, Hula Hoops, the colorful, disposable snacks of my youth. I feel like my husband must at Thanksgiving. It's a soothing ritual, reminiscing, and I so rarely get to do it.

But, no matter how much I'm enjoying England, I'm not sure it enjoys me, or people like me. Over the next few days, the country experiences a shortage of petrol, because they're down a hundred thousand truck drivers since Brexit, and supply chains are in crisis. The government dangles emergency visas to people they've shut out since the referendum, and a month in, twenty drivers have applied. Christmas is in grave danger, and the government seems puzzled that people aren't lining up to drive trucks all night for the whopping three months the visas last. "But everyone wants to come to England" is the puzzled response. "Don't they?" The country seems to be dealing with a severe misunderstanding of their reliance on immigrants, a surprise twist in what they thought was a familiar power dynamic, and I'm curious to see how the story unfolds now that a bunch of foreigners get to determine what happens next.

In the meantime, I've decided not to buy the Kashmir books. I have my own stories to tell, and Dad can read those. But I still check my messages, hoping for word from Oliver. In our last exchange, he had asked me to send over some questions that he could answer via email. Slightly exasperated, I do send them—"How did you get funny?" is one—but he's already warned me that his correspondence can be "a graveyard I try not to think too hard about." I don't expect a response, which is just as well, because I don't get one. But I don't need to meet Oliver anymore. I've gotten what I needed from England: between the language, the literature, the laughter, the snacks, a sibling—a foundation of happy memories I can come roll around in whenever I'd like. Yet, in the same way that my husband would probably never move back to Queens, the shapes I've shifted into since my time here are irreversible.

And I don't even know if it's London I want. I'm starting

to suspect that the place I crave, the home I've yearned for, is no more than a web of childhood memories suspended in time. They were so long ago and so precious to me that I can't be certain they were real. Were they something I should question? Bird milk, mosquito bones. But in the end, I don't think it matters. I might live with this feeling, of hovering between years and places, content in my own space yet craving another, for the rest of my life. So I suppose I'd better get comfortable with it. At the airport, I bypass slick restaurants to pick up two sacks of crisps, one for now and one for the plane. And as we take off, with enough fuel to get us across the Atlantic, I stare out the window, excited to get back to my real life, but missing my English one already.

Acknowledgments

A bottomless well of thanks to:

My agent, Erin Malone, who knew I had this book in me many years before I did. Jose Mogollon, Camille Morgan, and Alexandra Figueroa for handling every detail.

Fiona Baird and Laura Bonner at WME.

Diana Tejerina Miller, Reagan Arthur, Marisa Melendez, Pei Loi Koay, Andrea Monagle, Terry Zaroff-Evans, Zuleima Ugalde, Sarah New, Abby Endler, Laura Keefe, and the entire team at Knopf. Linda Huang for the gorgeous jacket.

The most wildly generous and supportive editors: Basharat Peer, Jane Marie, Silvia Killingsworth, Jessica Grose, Valerie Steiker, Rachel Arons, Adam Frucci, Megh Wright, Alan Sytsma, Richard Rushfield, Dan Saltzstein, Joanna Nikas. And Carrie Frye, the cutest, most enthusiastic word ninja.

Sharon Jackson and Jack Black, for showing me what it looks like to love the work.

Stuart Cornfeld, no longer with us, but with me always.

Jami Attenberg and Emma Straub, my fairy godsisters, who answered every dumb question I had over text and Marco Polo (it's very cool, too cool for regular people, don't even think about it).

Seyth Miersma, Reilly Brennan, and Sarah Schechter, who always knew I was a writer.

Evan McGarvey, Julieanne Smolinski, Tahmima Anam, my earliest readers and cheerleaders.

Jenny Maryasis, Amy Barham, Beth Morgan, Nora Cranley, Annie Miyao, Liz Dinerstein, Preeti Wali, Camilla Blackett, Bolu Babalola, my 24/7 text support squad.

Drs. Patti Martin, Anjali Alimchandani, and Cathy Quinn, my mental-health team.

Amy Friedman, the writing teacher who told me I should.

Malin von Euler-Hogan, for making sure I didn't embarrass myself with the proposal.

Joan and Howard Rothman, my spectacular extra parents.

MacDowell, for lavishing me with the time and space to create (and nap and dance).

Our beloved nanny, Ursula Martinez, without whom I would not have a career.

My real Masis, Mamus, Uncles, Aunties, and cousins. And my "aunties," "uncles," and "cousins" in the Kashmiri community at large.

Punit, my first best friend.

My brilliant, enchanting children: D, our giant-hearted, giant-brained, giant-haired firstborn; and L, the clever, spicy little empress of option C.

And Rodney. Thank you for dragging me into the elevator to a penthouse of happiness I didn't know existed.

Acknowledgments and Permissions

A portion of these essays first appeared, in slightly different form, in the following publications: "Goddess of Destruction" originally appeared in *The New York Times* on September 12, 2019, titled "We Never Moved Back to Kashmir, Because We Couldn't"; "Dotted Lines" originally appeared in *The New Yorker* on May 9, 2022, titled "The Pop Song That's Uniting India and Pakistan"; "On Language" originally appeared in *The New York Times* on September 18, 2020, titled "I Hate It with Both My Eyes"; "Sibling Revelry" originally appeared in *The New York Times* on April 17, 2020, titled "Is an Indian Holiday the Cure for Sibling Rivalry?"; a significantly different form of "Sixteen Kitchens" originally appeared in *Lucky Peach*; "Bildungsroman" originally appeared in *The New York Times* on March 25, 2020, titled "Everything I Know About Parenting in a Crisis, I Learned from My Mom"; "Mother Sauces" originally appeared in *The New Yorker* on July 16, 2020, titled "How to Extract a Mother's Rogan Josh Recipe over Zoom"; "Fed Is Best" originally appeared on *Grub Street* on June 10, 2020, titled "How I'm Teaching My Six-Year-Old to Cook for Himself"; "The Culture" originally appeared in

The New York Times on April 12, 2021, titled "Don't Mistake Silent Endurance for Resilience"; "Astrocartography" originally appeared in *The New York Times* on January 22, 2020, titled "Where Should a Scorpio Live? Ask an Astrocartographer."

Poems of Lal Ded reproduced by permission from the publisher, Penguin Random House India. English Language Translation Copyright Ranjit Hoskote, 2011.

Priyanka Mattoo is a writer, filmmaker, former talent agent, and a co-founder of Earios, a women-led podcast network. She is a contributor to *The New York Times* and *The New Yorker* and a recipient of a MacDowell Fellowship. Priyanka holds degrees in Italian and law from the University of Michigan and currently lives in Los Angeles with her husband and kids.

A NOTE ON THE TYPE

This book was set in Hoefler Text, a family of fonts designed by Jonathan Hoefler, who was born in 1970. First designed in 1991, Hoefler Text was intended as an advancement on existing desktop computer typography, including as it does an exponentially larger number of glyphs than previous fonts. In form, Hoefler Text looks to the old-style fonts of the seventeenth century, but it is wholly of its time, employing a precision and sophistication only available to the late twentieth century.

Composed by North Market Street Graphics
Lancaster, Pennsylvania

Printed and bound by Berryville Graphics
Berryville, Virginia

Book design by Pei Loi Koay